MY AMERICAN ODYSSEY
FROM THE WINDRUSH TO THE WHITE HOUSE

Roger Griffith   Volume One

SilverWood

Published in 2015 by SilverWood Books

SilverWood Books Ltd
30 Queen Charlotte Street, Bristol, BS1 4HJ
www.silverwoodbooks.co.uk

ISBN 978-1-78132-306-9 (paperback)
ISBN 978-1-78132-307-6 (ebook)

British Library Cataloguing in Publication Data
A CIP catalogue record for this book is available from
the British Library

Set in Sabon and DIN by SilverWood Books
Printed on responsibly sourced paper

To the women in my life, Mum and sister Laurice.
Without you both, I would have nothing.

To the spirit of the Windrush Generation *for giving us everything.*

To all my friends and family who have given me the spirit,
support and strength to keep going and tell my story.

Contents

Introduction

In my home, among the treasured pictures and memorabilia from my travels, is a picture of President Barack Obama. Underneath his smiling face are the words, 'I was there, January 20 2009', and I was indeed there on that momentous day.

When the first Black American president was inaugurated, I was standing on the Washington Mall with two million jubilant others, cheering and congratulating, and feeling truly blessed to be at this incredible occasion. On that bitterly cold sun-blessed winter's day, we were all part of history in the making. In possibly the most racially segregated country on earth, with its dark and violent history of slavery, there was now a Black man at the helm. It was something I never thought I would see in my lifetime, yet here I was witnessing it first-hand – even if he was only a tiny speck on the steps of the distant Capitol Building. Here, on the jam-packed Mall known as America's front lawn, people of all colours were united together in happiness and hope for the future.

President Barack Obama's incredible speech penetrated deep into my soul. Every word, phrase and cadence of the extraordinary orator carried a signal for us each to be or become a better person, and to do our bit for one another. His positive message was for everyone listening around the world, not just those of us who were there in person. It truly felt like things were changing, at long last, and you could really be anything you wanted to be.

After the tears of joy dried on my face, I was hugged and congratulated for being there, for what seemed like the thousandth time, by another total stranger. We all felt part of a select club, celebrating this amazing day. I thanked them warmly, and returned the praise, my English accent cutting through the sub-zero temperatures like a bullwhip.

11

'Oh, you're British?' they said, smiling.

'Yes,' I replied, sounding more like Prince Charles than Dizzee Rascal, or even Huggy Bear.

'Oh, we didn't realise there were Black people in England.'

I smiled politely, long used to this oft-repeated ritual in America concerning my identity. Rather than be upset or offended at the inaccuracy, I have learned to use it to my advantage. My accent has opened more doors in America than I care to remember, be it an extra helping of food from a silver-haired waitress, a discount in a shop or car rental agency, or getting my overweight luggage waved through by a smiling sympathetic attendant at the airport.

You see, I've travelled all over America, on twenty trips or more, since I was sixteen. At first I came to visit family who'd migrated from Guyana to the United States of America, rather than to the United Kingdom as my parents had – Dad in 1958 then, as was the trend, he sent for my mum and my sisters in 1960. I'd stay with my brother, cousins, aunts and uncles scattered along America's eastern seaboard, from Connecticut to Florida. Then, later on, I purposely planned trips to explore and witness everything about Black culture, from sport and music to religion and politics. From a young age, I couldn't help comparing how Black culture in the United States differed so much from that back home in the UK. I wrote my own version of *Letters from America*, as my personal American odyssey began to unfold.

As a Black child growing up in Bristol and London in the 1980s, with little of my own culture to look up to, and certainly no role models, I looked to the United States for inspiration. There I found heroes, leaders and a sense of pride. I was part of a new generation, born in Britain and searching for our identity. Before we'd fully acknowledged our African roots of heritage, we turned to America. In leadership we found icons such as my ultimate hero Dr Martin Luther King Jr, as well as Malcolm X, campaigning for civil rights, dignity and social justice. We gained strength and meaning in our lives from the likes of Rosa Parks or the Black Power movement. We saw the first images of successful Black people in sport with Jesse Owens and Muhammad Ali. In music we found pride from the success of Motown, followed by Hip-Hop which, when mixed with those Motown harmonies and RnB, became the biggest-selling music genre in the world, creating a new counter-culture with its own look and language. Finally, in entertainment personalities such as Sidney Poitier, Denzel Washington and Oprah Winfrey became trailblazers in showbiz.

Five decades after receiving the right to vote, and with some of the older generations in America still able to recall their time on the plantation fields, the first Black man is now in the White House, completing a remarkable journey from the plantation to the polling booth, then to the presidency.

*

Later on that evening, after the momentous events in the Mall, I sat in a bar on the famous Capitol Hill, where more shady deals have been completed than in the notorious drug-ravaged streets of Washington a few blocks away. Many of the day's throng had left to find warmth or to prepare for the evening's numerous balls, while I thawed out by nursing a medicinal supply of brandy.

I watched President Obama's speech again on a TV in the corner, not only with pride but also with newfound meaning and poignancy. Had the future, my future, really opened up? I wondered. I looked at the poised individual on the screen. No longer did Hollywood have to cast Morgan Freeman or Dennis Haybert from *24* in the role of a Black president – the real deal was in the chair. Here was a man without corporate sponsorship, family patronage like Kennedy, Bush and Clinton, or even lengthy political experience who had managed to get elected to White House on his terms. I reflected on my joy at witnessing this, how it was going to change the landscape of history for future generations, and also how it could change mine, too.

I listened more closely to the president's words. 'What is required of us now is a new era of responsibility...' he pronounced. The words swirled in my head. All of my personal history, and that of my parents and their forbears, seemed to converge and speak to me.

'You need to tell your story. What's the point of all those notes you've been making over the years?' I heard them say.

'I got a story to tell.' The beginning of the rapper The Notorious B.I.G's track started in my head.

'Tell their story. Your story. Our Story.' More voices swirled in my head. Not just the story of the fight against racism and social injustices; not just of American idiosyncrasies; not just of how my parents came to be in England in the 1960s, but put it together into a whole story from my own personal perspective.

My old negativity butted in. 'I'm not famous, a respected writer or a celebrity, so why would anyone want to read my story? Just stick to what you know.' But I knew if I had followed that logic, I would have been freezing somewhere else right then. Perhaps I would still have been painting the old Severn Bridge, which links England with Wales, as I had eighteen years earlier. Perhaps I would never have retrained to become a housing officer, starting a journey of hard work and study which led me to leave the cycle of unemployment, deprivation, violence and anguish in which I had been for so long.

'It's time to put away such childish things...'

President Obama continued his speech. I looked around the bar at its patrons, getting misty-eyed again. It felt as if Obama's words were aimed in my direction. I knew he could do almost anything, but now the president was reading my mind.

'Tell their story, your story, our story,' the voices chanted again.

It was time to find my own voice. I consider myself to be 'Black-British', a term I have only been comfortable with since the mid-nineties. Before that I was Afro-Caribbean, without having the maturity to understand that label, and before that simply 'second generation'. This was the term given to immigrant families' children who, after their parents had been invited from the British Commonwealth to live and work in Britain, were born within the mother country's borders. Our voice has struggled to be heard, much less understood. More often than not, I've felt I had more to add or corrections to make to patchy or plain incorrect commentary about the experience of Black-British life and society. Now I wondered: why shouldn't my voice be a valid one, as a Black-British man with his own stories to tell, and a curiosity about his cultural history and how it links with America?

President Obama was now striding down Pennsylvania Avenue on the way to his new home, hand in hand with his beautiful wife Michelle, savouring every moment of the adulation from the crowd. The world's expectations were on his shoulders, but for now he was basking in the achievement of his dream: the living, breathing, smiling embodiment that anyone can be anything they want to be.

I am not internationally famous, but I hope you find my family's story of interest. I am not an academic historian, but with a hunger for the truth I have religiously researched any facts as told to me, and have referenced my sources along the way. I am not a travel writer, but I love to explore and write about what I have seen, heard, experienced or felt.

'I got a story to tell,' I said to myself. 'My time is now.'

1

America and Me

Coming to America

I was as eager and inquisitive as any sixteen-year-old would be, flying across the Atlantic Ocean aboard a cavernous British Airways 747 jumbo jet in October 1981. I had been told by my mother to calm down and get some rest ahead of the long journey as I excitedly chattered away. Shackled by a seat belt and with roving stewardesses patrolling the aisles, I had no choice but to comply.

The next thing I remember was Mum gently waking me as we began our descent into New York City. I looked out of the window at the stunning scene below me which I had only seen in photographs and my daydreams. I had a bird's-eye view of the famed copper-lady – the Statue of Liberty – who had turned white-green from the elements. 'Wow,' I said as she welcomed us into her city, just as she had done millions of immigrants and visitors before me. I scrutinised her every feature. Sure enough, as the *Encyclopaedia Britannica* had informed me when I'd eagerly read it before my trip, she had one arm upstretched, holding a golden torch, and a book tucked under the other. Ahead of Lady Liberty, Manhattan's picture-book skyline rose up in the distance. The Chrysler Building's twisted spire, the majestic Empire State Building and dozens of other colossal buildings crammed into every conceivable visual space. The World Trade Center was still there then, standing proudly as we approached the south of the island of Manhattan. The skyline still looks magnificent today, although to those who can remember what it looked like before September 11 2001, the memory can never be the same after that grisly morning in New York. It reminds me of a beautiful woman who then smiles to

17

reveal she has had her two front teeth violently knocked out.

Although my parents were divorced, my father had contacted his American connections to help out with our stay. We were going to stay with my Aunty Daphne, Dad's sister, who lived in Brooklyn. I was fascinated by the fact that I had an array of cousins who would have funny accents, different attitudes and a completely separate understanding of the world to mine. However, we were connected by our bloodlines through the Griffiths (my father's family) and the Coleridges (my mother's family) who had migrated from Guyana at various times, from the late-1950s onwards, to the East Coast of America. As well as my father's relatives in New York, my mum had a sister in Maryland near Washington DC, a brother who was about to become the Bishop of Connecticut and my grandfather in New Jersey, who I was still yet to meet. Both parents had more siblings and extended family scattered around America who, sadly, we did not have time to visit on this occasion.

Due to this family connection, I was thrust into a different world across the ocean with conflicting feelings of anticipation and duty. It was not like visiting Spain or other foreign places for a holiday like some of my former classmates at Lawrence Weston School (that I had left without qualifications earlier that summer) had done. My strict mother reinforced this fact. I was there for a reason – to see family – and fun would be a secondary by-product if I was lucky. Of course, I would manage to achieve both, and I suspect this was my mother's intention all along.

This and other early visits to America created an insatiable wanderlust in me; a yearning to explore the world and its cultures, sights and sounds. I was fortunate enough to have visited four American states: Connecticut, New Jersey, Maryland and, of course, New York state by the age of sixteen, before I had even set foot north of the Watford Gap in the United Kingdom.

We were to be met at JFK Airport not by the yellow cabs that help give New York its romantic glow but, as most of my parents' generation were, by a willing cousin, friend or family member who had given up their afternoon, and a few more days to follow, to ensure our safe passage around their home town. On this occasion it was my Aunt Daphne's husband – a huge bear of a man with an American drawl who looked like he'd just stepped straight out of an episode of *Starsky and Hutch*. The Beckhams' progeny, the Clintons' latter home and a host of other celebrities were yet to gentrify Brooklyn's mean streets back in 1981, and yellow cab drivers were often a little choosy about whom they picked up, or, more to the point, where they dropped their passengers off. Besides, the taxi would not have gone from the airport through Manhattan to Brooklyn to 'show the boy some sights'.

Brooklyn

Being driven through Manhattan in my uncle's nondescript Cadillac, I got a closer look at its towering beauty. Eventually my young jaw closed, only to open again as we crossed one of the many beautiful bridges that span the Hudson River to arrive at Flatbush Avenue, Brooklyn.

In Britain, an avenue suggests a cute, leafy cul-de-sac with maybe forty semi-detached three-bed homes, located somewhere in suburbia. This was to be the first of countless Anglo-American contradictions. Flatbush Avenue is a long, winding street of over twenty miles, which back then, due to its width and mass of traffic, was more akin to a motorway with traffic lights and a subway running through it. It harboured many different ethnic communities, mostly poor and, certainly around where Aunty Daphne lived, exclusively Black.

This was my first experience of segregation, albeit for economic and social reasons rather than what was known as the Jim Crow laws of the southern states of America, about which I was yet to learn. I barely saw a single white face in Brooklyn back then, which I found odd having either lived in a ninety-nine per cent white area of Bristol with my mum, or visited my dad, my elder sisters and family in London, the multi-ethnic city of my birth. I was more intrigued to discover that Brooklyn looked similar to the overactive imagination of my excited playground classmates who had seen places like Harlem on TV – shabby and run-down. If Brooklyn looked this rough, what on earth would the Bronx look like, with the Bowery where dropouts, drug dealers and hustlers roamed? I wondered to myself with excited expectation. The seemingly obligatory broken-down cars and dilapidated buildings lining the road had replaced the elegance of Manhattan. To add to the sight of poverty, I saw something I was going to see often on my future trips to America: men and women pushing their worldly belongings in trolleys.

In over thirty years of visiting America, I have spent the vast majority of time staying with family or visiting urban areas to gain my own historical perspective. Within these areas, poverty can be seen everywhere with the ubiquitous presence of bag ladies, down-and-outs, dropouts, hobos or whatever unflattering description one chooses to use. The sight of the homeless in ill-fitting dishevelled clothing, wearing a combined look of helplessness and weariness, is a sight I have seen far too often in the richest country in the world, and one which never ceases to sadden me.

Aunt Daphne lived in a large brownstone public housing block of apartments and maisonettes, which in America are crudely termed as 'The Projects'. Kept scrupulously clean, her home appeared to have TARDIS-like qualities in order to fit her large family of five super-sized boys within.

After unpacking, I was quickly shunted away from the grown-ups to meet my cousins – Andre, Ivlor, Leonard, Steve and Colin, ages ranging from twelve to twenty. All of them seemed taller than I had been at their age, or bigger than I was ever going to be. My mother was wrong. She said if I ate all my greens I'd grow up big and strong, but it appeared all I required to reach the land of the giants was fast food.

My cousins asked me funny questions about life in Britain; about my friends, school, clothes, music and my weird accent. I think *ET* would have felt more comfortable being questioned about his planet by my cousins. My gang or 'tribe' in Bristol was Rude Boys, heavily influenced by Jamaican Ska music, a precursor to Reggae popularised by the record label 2 Tone and by one of my favourite bands of all time – The Specials. My dress in the early eighties was bizarrely half-skinhead – whom I hated as much as they hated me – and half-mod, who were cool. The punk era had left me sporting an earring in my left ear, but there was no chance of me donning any make-up like the New Romantic bands, such as Duran Duran or Spandau Ballet, which had become popular. Besides, being Black was enough to attract insult and injury.

Thankfully, being adolescent boys with a shared hereditary streak from our Griffith/Coleridge fathers – an interest in girls – my cousins and I finally bonded. Having lost my virginity a few months earlier, I felt I was experienced enough to give New York natives, and Agony Aunt Dr Ruth, a few tips in the area of sex, although I found my cousins' responses to the fact my childhood sweetheart was white a little unsettling. It was not expressed in a racist way; it was just beyond their shared comprehension to date outside of their race. They asked me what she looked like, as if seeking confirmation of alien characteristics or body parts. Intriguingly they asked me what her parents had said about their daughter dating a Black teenager. I shrugged, saying they appeared to give grudging acceptance, even if I hadn't quite got past the 'hello' and 'goodbye' stage with her father. I was later to discover that this was positively warm and friendly compared to the reactions of some of my white and Asian ex-girlfriends' parents. Sometimes I had even had to meet my girlfriends by old red telephone boxes or on anonymous street corners to hide the fact that we were dating.

The next day I was eager to explore the new frontiers of America, but how was I to get around? The adults were at work, my cousins at school and my mum, having visited her father here a few times previously, had little interest in seeing the sights of NYC again. So that left me to my own devices. I did not have to beg my mum to be allowed out alone; she knew her son was grown up enough. I'd already proved capable of getting around the London Underground alone on my regular trips to London for family visits and football; I'd been on summer holiday child-minding duties since I was eleven years old, looking after my beloved nephew Dominic and niece Ade to give their respective mothers a break; and when my transatlantic clan had visited the UK throughout my early teens, I was the one given the job as tour guide. More importantly, my mother was a working mum, which meant I pulled my weight around the house way before my peers, and knew how to load a washing machine, clean and rinse dishes, and generally ensure our flat had not turned into a neighbourhood squat by the time she'd finished a day's work.

'Mum, it's real easy,' I said reassuringly. 'I just have to follow the coloured lines, just like the London Underground.' She looked at me watchfully, probably sensing that my childhood was slipping away.

'Just be back before dark,' she advised with a raised eyebrow.

As shocking as it may seem to have let me out alone, my generation – Black or white (the Asian children with whom I grew up weren't to find their emancipation until the nineties) – were different to today's teenagers. We would announce that we were going out for the day on our bikes, and not come back until sunset. Mobile phones were a concept that belonged in our *2000 AD* space comics. We knew exactly where the local paedophile's house was, and carried out our own daily risk assessment based on the rumour mill's reports of his whereabouts. Wearing a safety helmet and knee-pads for riding a bike would have triggered a collective beating for being soft, ending up with the wearer suffering more pain than if they had scraped their own skin along the pavement. In any case, how would anyone improve their cycling skills without a hard landing or two? In short, we were streetwise, and understood that accidents, mishaps and bad stuff not only happened, but were an essential part of our growing-up, as a tough unforgiving world was around the corner. So off I went to the subway without a kiss or a watchful wave, but loved nonetheless by my mum. For Captain Dan Dare a.k.a. Roger Griffith had his first foreign solo expedition to navigate and where better to start than the grandeur of Manhattan?

As a teenager I lapped up American teen culture, from its films, including *Porky's* and *Grease,* to its music which had been followed by British teenagers since the days of Bill Haley, Elvis Presley and Nat King Cole, plus the clothes and street slang. Two other films, *The Warriors* and *The Wanderers*, about gang violence, were set in New

22

York and dominated our subculture, not to mention my thoughts that day. The image of baseball bat-wielding gangs waiting on street corners kept springing to mind, giving this day trip around the city a slightly dangerous feel, but the reality was that it was a day of hard labour not a movie set, and I had to stay focused on finding my way around.

The subway rumbled away constantly in the background; people scurried about like soldier-ants; cars tooted their horns at every perceived error. Smells of hot dogs, pizzas and tasty new treats drifted through my nostrils as I skipped along, savouring this new world, but it wasn't as shiny and clean as I'd imagined it would be. Grime and dirt covered the pavement. Garbage bags were piled high on the sidewalks. Signs of poverty were everywhere.

I continued walking, minus a yet to be invented iPod, or even a Sony Walkman cassette player, but strutting along to my own beat. I must have looked quite a funny sight to the native New Yorkers – striding down Flatbush Avenue towards the station with my freshly developed pimp-roll, dressed in Ben Sherman checked shirt, Harrington jacket and two-tone trousers well above my ankles, revealing my rude-boy white socks and Doc Marten shoes.

I began to sing 'A Message to You Rudy' from my favourite band of that era, The Specials, remade from a 1967 Dandy Livingstone Jamaican Ska classic. I was blissfully unaware that I was on the point of something memorable and life-changing, as this was to be the first of many global explorations. I felt every bit the king of New York. I was The Don; the main man; fearless, excited, and with a camera in hand ready to capture my dreams.

Manhattan's Magic
Assuming I could easily transfer my skill of memorising the London Underground to another city and the New York subway, I studied the map. The colours were similar: greens, blues and yellows, but the names of the lines – Victoria, Piccadilly and Circle – had been replaced by numbers and letters. Pah, this will be child's play! I confidently thought, which was exactly what it was.

I could hear the train rumbling towards me, and could see trains criss-crossing their way through the bowels of the city. As befits the world's first twenty-four-hour metropolis, the New York City subway does not even close to greet Santa Claus.

As I would find out time after time in future visits to America, its objects, buildings and people always seem to be more extravagant, louder and bigger than their British cousins, and this train was no exception. It burst out of its tunnelled tomb, and I grinned when I saw that a thoughtful artist had duly tagged the train with graffiti, just like in the movies and music videos I watched. I squeezed my way on-board, consulted my map and headed to my first stop: Uptown 34th Street, near the Empire State Building, which held a special place in my imagination.

I was fascinated by the sheer magnificence of the towering building, and couldn't wait to get to the top. The express lift rocketed through the building's many layers, up to the crowning beauty of its art-deco tower which beamed television pictures around the world.

Ask any Wall Street executive, and they will tell you New York is an easy place to feel like the master of the Universe, especially at the summit of its grandest building where I now stood. Scenes from the film *King Kong* came to mind: my view seemed a work of someone else's imagination. I surveyed every grand building around me, looking down at the Legoland-like vista around me in wonder, feeling every bit a man – or soon-to-be man – of the Universe.

Leaving the Empire State Building, I walked to the plaza of the Rockefeller Center, which was minus its signature ice-skaters as it was a mild autumn day. My fellow-travellers jostled for space with the worker-ants who were scurrying to and from their places of work. Next, I moved towards Grand Central Station, which sent passengers all across America; I'd seen its impressive architecture in film scenes. Nearby was the squat rectangular shape of the United Nations building, representing the hopes of many but the fruition of few of the dreams of its 192 member nations' citizens.

Just before I got on the ferry to the Statue of Liberty, I visited what was then the World Trade Center. I've now visited New York City a few times, and I regret never having stepped inside the Twin

Towers. Somehow I felt loyal to the splendour of the Empire State, and felt there was something cold and unwelcoming about the Twin Towers, which I now understand signified the naked pursuit of money and greed based at the adjacent Wall Street. On that first visit I still marvelled at their arrogant beauty, craning my neck upward to view storey upon storey of vast glass exterior from the pavement below.

I boarded a ferry and stared across to Ellis Island, which had processed over twelve million migrants to America between 1892 and 1954. People from all over the world had arrived here, expectantly waiting to make new lives and live the American Dream. My family came after that, but with hopes and expectations just as high as those who'd arrived before them.

From the air I had already been in awe of the sheer size and bulk of the Statue of Liberty, and as the ferry drew closer I saw the full 300-foot extent of her magnificence. One of Lady Liberty's feet was trampling on a pair of shackles as an expression of newfound freedom.

The Statue of Liberty had been a gift from the French to the city of New York in 1886 to mark the centenary of American independence in 1776. I later discovered that only a mere twenty-three years before the gift was given, President Abraham Lincoln had set the slaves free with his Emancipation Proclamation in 1863, with the Thirteenth Amendment, which officially abolished slavery, coming in 1865. Quite whether the ex-slaves were thought of as among the 'Tired, poor, huddled masses yearning to breathe free...', part of the inscription on a plaque inside Lady Liberty, remains a question to history.

At the time I was more excited by the fact that I could walk around her cavernous interior than by history, so I climbed up the dizzying steps and was out of breath when I finally reached her crown. Sadly the joyride thrill I got from this experience was banned by George W Bush after 9/11, but during his first ten days in the White House, President Obama announced plans to reopen Lady Liberty for the general public, and has duly kept his promise.

On the return ferry to Manhattan, I viewed the splendour of the island from ground level as we glided across the Hudson River. New York's bridges are as much part of the city's glamour as its famous monuments, and there are over 200 tunnels and arches connecting traffic and transit to the five boroughs of New York: Manhattan, Queens, Brooklyn, the Bronx and Staten Island. I marvelled at the magnificent water-crossings that carried people on foot, trains and buses, and in particular the bridge that connected my family's inner-city life in Brooklyn with swanky uptown Manhattan. The Brooklyn Bridge dwarfed the only other suspension bridge I had seen – the scenic Clifton Suspension Bridge that straddles the Avon Gorge back in Bristol.

Glancing at my watch I saw it was late afternoon, and the nightfall that would signal the end of my fairy tale in New York was approaching. I did not know when or if I would be back in the Big Apple again, so I decided there was enough time for a quick visit to Times Square.

Excited and giddied by the lights, flickering billboards and huge screens, I applauded warmly to myself as I noticed Broadway's famed theatres. Even though I had no idea what was showing, it meant another 'mission accomplished' on my tourist trail about which to tell my mates back home.

In need of some nourishment I bought a slice of famed New York pizza, washing it down with grape soda, savouring the taste of both as it was the first time I'd experienced either. I ate my street-feast right there on the sidewalk, the stringy cheese on the pizza snapping against my face like an elastic band as Times Square's neon lights began to outlast the daylight. I watched the endless ranks of yellow taxicabs weave their way through the bustling traffic along 42nd Street, their tooting horns only brought to a halt by red lights or another fare.

Wandering around Times Square, I suddenly realised I was completely unprepared for the illicit thrill of the many sleazy fleshpots that surrounded the area in the early 1980s. Sex shops and theatres were literally everywhere, and certainly not listed on my map. Intrigued, I eventually found one not bothered enough to question my youthful looks, which allowed me entry to my first pornographic movie. While I was watching my adult sex education lesson literally unfold on the big screen, a kindly elderly woman approached me and offered to relieve any tension I may have been experiencing after a hard day's sightseeing. Unsure of what therapeutic exercise she could perform in the half-full auditorium, and more concerned with hanging onto my treasured $10, I politely declined, especially as I had to get back to Brooklyn and avoid the wrath of Mum. Darkness was falling outside.

I scurried back to the subway, leaving the 'bright lights and big city' of Manhattan behind. Having more or less avoided trouble, I arrived back safely – and all before the big hand had reached 7pm. I felt exhilarated, as if I had outdone Cinderella with my curfew kept, even though my potential companion had looked more like an ugly sister than Princess Charming.

So this is how I established my relationship with America, and why, after giving birth to me, the second-best thing my mother ever did was to let me run free on the streets of New York that day. It's an act that today would not only have seen me taken into care but Mum vilified following her fifteen minutes of fame as that month's 'Bad Mother' exclusive, but I would not swap that freedom and those joyous early forays of exploration for the cloistered cotton-wool existence of young people today for anything. It is not a question of things being better or worse, but they were different times. Through such experiences, I became a different person: fiercely in-dependent, and more than capable of setting my own challenges and succeeding.

I still find travelling alone a joy, and certainly being alone is no reason not to travel to a new adventure. Looking back, I probably took a wrong turning or two, or got off at the wrong subway stop, but I always managed to find my way again. I'm pretty sure at some point I was close to an unknown danger as the curious locals surveyed me, but I would continue forward with a smile, choosing not to worry about what could happen, instead concentrating my efforts on deciding my own destiny. My love affair with America had begun – and no, not because of the half-naked prostitute in Times Square.

Once I could afford it, I became a complete travel junkie. I explored Europe, Australia and Asia, and made personal pilgrimages to the Caribbean and Africa, but I travelled to America more than any other country. It would always find new ways of luring me back.

Whether I am on the East Coast or West Coast, Midwest or Deep South, I always find myself intrigued and at ease within America's borders and with its people. That wonderful day exploring Manhattan became the blueprint for my future travel. Later on that trip I also visited tranquil Connecticut, and the historic Washington Mall that would provide the inspiration to write this book twenty-eight years later.

Before President Obama, America had a turbulent relationship with the rest of the world, which would make some people stare at me with either pity or scorn if I declared my guarded support for all things American. Perhaps they would have been impressed if I'd said I was a Francophile, but being an Americanophile does not sound the same, nor does it conjure up the same sophistication or glamour, so I just say I love Americana – meaning, for me, a liking for things American. My warmth for America is in its diversity and boundless positivity, but chiefly in how it can be so many things to so many different people who have reinvented themselves in a new world. As I've grown older, however, it has been America's other image – the latent dangers, contradictions and inequalities – that have caught my attention and became intertwined in my life.

Like many before me, I had been seduced by the idea of the American Dream, but the more I learned about the country and listened to the many different and disparate voices of its residents, the more I became acutely aware of how that dream could become the American nightmare. Just like any love at first sight, I fell for America's beauty and magnificence, but just underneath the surface I sensed and saw the darkness of its past struggles with racism, and its present and perpetual scars of poverty.

2

Back in Britain
A Question of Identity

The 1980s

When I returned home after spending nearly a month in America, it felt like society was changing around me. Hip-Hop culture was emerging, with its music, dancing, clothes and new language about to change the world. Rap music began to make its way into my growing music collection. These new sounds first emerged in New York, from rappers such as Grandmaster Flash, DJ Kool Herc and Afrika Bambaataa. Influenced by their West Indian heritage, which included sound systems at outdoor parties, they recreated this scene as block parties. They had listened to *toasting* in Reggae, which in its earliest form was a chant over music practised by African *griots* or storytellers. Its rhythmic speech pattern had found its way into music and poetry performed by people such as musician Gil Scott-Heron, and Muhammad Ali in his boastful taunts. Added to this were new and exciting images of people breakdancing to the sounds, and colourful graffiti, now known as street art, found around certain cities. It all made this new culture fresh, exhilarating and, most importantly for any self-respecting teenager, something your mum and dad would not approve of.

One of Hip-Hop's pioneers, Grandmaster Flash, was born in Barbados and emigrated to America with his parents. His seminal 1982 record *The Message* provided a blueprint for how to make a rap record with political and socially conscious lyrics. This influenced the likes of Public Enemy, Run DMC, KRS-One and an all-white crew called the Beastie Boys, and inspired a whole range of rappers of today, including Eminem and Jay-Z.

In the UK, songs such as The Specials' number one hit 'Ghost Town' (1980), Steel Pulse's 1978 album *Handsworth Revolution* and punk band The Clash's Ska-tinged 'The Guns of Brixton', on their 1979 *London Calling* album, all eerily prophesied the inner-city violence and uprising against the police and the state that was shortly to come. The cry went up in Brixton and Tottenham, London; Toxteth, Liverpool; Handsworth, Birmingham; and in my own city, Bristol, in the St Pauls area, in 1980, to rebel at the lack of opportunities, and protest against the constant taunts, glares and the daily stop-and-search campaigns of the heavy-handed and discriminatory police.

Although I was not directly involved, I felt an affinity and empathy with the rioters. As the decade drew on, I found myself forced to defend their response and my position, if not the violence. I had seen and felt at first hand the malevolent cocktail of racism, violence, police harassment, unemployment and utter helplessness that had pushed people over the edge, leading them to respond in the way the poor in Britain have been doing for centuries – they revolted. In inner-city Bristol the violence was not confined to race, as young white males joined their Black comrades in attacking the thin blue line of the police protecting society from the mayhem.

During Margaret Thatcher's ministerial reign, violence was not restricted to urban Blacks and the poor. The bitter miners' strike of 1984–85, and the poll tax riot in Trafalgar Square early in 1990, were symptoms of unrest and uprisings across social, political and class lines as the recession bit deeper and polarised the country into haves and have-nots.

The rise of the far-right parties, the National Front and British National Party, both thin veils for Fascist neo-Nazi sympathisers, stoked a campaign of hate against ethnic communities which went beyond right-wing politics. Football hooliganism added to the violence in society at the time, making a simple Saturday afternoon shopping trip trickier than usual while dodging roaming opposition fans looking for an enemy to fight. With stadiums such as Manchester City's old ground Maine Road in Moss Side, West Bromwich Albion's in Handsworth and my team Tottenham Hotspur's White Hart Lane all in the middle of communities housing the influx of migrants after World War II, the 'enemy' was clear to the racist supporters of many teams at the time.

When I first moved to Bristol from London in the mid-seventies I lived in Easton, which neighbours St Pauls and was not far from Bristol Rovers' then football ground at Eastville. Whenever a notorious football team, such as Millwall or Portsmouth, were playing Bristol Rovers, we used to watch the away fans herded in from the train station at Stapleton Road. My friends, Dennis and John Thomas, and I would gather behind the safety of their police escort, staring at them as we would animals at the zoo. We were greeted with monkey noises and chants of 'Sieg heil' from some of their far-right supporters. Occasionally coins would fly through the air, and after dodging the missiles we would scrabble among ourselves for the loose change on the ground.

The Falklands War

Six months after I returned from New York, Britain went to war with Argentina over the Falkland Islands, a country thousands of miles away of which I had barely heard of, nor could I locate it on a map. As battles broke out in April 1982, the football-mad sixteen-year-old me was especially confused about why we were at war, because Osvaldo 'Ossie' Ardiles and Ricardo 'Ricky' Villa, who were both Argentines, played football for my team, Tottenham Hotspur. Together we had rejoiced over Tottenham's Wembley FA Cup final win, in which they had played a massive role, only the year before the war began. Now they were supposed to be my enemies? It didn't make sense. The Falklands War felt like it had nothing to do with me. I was indifferent towards some place I knew little about. Pictures of 'our boys' in battle only made me think it was a shocking waste of life. However, I was aware enough to know that Thatcher was playing a political masterstroke, using the Falklands War as a strategic propaganda piece.

For the first time, I was forced to declare that I would not fight for my country if we – the unemployed – were conscripted. This had become a national talking point and, for some, seemed a ready-made solution to what to do with the three million plus out of work. The debate, and accompanying taunts of being a coward and unpatriotic, drove a further wedge between me and the people with whom I'd grown up, and added to my increasing internal dialogue which was busy examining every facet of who I was.

At the same time, I learned that two of my formative heroes, Dr Martin Luther King Jr and Muhammad Ali, had gone through bouts of moral consciousness sparked by America's war with Vietnam. Dr King had made himself an enemy of the state by criticising the US government's invasion. Muhammad Ali had been banned from boxing for refusing to take up arms against the Vietnamese while he felt his people were 'treated like dogs and denied simple human rights' in his home city, Louisville, Kentucky. In the days when politically charged pop music rode high in the charts as well as in my consciousness, UB40 released their second album, *Present Arms* (1981). Its opening title track, with blazing horns and anti-war lyrics, was an antidote to any talk of military service.

Did my beliefs mean I was being disloyal to Britain? I didn't think so – this was the country in which I had been born, which meant something. I didn't even mind the monarchy, despite any latent socialist feelings I was developing. I understood from a young age that the Royal Family had an economic and cultural value to Britain; I'd even taken many American relatives to visit Buckingham Palace and the Tower of London (at their request).

Was I a pacifist perhaps? Hardly! Far from being able to turn the other cheek, I was having bar-room brawls every other week in Bristol, plus regular run-ins with the police, fuelling my anger further (although firing a gun is something I've never chosen to do).

Was I being ungrateful, then? Former friends and media acolytes of the government had united in an unholy alliance to claim that I should be paying back a debt of gratitude for being allowed into the country. They'd clearly forgotten that my parents had long since paid that debt back, on my generation's behalf, by sweeping their dirty platforms clean, changing bedpans, and worse.

Thankfully, I was not asked to test my principles or resolve by going to prison rather than signing up for war duty, as the conscription debates proved false rumours. On 14 June 1982, Britain rejoiced in its victory of the Falklands, sweeping Thatcher back in power for another term. The conscription debate, however, had raised important questions about my character, heritage and the land of my birth as I sought my identity throughout my adolescence.

Dealing with Racism

As my skinny frame belatedly began to fill out, my mind also began to grow. I was becoming more frustrated and confused by the people around me. Many people kept saying to me, 'Race makes no difference, we are all the same underneath' and other platitudes, but on the news, at home and all around the globe, I saw people being treated differently because of the colour of their skin.

What was so difficult, I wondered, about giving fellow human beings respect and to stop using racist language? Why was it so socially ingrained in the white area I called home to call Black people *niggers, coons, wogs* and *darkies* so casually? I protested against this racist language vehemently, and sometimes violently. Where once I would have ignored being called racist names, I now answered back defiantly or lashed out with my fists, despite sometimes being outnumbered or lacking the fighting skills. One night this became costly. As I stepped alone off the last bus home, I heard the familiar wounding call of 'nigger', and turned around to meet a fist and then flying boots. I still bear the result of that attack, as a deep wound turned into a scar on my upper lip. Initially I was traumatised by the attack but, after a while, I rationalised it, put it down to being alone in the wrong place at the wrong time, and moved on without a word to the police. Many such racist attacks went unreported due to a lack of trust in the authorities. Ironically later on, during my housing career, I would work with the police to tackle racial harassment and hate crime with SARI (Support Against Racism and Inequality, renamed Stand Against Racism & Inequality in 2013).

Eventually I persuaded people around me to refrain from using racist remarks with words, not violence. I was pleased that my hard-fought campaign had partially been won; however, in later years I was informed by friends that, out of earshot, the use of racist language continued unabated, which sickened me.

I grew equally uncomfortable at the regularity of insults and jokes against Asians. In the local bars I visited, the people I had grown up with called Asian people *ragheads, chinky, slit-eyes* or *Paki*, casually lumping a third of the planet's population into a vile grouping stirred up by opposition to immigration, rife in much of the media at the time.

For speaking up against racism, people said I had a 'chip on my shoulder', a term that has succeeded in angering me ever since I first heard it, aged eleven, in my first year of senior school. I assumed anyone saying it to me was trying to put me down. In time a new taunt emerged: I was dubbed 'Malcolm X' because of my growing militancy. He was a man I'd known little about, other than that he had derogatory views about white people, before I discovered that he was 'the hate that hate produced'. Unlike Dr King, with his non-violent strategy of uprising, Malcolm X was prepared to fight for his equality. I had seen the famous picture, reprinted many times on T-shirts and posters, of a suited Malcolm X cautiously peering out of a window, looking for assailants with a rifle in one arm, and the words 'By Any Means Necessary' stamped across it. I learned that this hate and some of his ideology had come from having his early life destroyed by racism, including the murders of family members.

All these slurs didn't help me get any nearer defining who I actually was. What was this 'identity' thing anyway? Where was I from, and what did it all mean? I constantly wondered. My well-being would have been at risk if I'd declared myself American – a fleeting desire to sound more glamorous to my gang of mates, a mixed collective of white, Black, Asian and mixed-race boys who were literally my surrogate brothers in arms. We resembled the musical bands we worshipped, The Specials, UB40 and The Beat. Their down-to-earth attitudes kept me sane and ensured my views were rooted in reality. I couldn't just make up where I was from, so I needed to get to the bottom of it.

From the playground onwards, I had been taunted and repeatedly told to 'Go back home to your own country!' Often this was even shouted at me from a passing car as I waited to cross the road. I was stung at first to rage, then reflection.

I was born in England, and carried a British passport, but my parents were West Indian. So was 'home' the Caribbean, and did that mean I was West Indian? This ideology was fine and sat comfortably within me – until I visited the Caribbean and was teased warmly by the locals for my *Englishness*. Once again I felt like an outsider; not knowing my true self; rootless, if not homeless. My two older sisters Laurice and Marilyn had been born in Guyana, and had travelled over with my parents when they were aged six and five. They would not let me forget that *they* were the ones with the authentic badge of honour of having been born there, and not in the UK as I had been. Was I African, then? Well, apart from the Pyramids, the only thing we learned at home or school about Africa was the negative stereotypical image of mud huts and starvation. Who wanted to say they came from there? It was hardly empowering.

'Afro-Caribbean' was the label with which I was profiled by the state, but what did that term actually mean to me? My heritage was from Africa and my people were from the Caribbean, but these monikers didn't take into account the country in which I had actually been born. Mind you, back then that wasn't a club I either wanted to join or of which I was being offered membership.

My skin colour posed more dilemmas and contradictions. I knew I was definitely not 'coloured' as in a rainbow. Brown was my natural skin colour, but I was equally uncomfortable with that as a term. As for having no skin colour at all, or being colour-blind, well, for as long as I could remember I had been made to feel different, from being the last one to be picked for kiss-touch by young white girls to being placed on the wing in football matches by ignorant teachers who'd say it was because 'Your lot are really fast!' That left 'Black' with the B capitalised and used as a political term and not merely a colour. It was popularised by activists from America who wore Afros that were works of art, accompanied by dark sunglasses and Superfly clothes. They had an attitude and a message that was inspiring and empowering to a generation and best summarised by James Brown's 1968 anthem, 'Say it Loud, I'm Black and I'm Proud'.

Throughout my teenage tearaway years and into my maturing twenties it was Black America, not Africa, which was the major inspiration for us, the first generation born in Britain, but termed as second generation. We admired America's icons, heroes, sport stars, actors, musicians, writers and entertainers. There was a plethora of images and sounds to be proud of and inspired by. Once we'd learned, absorbed and understood these examples of how our American cousins had forged their pride and identity from their own joint African and American roots, we could begin to create our identity through our own history and experiences. This rich culture coming from across the ocean made me long to visit again, but unfortunately I could only observe at a distance as the lack of a job meant America would be unaffordable to me for over a decade.

The Early Nineties – Divided Societies

Since Margaret Thatcher had come to power in 1979, instead of practical, useful apprenticeships, my generation had the vastly inferior Youth Training Schemes to supposedly help us into employment. I trained as a warehouseman, ground-worker and general builder to no great effect or aptitude, leaving me ill-equipped for any decent career. Years of fruitless labour and unemployment wore on, leaving me jaded with life. Along with these policies, which put and kept the poor at the bottom of society, the prevailing haughty attitudes towards the unemployed and impoverished didn't help our cause by suggesting it was somehow our fault that we didn't have jobs. We were work-shy or too lazy. This was illustrated by Norman Tebbit's request to 'get on our bikes' and find non-existent jobs – or maybe he just wanted us to get healthier...

Thatcher compounded the common view at the time that it was everyone for themselves when she famously declared, 'There's no such thing as society' in an interview with *Woman's Own* magazine in 1987.

Across the pond, things weren't much better. Thatcher's buddy, President Ronald Reagan, and his Reaganomics were dividing America along class lines, creating a tinderbox in poor – and usually Black – communities. This added to the anger seen in the Los Angeles race riots in 1992, which were incited by police brutality after amateur footage of Rodney King being beaten repeatedly by four Los Angeles Police Department (LAPD) officers while he lay on the ground, was beamed around the world. The acquittal of the LAPD officers following their trial led to six nights of rioting, looting and carnage, including fifty-three deaths and billions of dollars' worth of damage.

The Re-Education of Roger Griffith

For me, music was always the light in the darkness, in the United States and UK. At home *UB40,* a multicultural Reggae band from Birmingham, named themselves after the form used to register for unemployment. They called their first album *Signing Off* (1980), a term that meant coming off the unemployment register, or 'dole' as it was known. They also had a hit a year later with 'One in Ten', which was the government statistic of the number of unemployed adults in the United Kingdom; a statistic that was, and sadly still remains, much higher in the inner cities.

Alongside unemployment, the government's policing policies targeted Black youth with the 'stop and search' (SUS) laws, allowing the police to stop and search anyone they suspected of committing a crime. SUS allowed the police misguidedly to target a large proportion of Black youth, disrupting their daily lives and merely succeeding in increasing hostility and animosity on both sides. Whether innocent or guilty, a worryingly large proportion of people who died or were injured in police custody were Black men, a statistic which was met with indifference from the authorities.

Injustice, heavy-handed policing and a lack of opportunity were daily factors in inner-city Britain and America, so it was a surprise only to the establishment when the lid blew off the pressure cooker and exploded into riots on both sides of the Atlantic. These factors of life around me challenged me to explore myself and begin to shape my own identity. It also made me want to understand how people had overcome similar inequalities in other countries. I sought new knowledge and became eager to explore civil rights stories from America, and then South Africa.

With a paucity of Black British role models, I devoured Black literature from around the globe. I read about the abhorrence of South African Apartheid, beginning with Nelson Mandela. I felt that anyone who was an enemy of Margaret Thatcher – who branded Mandela a terrorist – was definitely a friend of mine. His struggle for freedom was beginning to make him a cause célèbre around the world, as the *Free Nelson Mandela* campaign, led by Amnesty International and accompanied by a hit song of the same name by The Special AKA, attracted attention and finally led to his release in 1990.

Watching Richard Attenborough's epic 1987 film, *Cry Freedom* about Stephen Biko, starring my favourite actor, Denzel Washington, led me to uncover more about the ideology to end Apartheid that had cost Biko his life. I read more stories about the horrors of Apartheid, including the Sharpeville Massacre of 1960 where sixty-nine unarmed protesters, including ten children, were shot down for refusing to carry their pass-books. In Allister Sparks's book, *The Mind of South Africa*, I discovered how the evils of Apartheid were not only created but also re-enforced and supported by governments around the world, including the one that was making my life a misery.

I added Black literature to Black politics, reading novels by Toni Morrison, Maya Angelou, Alice Walker and James Baldwin which enriched my mind and my soul. I devoured *The Autobiography of Malcolm X* as told to the late Alex Haley, detailing the demonised and misunderstood man after whom I had been nicknamed, which gave me pride and strength.

The powerful street poetry, otherwise known as rap, and in particular the Hip-Hop group Public Enemy who emerged in the late-eighties, was like listening to a Black encyclopaedia, where I seemed to find new Afrocentric references on each listen. This new knowledge did not turn me against white people, or even make me feel anger towards them, despite my experiences of violent encounters, abuse and mistreatment at the hands of some. Instead I found meaning in the conclusions of Dr Martin Luther King Jr and Malcolm X: that violence, though an understandable reaction, was not a solution, and would do nothing to solve the race issues of the world. I also found plenty of people willing to help me help myself as I began my career in housing.

For the first time, education became fun and enjoyable, and I was developing a desire for more of it. The search for my identity was not only being forged, but was proving to be elevating my life and my soul. Closer to home, I was starting to understand fully the legacy I had been given from the first group of explorers to arrive en masse from the Caribbean – the *Windrush* Generation.

3

The *Windrush* Generation

My parents are part of the *Windrush* Generation, named after the ship that began the mass influx in 1948, continuing through the fifties and sixties, of people from the Caribbean, and then the wider Commonwealth, travelling to England to start a new life. Their arrival would change not only the face of a nation, but also its very identity.

My father left Guyana's capital, Georgetown, for England in 1958, travelling for thirty days via plane and boat through the Caribbean, and then via ship across the Atlantic. As was common at the time, he sent for my mother and my two sisters two years later, before I was born in the United Kingdom. Having paid his fare to Britain for £65, he joined his two elder brothers, including my Uncle Varney who had already been in London for two years.

Passengers paid around £28 for their passage on the first boat, the *Empire Windrush*. It had been used for carrying troops in World War II, but on 22 June 1948 it brought 492 people travelling from Jamaica to Britain. The largest group of West Indian immigrants to arrive in the UK since the war landed at Tilbury Docks, near London, to help rebuild a country ravaged by war. Although Britain was victorious over Germany in its fight for freedom, it had lost a lot of its menfolk, and its infrastructure was badly damaged. There was much work to be done and not enough people to do it, so the British government placed advertisements in West Indian newspapers, and word-of-mouth spread fast about the new opportunities abroad to make money and begin a new life. The migrants were invited guests, given full rights to enter Britain by the 1948 Nationality Act, which made all the people of the former colonies of the British

Commonwealth into British citizens. This, and a less than idyllic life in their home countries, sparked many to leave the land of their birth in search of the new Promised Land and Jerusalem.

The History Behind West Indian Migration

The images of the first migrants filing off the *Empire Windrush*, dressed in their 'Sunday best' suits and ties or dresses and smart shoes with an array of hats, have become an important landmark moment for future generations of Black Britons. It was a key event in the history of multiculturalism in the United Kingdom, which is now imprinted on everyone's consciousness after much work to keep this crucial piece of the history of these isles fresh in people's minds. Maybe because it was then relatively recent, I was never taught about it in school. It was only in my late-teens that I began exploring more about how I came to be in England, and how this story changed society forever. It is an inspirational tale of hopes and dreams, frustration and fear, which needs to be shared through the generations.

As the first pioneers strode apprehensively off the ship, their feelings must have been all over the place as they encountered customs with which they were familiar and a country they felt loyal towards. Speaking the language was not only an advantage, but also part of their upbringing, plus they had also been taught many aspects of British life and society. The grip of British colonialism was strong in the Caribbean, and had been in place since the establishment of the West Indies during slavery. Most of West Indian social structures, governance and commerce came from Britain, which presided regally over its subjects. They had only ever known European rule and referred to Britain as 'the mother country', with London the metropole or centre of the Empire. King George VI, and latterly Queen Elizabeth II, were recognised warmly as the heads of state for the region. Many men had already fought for Britain and the free world in the war against Hitler, whose ideology would have readily exterminated them with the same irrational pathological hatred used against the Jews.

Victorian values prevailed among the residents in the Caribbean, and Christianity, through Anglicism and the Church of England, was the dominant religion. Gifted West Indian students had enjoyed scholarships to the UK since the early part of the twentieth century. In busy Caribbean cities a person would be likely to see a policeman directing traffic wearing full uniform, including white gloves, just like his counterparts in the UK. Some of the Caribbean capital cities take their name from the Crown such as *Kings*ton and *George*town. Some countries, parishes, capitals and districts were named after Christian saints, including St Vincent, St John (Antigua) and St James (Barbados); some after The Queen herself – Victoria (Jamaica) – just like its Commonwealth cousins in the Antipodean islands. High commissioners, governors and diplomats ran the Caribbean under successive British governments. The education system, infrastructure, rules and governance that existed throughout the English-speaking chain of islands that stretched from Jamaica through the Caribbean Sea to Trinidad, and on to mainland South America to include Guyana, had been developed through colonialism, and became an integral part of the British Empire.

During the eighteenth and nineteenth centuries, much of Britain's power in the world came through its colonies, which Britain harvested, much like any diligent farmer, to meet its own specific needs and demands, extracting raw materials or growing specific crops where required. This interrupted the natural development of many islands in the Caribbean, leaving the colonised countries with land not fit for growing a variety of produce, and just a few crops per island, such as sugar, rice or wood, for exporting. Now, the empire was coming for its people, starting a mass brain and talent drain with the willing help of West Indians eager to escape the lack of opportunity at home and build an exciting life somewhere new. This relationship, for better or worse, certainly gave Britain a massive boost in rebuilding the nation after World War II, and a huge labour advantage over its European neighbours.

These historical, social and political factors were all a familiarity of life for the residents of the Caribbean Islands. It is easy to under-estimate their sense of loyalty; of 'doing their bit' for the motherland who had requested their help. Life in the Caribbean was a struggle, with limited prospects for advancement. Remarkably, the latent racism based on skin colour, as practised since the days of slavery, was still as rife and as common as in a Georgia cotton field, meaning the lighter someone's skin colour was, the better their overall prospects would be. Thus the push factors to leave were established, and coupled with the chance of adventure, the attraction of personal wealth and family connections across the ocean, they meant most were happy to leave. West Indians had a dream of living in a place that would be welcoming, with plentiful, varied and fulfilling work; a nation of which they already felt an extended part. Hopes and expectations were high, and new frontiers in Britain and also America were being established as the different peoples of the Caribbean sought their fortunes abroad. However, just like any gold rush in history, a degree of disappointment was inevitable, and in the beginning there were always going to be more losers than winners.

Arrival on *Empire Windrush* and Beyond

The first pioneers found the streets were not paved with gold, as had been mythically represented, but instead with a harsh coldness that emanated from the climate as well as from the local populace. While successive governments had encouraged the migration, no one, it seemed, had talked openly to the nation about the new arrivals. Britain, though liberated, was just emerging from rationing and coming to terms with the brutal consequences of war. The war spirit had held the country together, but life was about to change again, and the people needed to be, at the very least, informed of the newcomers' arrival and what they could do to help create harmonious relations. Instead, the unfriendliness and hostility the Caribbean pioneers received from their hosts was as much a shock to their system as the often bleak and bomb-damaged landscape. Hitler's Luftwaffe had decimated many British cities' skylines, leaving destroyed buildings and roads, on top of which heavy smog clung to the air. Endless rain and harsh winters found many newcomers unprepared for weather and conditions beyond their shared comprehension.

For these West Indians, and the many that followed, the only sight they had previously seen of white people was of landed gentry or royal subjects in the Caribbean. The sight of poverty-stricken, illiterate white people living in squalor, and in some areas in worse conditions than in the Caribbean, was a shock to the system. Accents were different to The Queen's English; people spoke with various colloquial dialects, such as *cockney, scouse* and *brummie,* adding to the misunderstanding. Few of the local populace could identify from which island the newcomers had come, or worse, even differentiate between Africa and the West Indies. They seemed more interested in when the pioneers were going back 'home' than in the contributions they could make.

Despite African-American and West Indian servicemen being stationed in the UK during the war, for many British people it was their first sighting of Black skin. Verbal abuse, harsh stares and ostracism were commonplace. It was a metaphorical, and sometimes literal, slap in the face for those brought up with the idea of British fair play, nobility and (apparently not so) common decency.

How My Family Found Their New Home

My parents joined the quest of so many to build a new life for themselves, and became preoccupied with negotiating the difficulties of this new land where racism was always in the background. Theirs was a stoic generation, ironically and indelibly imprinted with the British stiff upper lip in their armour for braving a new environment. They rarely talked openly or publicly, or bemoaned their treatment, and never complained to their children about their experiences; however, we couldn't fail to notice their brooding sense of resentment and frustration.

My father had a wide range of skills. Before he came to England he had been a tailor, made repairs at the harbour and worked at the bank in Georgetown. 'You turned your hand to anything you could, to either help or make a shilling,' he readily recalled. I remember he was a trained barber, and would cut his brothers' hair and my own, before the age when 'high-top fades' and 'No 1' haircut designs became fashionable for Black youth. For him, coming to England was a chance to learn a full trade and gain prestige. He saw it as an opportunity that couldn't fail to make a better life for himself and his young family.

My father, being of dark skin like me, was a victim of the bizarre caste system in the West Indies. This was a relic from plantation life based on colour pigmentation, which is sadly still around in parts of Brazil, America, Africa, Asia and the West Indies. Needless to say, he was glad to get away and have the chance to make something of his life rather than be held back by old prejudices.

The sense of pride of those who remained in the Caribbean cannot be underestimated. On learning that one of his nephews was coming to Britain, my father's uncle naively wrote to Winston Churchill to announce the Griffith role in helping the motherland. To his credit, Winston Churchill's office replied, and my father carried the letter with him to England, proudly presenting the document to his older brother, my uncle Varney, along with strict instructions from their father to pop in and say hello to the prime minister, Winston Churchill. Clearly the Griffiths and the Churchills were now pen pals and friends. Tears of warmth still spring to my eyes when I recall Uncle Varney laughing about this, and lovingly recounting how my father, the green 'bwoy' from the bush of Guyana, clutching only a letter and a suitcase, would ask for directions to number 10 Downing Street, thinking he could have an audience with the great Winston Churchill.

These, then, were the often repeated push-pull factors that brought my parents to Britain, and the answers given whenever friends asked why my parents and their ilk left all the natural beauty of the Caribbean behind to come to Britain and start life at the bottom of both the employment and social ladders.

Employment for All
Although joining at the very bottom, my father was pleased to join the ranks of the London Underground at Archway station in 1961. He felt proud to don his uniform, including a blue and yellow striped cap which made his head hurt. His first assignment was sweeping the

station, and he recalls at one point scuttling back into the shadows in shame as he recognised a female friend from Guyana. Like many Black and brown people of that time, he did what he could to provide and maintain, as he put it, 'in supporting his family'. He began to rise through the colour bar of London Transport, moving from sweeping the floors to ticket collector, then guard. 'Mind the closing doors!' he would bellow at me when I was a boy in a parody of himself. He progressed to driving trains, and eventually his people skills led to a move 'upstairs', as he put it, into management. Born into a loyal family of royalists, he was never prouder than when, as station manager for Green Park station, he greeted Prince Charles at the opening of the Jubilee line on 30 April 1979, the day after his forty-sixth birthday.

Many newcomers found employment in national institutions, such as the newly established National Health Service, public transport services and the Post Office, all of whom recruited extensively from the new migrants. In the Midlands and northern England, industries clicked into action; no longer geared to producing instruments of war, they now restarted manufacturing textiles, cars, steel and coal. Although work was plentiful, it was hard and unrelenting, and often the jobs that the locals did not want to do, meaning the pay was poor. Colour bars existed in white-collar and skilled jobs, forcing migrants to take unskilled labour. The recruitment drives in the Caribbean, which had helped fuel the gold rush, were invitations to take generous employment, but when the workers arrived they found themselves placed on the lowest rung of the employment ladder, regardless of ability. The new migrants began life in the UK as factory workers, nursing assistants or glorified cleaners, emptying bedpans or sweeping up mess, so the money earned was certainly not enough to return home with a king's ransom. Besides, the *Windrush* Generation and those that followed were here to help rebuild the nation and to help their families 'back home'. Money earned, however minimal, was set aside to send home, or for future housing projects such as 'pardnering': a form of mutual co-operative savings bank to pool money together. This meant that for modest outlays relatively large amounts of cash were available for essential large outgoings, such as deposits on homes. What money remained was used for food and lodgings.

Housing

The first settlers from the *Empire Windrush* were temporarily housed in Clapham, south-west London. They would later move on to establish a vibrant community in nearby Brixton, which would become synonymous with the image Britain, and indeed the rest of the world, has of West Indians living in the UK. Other towns and cities in England were also beacons for the migrants, who settled in inner-city areas which were generally already notorious, or run-down and became demonised as ghettos. These included Moss Side in Manchester, Chapeltown in Leeds and Burngreave in Sheffield; Handsworth, Birmingham and St Ann's, Nottingham; Whitmore Reans, Wolverhampton and, in southern England, St Pauls in Bristol. In Butetown/Tiger Bay, Cardiff, and Toxteth, Liverpool, migrants joined established communities with a history of a Black presence from African seamen who had settled there since the nineteenth century.

Although the migrants found employment, finding shelter proved more difficult. With the basic human need of providing a roof over one's head being the overriding concern of the day, many were forced to accept substandard accommodation. There was no central provision or planning made, and local authority housing lists were based on residency in the country, criteria which the migrants clearly could not meet. No extra housing was provided, and they were left to fend for themselves in a hostile environment, enduring intolerance and racism from the local white population. Many of the locals did not want the newcomers as neighbours, or in the country at all, and did nothing to hide their displeasure. The signs reading 'No Coloureds! No Irish! No Dogs!' that were placed in windows endured as an everyday reminder of the latent hostility for the *Windrush* Generation, and have gone down in folklore.

Housing was in short supply following the wartime bombings, and many slept several to a room wherever they could find space.

Conditions were harsh and overcrowding rife. With deprivation exacerbated by uninsulated and poorly heated properties, the newcomers also endured diseases and respiratory illnesses, including tuberculosis, which helped to demonise their reputations.

Exploitation was rife, with the slum landlord Peter Rachman's name being synonymous with sub-standard housing and unscrupulous landlords – the inspiration for Rachman Housing, which I would later study as part of my housing career. Rachman got around the problem of statutory sitting tenants, who had been given the right to stay in their properties at a fixed rent for the duration of their lives, meaning that property developers like him could not increase rents and boost their profits. He intimidated the sitting tenants by carrying out building works around them, including taking the roof off properties, and installing the new migrants, or even prostitutes, as neighbours, resulting in 'white-flight'. Rachman was the one who did make a king's ransom from the new migrants, amassing a huge fortune by expanding his empire on the basic principle of supply and demand. He abused the then unregulated housing market by buying up large mansion houses in west London and converting them into flats and rooms, then renting to the housing-starved newcomers who could not find homes elsewhere, and who would not complain to the authorities at the inflated rents as they felt fortunate to have a roof over their heads. However, despite having shelter, their conditions inside were restricted to an outrageous degree. Cooking is as much a part of West Indian culture as the sunny climate the migrants had left behind, but if they wanted a freshly cooked meal, they would have to queue for a place on the stove with their pot parked on the stairs and their money ready for the meter. In some cases, kitchens were removed to make an extra room in which to cram more paying tenants, with the bathroom doubling up as a kitchen.

Paraffin heaters or one-bar electric heaters would struggle against the cold, and the smell from the fumes would seep into clothes. The early pioneers readily recollect that smell, which would be apparent to everyone when they travelled on public transport. Accompanying passengers would immediately be able to detect the type of conditions migrants lived in.

Those happy to house the migrants were pressured not to, or felt ashamed of having 'coloureds' living in their homes and would hide their new intake away from their friends. The migrants faced restrictions on bathing, cooking, whom they had as visitors, or the time they had to come home, much like a child would be treated by an adult.

Social Life

Very few children travelled over to the UK until their elders felt settled enough. Initially there was a larger ratio of men to women, around three to one, travelling to the UK. Many had transient lifestyles, and did not feel it was safe or fair to raise children in foreign lands until they had found out more about the new country, where life was proving tougher than expected.

In addition to a hostile welcome in the world of employment and housing, even when they turned to a range of social activities to relieve the stress and join British society, Caribbean migrants faced discrimination and exclusion. Simple courtesies that were an everyday occurrence in the Caribbean, such as saying 'Good morning' or 'Hello' with a smile, were not commonplace in the United Kingdom, and were sometimes met with a stony silence or an aggressive glare.

Many men and women who were used to the Sunday morning ritual of going to church, and the comforting sense of belonging to a religious community, found that they were not even made welcome there. My mother remembers the local vicar pretending to be busy and refusing to acknowledge her as she queued to meet him after the service. Other churchgoers would refuse to use the cup of Communion after them, which stung these Christians deeply. These less than subtle slights led to the growth of the Black church in the UK through evangelical churches, such as Seventh-day Adventists, New Testament and Pentecostal churches, where people could congregate and meet for support.

Another bastion of society and fair play, which held the unity of working men's and women's rights at its core, was the trade union movement. This blocked the employment path of the new migrants. The trade unions, driven by a fear of the use of cheap labour to replace their workers, began practices of protectionism or closed shops. There were restrictions placed on the grade and level of employment for the migrants, and even industrial action was taken, with union members walking out on strike when Black or Asian people were employed.

Going to nightclubs or pubs could be met with further ostracism or intimidation. Physical violence could be meted out to those who roamed the streets alone, particularly from the Teddy Boys who formed that generation's dominant male adolescent street gang.

Faced with this hostile environment in employment, housing and within their social lives, an extraordinary spirit emerged as the new arrivals created their own social institutions. Support systems grew, and a burgeoning sense of collectiveness, pardnering and new communication methods were introduced. The barber's shop then, as now, became a fundamental institution of Afro-Caribbean life, spreading news of work, travel details or gossip from the Caribbean.

Two other major areas within socialisation and culture were to leave a lasting impression on Britain. They would entertain many, and boost the economy and reputation of the country. This happened with sport, initially through cricket, and then through football from the 1980s, and the creation of a vibrant underground music and nightlife scene, which is still thriving today.

Cricket, Lovely Cricket

The empire of Great Britain's dominance over its colonies has long since subsided, including the loss of America. But throughout the world, Britain still holds an influence, consistently punching above its weight for a nation of its size. One example of this is through its invention of sporting games, and one in particular which has had profound cultural, social and political influences much greater than a mere game, is cricket. The phrase 'that's not cricket' has a global significance, meaning something underhand or crooked, and also something at the heart of Englishness in terms of fair play and decency. Cricket is played predominately in the former British colonies of Australia, New Zealand, Pakistan, Bangladesh, Zimbabwe, South Africa, Sri Lanka, India and, of course, the West Indies. It is extraordinary how this bastion of Englishness took root in these alien lands, and not only was embraced, but also became a part of the fabric and culture of all these Test-playing nations. Each one of these colonies has given the game a new flourish and added to its rich history, and in England, cricket has helped break down class and social barriers.

In the West Indies, cricket holds its own political and social significance, and is arguably the one single institution that bonds the region of separate countries together. Originally, following the introduction of the game to the West Indies in the eighteenth century, Black players were only allowed to fetch the ball back from the cane fields beyond the boundary, before eventually being invited to join in. However, until the turn of the twentieth century, only white players were allowed to represent the West Indies, as a collection of bankers, merchants, landowners and noblemen took to the field under the region's banner. When Black players did enter the team, they faced an unofficial apartheid in terms of which position they could play and which cricketing clubs they could join. Most significantly, the region's team was not allowed to have a Black man as its captain and leader.

Over time, within the Caribbean it was felt a Black cricket captain would prove a true distinction of meritocracy. It would also reflect the growing calls for independence emanating from the Caribbean islands that wanted to determine their own future, as was championed since the 1930s by the first recognised great West Indian player, Learie Constantine from Trinidad.

The Lord's Test, 1950

In 1950, two years after *Windrush's* arrival in the UK, a West Indian team which would reflect the true diversity of the West Indies, including East Asians like Sonny Ramadhin, arrived to play a Test in England. The British had taken large numbers of Asians to the West Indies as indentured labour, particularly to Trinidad and my parents' home of Guyana, altering those nations' identities, and latterly their politics. This groundbreaking test series was widely followed throughout the Caribbean, and for the first time by West Indians in England. The plight and hardship of the migrants from the various islands created solidarity, and they now united under the West Indies cricket team flag. It is still a unifying force today. No more Trini, Jamaican, Bajan, Guyanese or small islander; they were now West Indian, a fact they faced every day on the streets of the communities in which they lived.

The West Indies won the series three to one, inducing parties and jubilation of carnival proportions in the West Indies and, for the first time, in England. After the first victorious West Indian team ever to win a match on English soil at Lord's, London, calypsonians Lord Kitchener and Lord Beginner were said to have led a dance from the ground in St. John's Wood to Trafalgar Square, followed by many spectators and revellers from both sides. The respect earned after the victory was new. If the West Indians could strategise, play to set fielding patterns, abide by moral codes of sportsmanship and show teamwork and leadership, then the migrants could be better respected and trusted in roles worth more than sweeping floors.

The West Indies had beaten the motherland at the home and headquarters of cricket. Independence from Britain followed during the fifties, and after a long campaign led by the author CLR James, Frank Worrell was finally granted the captaincy for the 1960 series against Australia. Due to his leadership, a united team representing the diverse regions of the Caribbean would play exciting cricket around the world. After a narrow, entertaining defeat, his team were given a ticker tape parade by thousands of their hosts in Melbourne, and the accolades continued when they arrived home. Worrell and his teammates, the legends Clyde Walcott and Everton Weekes, were known collectively as the 'Three Ws', and also Garfield Sobers, would all be awarded knighthoods by The Queen. Together, they set the template for a period of cricketing domination that was to last for nearly twenty years, and help forge West Indian identity and pride.

Just as Jesse Owens had done in front of Hitler on the running track of Berlin at the 1936 Olympics, these sporting greats had reshaped the context of how a Black man was perceived in the world with ramifications far wider than a playing field, showing that sport was more than just a game.

In the UK, a number of local cricket clubs were started as social support structures within Black communities. One, the Bristol West Indies Cricket Club, would later produce David 'Syd' Lawrence, who represented England at international level. Indeed, the children of these West Indian supporters may have failed Norman Tebbit's 'cricket test', but they would play major roles in an array of victorious British sporting teams, from cricket to football, and also helping British success in athletics, and both Rugby Union and League.

Nightlife

The first arrivals being predominately male, and having none of the social constraints to hold them with families not arrived or established as yet, they did what many a single male had done in any frontier town – they had a good time. A network of unregistered clubs and dances, known as 'Blues' or 'Shebeens', sprang up to serve their needs. Word spread throughout the cities that these were the places to be to have a good time, and none was more so than Notting Hill, west London, within the same area that Peter Rachman had built his empire and notoriety. They even used some of his houses. Alcohol, gambling, smoking, dancing, recreational drugs and music were in abundance, as was a notoriously ready supply of female company of all races and backgrounds, eventually causing a government crisis, international scandal and headlines through the Profumo Affair.

My uncle Varney came to London in 1958, two years before my dad, and worked in the West End of London during the Swinging Sixties. Back in Guyana, one of his many jobs had been working in the jungle in the heart of the Guyanese interior, mining one of the country's chief products, bauxite ore, for use in aluminium. Now in the United Kingdom, Uncle Varney became a telephone engineer, installing new landlines to homes and businesses in London. He would reminisce and chuckle about the good times in the sixties, when nightclub owners would plead with him to install their telephones earlier than their competitors in return for free entry at the head of the queue. He would take full advantage of his host's generous hospitality. He was a keen dancer, before an operation left him housebound and confined to a wheelchair. When I used to sit with him and he talked of this era, his face would light up with the mischievous Griffith devilment that I have been fortunate to inherit.

The West Indian parties flourished in the tight, confined, dark spaces, and attracted many others. People travelled from nearby Soho in London's West End, knowing they could get all the illicit entertainment they required with near impunity. Unable to get a firm foothold on the employment ladder, they found the fruits of crime began to pay and, although exaggerated at the time, Black men began to date white women, and acquired a reputation for pimping and prostitution. Inevitably, resentment, negative stories and hostility grew about the new settlers, who were caught in a vicious circle of competing with the poor white working classes for scarce housing resources and job prospects, all the while living in conditions that were not of their own making. These harsh early experiences were to mark West Indian relations with the wider community for a number of years, and marred relations between the races.

The authorities overlooked the new frontier spirit that had been created, until the pressure keg exploded in 1958 when riots broke out in Notting Hill and Nottingham following attacks by white youths on the Caribbean community. Over the August bank-holiday weekend in Notting Hill, gangs of mostly Teddy Boys, who had been urged by Oswald Mosley's Blackshirts from the Fascist Union Movement and other far-right groups to 'Keep Britain White', armed themselves with sticks, knives and bottles. They gathered, seeking to cause havoc and to mirror some of the violent beatings their Nottingham counterparts had meted out to the St Ann's West Indian community, where thousands had rampaged a week earlier. The West Indian community was not prepared just to sit back and accept the unofficial occupation, and fought back, seeking to defend themselves. Fuelled with years of abuse and harassment, people came from all over London to help defend the Notting Hill community. Molotov cocktails were exchanged and bloody beatings handed out on both sides. The police were ineffective and were caught squarely in the middle of the two sides, but did manage to arrest 140 people from all warring parties.

Following the riots, local community and civic leaders met, led by Trinidadian Claudia Jones, who was the founder and editor of one of the first newspapers for the new community in Britain, *The West Indian Gazette*. They began the annual Notting Hill Carnival in 1959 as a positive response of the Caribbean community to the violence that had preceded it. The aim was not only to unite forces, but also to represent the magic, atmosphere and revelry from back home, and show everyone not only that were Black people peaceful and could throw a great party, but also that Black people in Britain, with their various cultures, were here to stay.

Movement of a People: An Overview of the *Windrush* Generation

Over 60,000 people settled in Britain from the Caribbean between the *Windrush's* arrival in 1948 and 1962, and, although many had not intended to stay for long, Britain became 'better the devil you know' and many did not return home. With the riots of the late-1950s, and more people arriving from the subcontinent, Britain began to take notice of its so-called 'colour problem'. The total number of new migrants was relatively small in comparison to the overall population figures at less than one per cent of the UK population, comprising approximately 500,000 Black and Asian people. By 1962, that figure had doubled in two years, with the West Indian total being approximately 250,000, according to Home Office figures. The issue of immigration began to take more prominence and came to the attention of leading politicians of the day, who ensured it would be, and is still, a national issue of debate.

With a huge dose of irony, one of the people responsible for the migrants' invitation to the UK, Enoch Powell, became a figure whose political career would become embroiled with controversy and allegations of racism. The invitation to the mother country had come post-war, following the loss of so many men and women in World War II. Enoch Powell as the then Health Minister for the government, and a man who had spent several years in India, had encouraged migrant labour from the Caribbean, Africa and Asia. The *Windrush* Generation saw this as not only their duty, but also their right as a part of the Commonwealth family.

The Commonwealth Immigrants Act of 1962 introduced immigration controls under Harold Wilson's Labour government, based on whether an entrant had ancestry from the UK, and excluding those whose families did not stretch back centuries. This marked the start of the closure of the open-door policy for those from the New Commonwealth, which was little more than euphemism for separating those from Asia, Africa and the West Indies from those from Australia, New Zealand and Canada. In some quarters, it was felt that the controls did not go far enough, and as the Conservative MP for Wolverhampton South, Powell's *River of Blood* speech would firmly bring the issues of race, identity, immigration and politics to the nation's attention.

Enoch Powell and the Rivers of Blood Speech:
The Voice of Babylon, April 1968

The Labour government's 1968 Race Relations Act finally provided new standards of equality, plus a legislative framework to protect Black and Asian people from discrimination in employment, housing and society. In response, Powell delivered his speech just sixteen days after the assassination of Martin Luther King Jr on 20 April 1968. It widened the divide in race relations, which has never been fully repaired, at a time when the nation, through the new legislation, had an opportunity to practise what it preached about decency and fair play.

Powell had been faced with rising complaints from his Wolverhampton constituents about the numbers of Black and Asian immigrants and their impact on local society. He responded with a speech containing the most provocative rhetoric on race in Britain ever heard from a modern parliamentarian, calling for an end to non-white immigration and for repatriation. With the prediction of violence punctuating his speech, in which he declared Rome's River Tiber would be 'foaming with much blood', Powell inflamed the nation further by stating, 'In this country, in fifteen or twenty years' time, the Black man will have the whip hand over the white man.' He accused immigrants of attacking an elderly woman, pushing excrement through her letter box and smashing her windows. Despite the noble efforts of the British media, the woman in question was never found.

Immigrants as a whole were perceived as knowing little of British culture, despite having been immersed in it from colonialism. Powell referred to Black children as 'piccaninnies', a derogatory term from the Deep South of America meaning caricatures of children of African slaves with thick red lips, bulging eyes, unkempt hair and few clothes. Once again, and not for the last time, the tinderbox of race relations exploded. Powell was expelled by Edward Heath from the Conservative Shadow Cabinet at a time when he was seen as a potential future prime minister. He became a martyr for his constituency, who two years later, in 1970, voted him back in for a seventh term as MP with an increased majority of nearly two-thirds of the vote. His words undoubtedly struck a chord with the ordinary man in the street who believed that Powell had only expressed the feelings of many, especially those of the working class, some of whom marched in protest at his sacking.

My mother was a nurse at the time, and not a political firebrand in her views like my father, preferring the quiet dignity, social conscience and local actions the Coleridge side of the family pursued through the Christian Church. She recoiled when I asked her what things were like after Powell's inflammatory speech, and she remembers being met with increased hostility and coldness on her wards in the days that followed the *Rivers of Blood* speech. Her experiences were similar to those of many of the *Windrush* Generation, and such indignities remain a hurtful, hidden scar, never spoken of or shared with us as children. It wasn't until much later in life, when reading about their rough passage, and watching programmes such as BBC Television's award-winning 1998 documentary *Windrush,* produced by Trevor Phillips, a Black Briton born of Guyanese origin, that I discovered I had been sharing a roof with a living piece of history all along.

Powell would continue to raise the issue of immigration, becoming a figurehead for the far-right, and legitimatising propaganda which had its roots embedded in the same philosophy against which Britain had gone to war to protect the world and itself. He gave credence to their message with his undoubted intelligence, and helped to give the far-right a national platform upon which it would build with disturbing consequences.

When Heath's Conservatives defeated the Labour government in the 1970 General Election, it was said that the soft stance by Labour about immigration and race had been a factor in the result. Heath's government introduced more immigration controls following Idi Amin's expulsion of Ugandan Asians. By 1972, only holders of work permits or people with parents or grandparents born in the UK could gain entry, effectively stemming most Caribbean immigration. In the face of growing hostility from the locals and calls to 'Send them back home!' the migrants could always respond with 'We're here because you were there', referring to the time when Britain had amassed its wealth and superiority complex from its colonies.

People from the Caribbean also settled in America due to the proximity of the West Indies to the United States. West Indians made the trip across to America for work, or through entry to the universities as students. However, the McCarran-Walter Act in 1962 also tightened up entry requirements, only admitting immigrants from across the globe with special skills, and placing strict limits per country through quotas.

Both my parents had friends and family who'd migrated to America. They arrived in America to complete contracted hard labour, such as farm labouring or fieldwork. There, if they 'skipped contract' from the employment into which they'd entered, they could be tracked down and beaten to return to work, much like the labour conditions that the slaves had endured several years earlier. Other family members, however, did travel to America to successfully gain an education through scholarships.

The Legacy of the *Windrush* Generation

Thus the colonial dependency cycle of wanting to create a new life and having little reason but climate and family for which to return home was well and truly established. With the monarchy having strong support in the Caribbean, and The Queen being revered throughout her New Commonwealth, the new settlers had a connection to the

UK, unlike in America where West Indians were simply employed as labour. Despite the hostility and racism experienced in the UK, most Caribbean immigrants still felt British, and were better off holding British passports. As the home of the empire, with a schooling system and language Caribbeans had known since their cradles, much hope was invested in Britain for the next generation.

Upon reading some of the accounts from the *Windrush* Generation in *Windrush – The Irresistible Rise of Multi-Racial Britain* by Mike and Trevor Phillips, one can only admire their remarkable durability and restraint. The conditions documented in employment, housing and within their social lives created a siege mentality of staying put and toughing it out. Tensions were inevitable. I am proud of their resilience to ignore the odd brick crashing through their windows, verbal abuse on the streets and in the workplace and resisting intimidation everywhere they went. It surprises me that more didn't get the next vessel home to escape all the UK had to offer. So many stayed to build for their children's future – the first generation to be born in Britain, but known as the Second Generation.

The arrival of those from the New Commonwealth was a Pandora's box for Britain. The gifts of cheap labour and someone to do the jobs that nobody else wanted to do had to be balanced against the loss of identity of a nation. Then, as now, the far-right parties stated that immigration was the reason for a variety of ills, including crime and disease.

In the UK today, the latest demonised set of migrants have arrived from Eastern Europe after the fall of the Berlin Wall and the expansion of the European Community, and also from East Africa following civil war in the region. Support for anti-immigration parties has grown throughout the UK and Europe, with increases in the share of the electoral vote and a number of European seats gained in the last two decades in local and national elections.

This seemingly perpetual spectre of suspicion and dislike of immigrants to Britain is particularly perplexing, since 'foreigners' have been calling Britain home since the Saxons' conquest of these shores, soon followed by the Vikings. The quintessentially English novelist and playwright JB Priestley wrote in his 1934 travelogue, *English Journey,* 'The England admired throughout the world is the England that keeps an open house', and history shows that countries that have opened their doors have gained greatly.

After the Civil War and World War I, the United States turned to non-Americans and developed a policy of immigration to keep up with the growing industrial revolutions of the age and advance the nation. America sometimes describes itself using the phrase, 'We are a nation of immigrants', from a 1963 book by President Kennedy, but it also has its detractors to integration, prompting the formation of the Ku Klux Klan in 1866 by defeated Confederates after the American Civil War.

Black and Asian people were not alone in their migration to Britain. Large numbers from Europe, especially Poland, Italy, Greece and Cyprus, also arrived after World War II. From South-East Asia, including the British colony of Hong Kong, people came with skills to help with reconstruction. The contributions of all these migrant communities to Britain have helped greatly in developing its culture, food, language and even identity. There is little evidence, given the vastly different and diverse skills of the immigrant communities that have settled in the UK, that the fears of British officials have been realised. Ian RG Spencer wrote in his book *British Immigration Policy Since 1939 – The Making of Multi-Racial Britain* that 'the creation of communities of different racial origins living side-by-side would almost certainly result in racial tension and a colour problem on American lines'. Uprisings have occurred, but these, as we'll see later, were due to frustration at the social and economic conditions and policing policies rather than a repeat of the race wars that occurred in Nottingham and London in the late-1950s.

The *Windrush* Generation's offspring have now assimilated into British culture, which in turn has gained a more tolerant attitude to race over the last twenty years, with less openly racist views being expressed. In part this is due to legislation, but I believe it is more to do with the abhorrence of racism generally, compared to the acceptance of racist comments when I was growing up. At least three generations of Britons with African-Caribbean heritage now exist, contributing to British society in virtually every field. The number of British persons born from West Indian parents increased from 15,000 in 1951 to 172,000 in 1961, and went up to 304,000 in 1981. The total population of British persons claiming West Indian heritage today has remained at just over half a million throughout the twentieth and twenty-first centuries, according to the Office for National Statistics.

Recently the Census made provision for those, like myself, wishing to be known as Black-British, which for me represents my heritage as well as the nation into which I was born. Previously, the categories listed were Black Caribbean, Black African and Black Other. Whether we are African, African-Caribbean, West Indian, Mixed-Race/Heritage or now Black-British, this small proportion of the nation has contributed greatly to Britain's recent history and its global prestige around the world.

This claiming of my identity as opposed to the one with which I had been labelled by the authorities – Afro-Caribbean, or had thrust upon me by Pan Africanists – African, has taken many years of private study and journey. I certainly felt that my identity could not be fully understood before I'd looked at my African ancestry, via the Americas and Britain's role in the transatlantic slave trade.

4

Discovering My Roots
via the Transatlantic Slave Trade

Land of the Free, Home of the Slaves

One year after Obama's election, I travelled America searching for answers to major historical questions about slavery involving many places and people across the globe. It troubles me that two of the first three American presidents, George Washington and Thomas Jefferson, kept slaves. They also fully utilised the income their tobacco plantations brought them in their roles as revered patriots and freedom fighters in the new America – ultimately leading to freedom for the slaves. To someone like me who has the blood of African heritage running proudly through my veins, yet knows that my ancestors chopped sugar cane in the heat of the South American sun in Guyana, the issues of freedom and slavery are as contrasting as the difference between light and darkness. My search for some answers to these historical puzzles began at President Jefferson's plantation Monticello in Charlottesville, Virginia.

Monticello is the president's former home, built on a mountain-top with a panoramic vista across Virginia and the nearby university town of which Jefferson was a patron, Charlottesville. His sumptuous twenty-one-room, three-storey neoclassical mansion house – which President Jefferson designed, and which is replicated in his monument on the Washington Mall – dominates the thousands of acres that encompass it. The plantation is a network of gardens, buildings and farms that grew a variety of crops and housed animals tended by over 200 slaves. There is plenty of evidence that Jefferson was a benevolent owner. In keeping with the thinking of the day, he viewed slaves as we would children: unable to live independent lives of their own. As I walked among some of the slaves' quarters – built below ground so as not to spoil the stunning views – I could begin to piece together how such a system existed and flourished.

Plantation owners ruled over millions of lives from the cradle to the grave, and sustained the growth of the transatlantic slave trade. Though British colonial slavery was first used in Virginia, the 'peculiar institution of slavery', as it became known, was assisted by British settlers from Bristol, who brought their African slaves with them from the British colony of Barbados into the then royal colony of South Carolina. Through Charleston, South Carolina's major slave trading port named after King Charles II, a large-scale importation of African slaves arrived and successfully began to cultivate rice on its plantations. Slavery spread to Georgia and throughout the southern states of America, establishing the power and grandiose ways of the plantocracy.

Slavery became entrenched into the southern way of life, which it would take bloodshed and civil war to bring to an end. Tracing the links between the Piedmont tobacco plantations and the newly formed southern plantocracy, I found both spiritual and emotional connections between my home in Bristol, my parents' origins in the West Indies, their family's migration to America, and our shared heritage from West Africa. Like many before me, I began to connect my own past on a vast continental scale via the transatlantic slave trade, from Africa to the Americas, and through to the role of the Europeans.

Slavery and Me

Like many of my generation, my first conscious experience of slavery was through the 1977 television series *Roots*, based on Alex Haley's epic novel. This was when I began to connect the dots of my heritage to the world around me. I experienced a number of emotions, including rage and guilt, but more importantly I was left with a legacy of an awareness of history from this powerful visual testimony. It was compelling family viewing, in addition to my treat, aged eleven, of being taken to the cinema to see the latest James Bond movie (I was named after Roger Moore, who back then was a debonair action hero). I remember watching *Roots* intently every Sunday evening with my mum. As its story unfolded, *Roots* became my story and our shared story. I don't remember wanting to kill white people, or do any of the other things that the media feared might happen at that point in time, but I was engrossed in a story about which I knew absolutely nothing. Having to watch 'your backstory' explained on a TV programme was a deeply unsettling experience.

My mother and I had moved from London to Easton in Bristol. All the environments in which I had lived until then were multicultural and were no preparation for where I was to grow up and live my teenage years – in a ninety-nine per cent white working-class suburb called Lawrence Weston in Bristol. Lawrence Weston was a place where one could count the number of Black families on two hands, and all were known by their surnames, like the Whites or the Dixons. With the overall numbers that low, Black families in the area were not perceived as a threat – or, to borrow a phrase from the Deep South, as 'uppity niggers' like the ones in St Pauls, Bristol – but the N-word was still heard far too frequently for my liking. As the journalist Gary Younge testifies in *No Place Like Home,* 'The playground taunts began the day after *Roots* aired and would continue for years'.

One of the few Black girls in my school year was given the dubious title of 'my wife' after the *Roots* character Kizzy. Chicken George would provide laughs aplenty for his showmanship, fine attire and cockfighting skills, but it was the rebellious Kunta Kinte, who constantly ran away and was beaten, whipped and eventually had his foot cut off, who resonated most with me. He also refused to acknowledge his 'slave name' Toby, and with my quick temper and hot tongue it was very easy for me to make the connection to what life would have been like for a rebellious young Black man back then. I banished the memory of Kunta Kinte being trapped in a net by fellow Africans, and erased the uncomfortable feelings that came with his capture. *Roots* was my only early recollection of slavery until my mid-teens. I was naively unaware that the city to which I had moved had played such a major role in the slave trade.

I know now that slavery has been in existence for centuries, with references in the Qur'an and Bible used to ease any consciences or lapsed morals. During the centuries of slavery's existence, its proponents would often quote phrases such as: 'slaves, obey your earthly master with respect and fear' (Ephesians 6:5). Great ancient civilisations, such as the Ottomans, Vikings, Egyptians, Greeks and Romans, all benefited from slavery to advance their empires, using slaves in everything from construction to domestic service, and many were used in wars. African slavery existed throughout the continent, with Cairo being a major trafficking centre, and some African tribes made their principal incomes from transporting people to other cultures as far away as Asia. For centuries, people had worked for others, and could not be classed as 'free' in the modern sense of the word.

In his book, *A Darker Side of Bristol,* local historian Derek Robinson says:

> Long before Bristol made a fortune out of Black slavery, the city ran a thriving business in white slavery. By the time of the Norman Conquest [1066], Bristol was the most important centre in England for collecting, selling and exporting slaves, especially attractive young women. In those days the actual practice of slavery was fairly common everywhere.[1]

The ownership of other human beings was a practice established across the globe and a part of many cultures and societies long before the Portuguese ships began to secure territory in Guinea off the West African coast during the fifteenth century, which began the transatlantic slave trade.

As the Portuguese overcame African resistance, they seized more land and began moving slaves to their other territories in Madeira, Cape Verde and the Azores. After a period of war between the Iberian superpowers of Spain and Portugal, the Treaty of Tordesillas was signed in 1494, handing Africa to Portugal. The Portuguese moved to protect their African assets, building forts along the profitable West

Coast of Africa where they had plundered gold and slaves. Portugal had also colonised civilisations in Central and South America where, after Columbus's intervention in 1492, Spain had gained an ascendancy over its European rivals. Spain introduced slavery to its conquered lands, and with the introduction of the Asiento System, granted merchant traders from around the world a royal licence to sail and trade enslaved people to and from countries now known as Peru, Colombia and Chile in South America, and also the Dominican Republic and Cuba in the Caribbean.

Portugal claimed Brazil in 1500 and during the 1530s began the largest transportation in history of African slaves to a single nation in history. The Portuguese used the slaves to work the land for sugar cane, which needed a tropical climate to grow, and in so doing created the blueprint for the transatlantic slave trade. Other European nations, such as Denmark, Sweden and Holland, had captured territory and traded slaves across the Atlantic, and the superpowers of France and, increasingly, Britain were growing envious at the increasing wealth being gained from Africa by their rivals.

The Capture of Africans by Africans

The Iberian superpowers could not have successfully established these foundations, which created the infamous Middle Passage, without the involvement of other Africans. Europeans rarely ventured into the interior of the 'Dark Continent', as they dubbed it, due to the high risk of disease and their fear of the ruling tribes. Most Europeans would wait patiently at sea, and sometimes held members of the African slaver's family as a bond for the goods they had traded before they received their human cargo to load on-board the vessels. African slaves were kept together in leg-irons, and marched hundreds of miles across the African interior to the west coast of Africa. This region covers an area of over 4,000 square miles, and includes Senegal, the Gambia, Guinea, Sierra Leone, Ivory Coast, Ghana, Togo, Nigeria, Angola, Congo, Mozambique and Madagascar. The slaves were held in specially prepared barbaric holding camps, known as forts or factories.

Britain's Entry to the Transatlantic Slave Trade

Up until the 1560s, British involvement in the slave trade only amounted to a few individuals, such as West Country-born seaman John Hawkins who, in an act of piracy, seized 300 slaves from Portuguese slavers and sold them into what we now call the Dominican Republic. After originally opposing the trade, Queen Elizabeth I not only granted Royal Assent but also invested in Hawkins's second voyage in 1564,[2] turning the individuals who were involved in slavery into a trade that would grow into one of the first global economies. On his second journey, Hawkins was accompanied by Sir Francis Drake in what is widely acknowledged as Britain's first formal entry into the slave trade.

The seventeenth and eighteenth centuries were notable for large-scale migration by Europeans, who journeyed around the globe, often removing, and in some cases nearly exterminating, all the indigenous people from their lands. Britain established important holdings in Barbados (1627) and in the largest slave colony, Jamaica (1655). Increasingly, Britain's role in the slave trade was being driven by economic factors.

The transatlantic slave trade was a huge enterprise on a global scale. Black, brown and white hands were all fully complicit in seeking profits from the trade. Alongside the African, British, American and colonial West Indian slavers, financial institutions, credit brokers, weapon manufacturers, ironmongers, shipbuilders and fitters, market traders and many other subsidiary trades were involved over centuries.

The Middle Passage

With the capture, transfer to the coast and storage completed, chiefly by African slavers, the next phase was to transport the captives across the ocean on slave ships. This second leg of the voyage became the notorious Middle Passage, in which horrific conditions were endured for between four and six weeks until the slaves reached the Americas. The slaves were chained together on the ships with limited food, water or air, often in sweltering or stormy conditions. Your bathroom was where you were shackled, and diseases such as dysentery were rife, causing many deaths among slaves and crew alike. When you were allowed out for restricted exercise while still manacled, any disobedience would be severely punished. During exercise, some slaves took their own lives by leaping overboard, preferring death to the living hell they were experiencing.

The famous slave Olaudah Equiano was the son of an Igbo chief in Nigeria before he was captured, aged just eleven. He described the horrendous conditions of the Middle Passage:

> The stench of the hold while we were on the coast was so intolerably loathsome that it was dangerous to remain there for any time, and some of us had been permitted to stay on the deck for the fresh air; but now that the whole ship's cargo was confined together, it became absolutely pestilential. The closeness of the place, and the heat of the climate, added to the number in the ship, which was so crowded that each had scarcely room to turn himself, almost suffocated us. This produced copious perspirations, so that the air soon became unfit for respiration, from a variety of loathsome smells, and brought on a sickness among the slaves, of which many died, thus falling victims to the improvident avarice, as I may call it, of their purchasers. This wretched situation was again aggravated by the galling of the chains now become insupportable; and the filth of the necessary tubs, into which the children often fell, and the groans of the dying rendered the whole a scene of horror almost inconceivable.[3]

The stench from the slave ship was said to drift ashore, heralding its arrival for miles before its docking at one of the various ports within the Americas. There the scramble for purchase would begin. Notification of a slave sale would have been advertised, and the slaves were sold in lots at auction like cattle, prized on their physical attributes. Ratios of two males for every female slave, as well as those for adolescent children and babies, would have been procured and arranged pre-sale without regard to the family structures that had been established in Africa.

As well as the human cargo, ivory, gold, silver and other precious items gained from African slavers and merchants were also sold. With the risk of slave insurrection at the end of a voyage ended, the crew would be reduced and paid, mainly with the use of merchant houses and financiers, at the ports. The ship would now be scrubbed clean of its vile human slurry and prepared for its final four-week leg of the triangular route: to transport the goods cultivated by the slaves in the Americas, mainly tobacco, rice, indigo, cotton, sugar and sugar-related products such as rum and molasses, back to their British commercial bases for their dispersal throughout the world.

Establishment in the British West Indian Colonies

The British colonies in the West Indies expanded rapidly, directly enhanced by the increasing transatlantic slave trade. The fertile lands and tropical climate of the Caribbean were ideal for growing certain produce, and with sugar consumption in Europe increasing, the region was prepared for slavery. Nearly four million Africans were transferred to the British colonies between 1551 and 1870.[4] The slaves were distributed to each of the British-owned islands, and the former land of the Native Americans became the home of the first plantations, and the planter aristocracy who enjoyed burgeoning wealth and nobility.

My ancestors began life in the territories of Berbice, Essequibo and Demerara, which were acquired from the Dutch in 1797, and they would provide the water to harvest the tonnes of sugar cane which would produce the fine brand of Demerara sugar. Those three territories would become British Guiana renamed Guyana after to reflect its independence into a republic in 1966 and taken from the Native Amerindians meaning 'land of many waters'.

On many islands in the West Indies, there were notorious seasoning camps designed to introduce the slaves to the rigours of the work they would endure. Much as a rider would break in a horse, the camps prepared the slaves for their future existence by putting them to back-breaking plantation work with little food or rest, and with torture being used as a means of governance.

For the more fortunate slaves, work in the Caribbean was in

servitude to the plantation houses, cultivating coffee or ginger, or tending to animals needed for working the land and as food. The overwhelming majority of slaves, however, worked in the fields, harvesting crops. A single sugar cane is between six inches and a foot thick with a hardy surface, and grows to six feet high. Cutting it down would be hard, back-breaking work, which required fitness among the gangs of men and women who had to chop it down, putting in long hours in sweltering heat. Once it was cut and loaded onto the carts, it was transported to the sugar factory on the plantation. The sugar was then sent back to Britain for the final refinement in London, Liverpool, Glasgow and Bristol to make sugar loaves for sale, and used especially for sweetening tea.

Establishment in the British Colony of America

Slavery was used in the thirteen British colonies stretching along the eastern seaboard. Work in the South Carolina rice fields was also hard and unrelenting. Slaves stood in waterlogged, swampy lands full of mosquitoes and reptiles to reap an elaborate system of sowing, threading and pressing rice seeds. As with harvesting sugar cane, this was done in gangs, mostly by hand, and was also physically punishing on the body. In order to keep the fields wet for the production of the rice, a system of dams between canals, which were also built by the slaves, was used to irrigate the paddy fields.

On the tobacco plantations of the Chesapeake region, the work was less physically taxing but more complex. Land was prepared for planting in January, then the seed was sown and the ground regularly tilled and weeded until harvest of the tobacco leaves during autumn. Due to its method of cultivation, tobacco damaged the soil, which could not be used three years consecutively, so the slaves were sent further into the interior to clear more land within the forests for tobacco farming.

Black and white overseers supervised this arduous work, sometimes carrying out their masters' instructions brutally. Fear and punishment were seen as the best ways of controlling the large numbers of slaves, and these control measures could take the form of mutilations and torture. The Black overseers, keen to enhance their reputation with their white masters or gain extra privileges, would show no mercy to the slaves. The slaves, however, were not accepting of their fate, and tried to have some form of control over their lives by carrying out many acts of rebellion. The house servants of the plantation held the most-prized jobs, but they would still be at the beck and call of the master and lady of the house. The house servants' tasks would range from cooking to cleaning, and even breast-feeding the plantation owner's children when the lady of the house was tired or could not produce milk herself.[5]

The Life of a Slave

It was in these West Indian colonies that the practice of using slaves as chattel, owned for their entire lives, was widely exploited. This practice, which had begun in the British colony of Barbados in the 1600s, expanded during the eighteenth century, especially to South Carolina and Jamaica. In both America and the Caribbean this meant generation after generation of slaves were born, reared and died on a plantation, and were branded physically and mentally as the property of an owner: a patriarchal hereditary figure whose name they would have known only as *Master.*

This total ownership of another human being as a commodity, known as chattel slavery, was one of the key differences to the slave systems that pre-existed the transatlantic slave trade. Slaves were treated as property, listed in deeds alongside cattle and horses, and branded with their owner's mark. Their treatment would depend on their masters' benevolence, for which they literally prayed. Just whom they were allowed to marry and raise children with, or to what religion they converted, would require the permission of their master. Children of the slaves were bred to be sold, and the master would take his pleasure from what he deemed his stock, including female slaves, not recognising any of the resultant children as his own. These children could also be sold as slaves. Benevolent masters did allow small privileges such as keeping smallholdings or farms to rear animals, and grow crops and vegetables. Founding Fathers and later presidents, George Washington at Mount Vernon and Thomas

Jefferson at Monticello, whose fortunes were enhanced by their tobacco plantations, were said to be among these benevolent masters, ruling as paternalistic patrons. They were viewed to treat their slaves kindly, but never, of course, as equals. Two of Jefferson's children, born to his slave Sally Hemings, trained as carpenters.[6]

Evangelical revivals sweeping America during the antebellum period, the period between the War of Independence and Civil War, saw the rise of religion, especially Baptist and Methodist faiths. This eased the lives of slaves who were generally given Sundays off to attend church. Churchgoing was a key tenet of many Western societies and seen as a way of civilising the so-called pagan Africans, who, quickly recognising the benefits and the temperance that came with religion, converted to Christianity. However, many slaves kept the African traditions which had crossed the Atlantic with them. Their customs were observed publicly at burials, weddings and births, and privately in their own language, such as within the Gullah community in South Carolina.

The growth of slavery in the northern states slowed, and was eventually outlawed as the Americans freed themselves of the remnants of colonial Britain to become the United States of America, creating an economic model based on free labour. However, slavery continued unabated in the Deep South during the antebellum period. This led to conflict through the pivotal Civil War, where the victor would determine whether its lands would be, as President Lincoln termed, 'slave or free'. The growing use of slaves as disposable commodities was by now a way of life in the southern states, and also for many individuals in Britain who held business interests in the Caribbean.

The Business of Slavery

Early British Slaving Forays and the Rise of the Planters

Following the British explorer Sir John Hawkins's early slaving and pirating missions along the West African coast during the 1560s, the British did not enter the slave trade on a grand scale for many years. However, when they did, they expanded slavery into a major business, exploiting their naval superiority, trade links and seafaring knowledge and skills. Pre-1660 Britain only traded approximately 2,000 slaves per year through private merchants.[7] By the end of slavery, over 200 years later, anywhere between twelve and twenty million slaves had been taken from their homeland in Africa. Many wealthy white families entered into slavery by setting up their plantations in the West Indian colonies and passing their wealth down through generations, creating dynasties. With a hot Caribbean sun and fear of disease from the tropical climate, there was a lack of available wives, with few British women prepared to move there permanently. This created a limited social scene, and white males were less than ten per cent of the population. There existed a constant anxiety over slave revolts in the West Indian colonies, and often the absentee planters stayed in Britain once their fortune had been established, hiring managers to look after their interests. In America, where slavery expanded rapidly during the antebellum period, several large plantation homes were acquired in the grand cities of the South, such as Charleston, Savannah, Atlanta and New Orleans.

British Slave Trading Companies and Rise of the Merchants

The most influential slave trading operation was begun as the Royal African Company (1672–1821). As its name implies, it enjoyed a royal charter from King Charles II, and a monopoly in the late seventeenth century. It also built protective forts and the dreaded factories where slaves were imprisoned, plus had interests in the lucrative gold trade. Its investors included prominent patrons such as Sir George Carteret, who was one of the first landowners and lord proprietors of the colony Carolina, the philosopher John Locke, and the Bristol philanthropist Edward Colston, who would later become an MP. The British Crown ended its monopoly in 1698, allowing private merchants to benefit from the trade. During the 1750s the Royal African Company restructured to reform as the Company of Merchants Trading into Africa, and stretched its influence over three centuries.

Alongside these slave trading companies were a number of individuals, known as merchants, who expanded the business of slavery.

Though returns were healthy and lavish lifestyles enjoyed, costs of the slave trade were high. However, the merchants were supported in maintaining their slave trading business by the West India Interest, who held social and business meetings across the country, including at the Jamaica Coffee House, St Michaels Walk, and Bishopsgate Street Tavern in London. This cabal of parties interested in slavery and its powerful commerce and products united the main private investors, financiers and merchants with influential lobbyists, and, importantly, made strong links to gain political influence to support the trade. Their self-protectionist interest in maintaining the slave trade would include attacking Parliament's decision to ban American ships from docking in the Caribbean during the 1780s, following the War of Independence, and during the 1790s it denounced Britain's decision to arm slaves who were rebelling against Britain's mortal enemy, France, in Haiti. This collective of vested interests fought the abolitionists' opposition to slavery. They also helped to delay its abolition in Britain, and prevented full emancipation for the slaves in the British colonies until 1834.

Britain's Major Slave Trading Ports and Cities
London, Bristol and Liverpool

Three of Britain's biggest ports in major cities had defining roles in the slave trade, becoming some of the biggest slaving ports in the world during the eighteenth century. London exploited its size and eminent financial base; Bristol used its global trade links; and Liverpool grew from a small town into a major city, creating wealth for an elite that was passed down through generations, sustaining an economy for many others.

Historian David Richardson has written several volumes regarding Bristol's prominent role in the transatlantic slave trade, meticulously listing each ship that left its docks. He states that London was initially the largest slave trading city, but from 1730 to 45 Bristol overtook London, and was 'responsible for over forty per cent of British voyages to Africa, fitting out on average thirty-six ventures per year or almost 550 during the whole period.' Ships that reflected the region, like the Bristol Merchant, Bath Snow and the Clifton, sailed out of the Bristol Channel to Africa before reaching the Americas.[8] Bristol's slave merchants fully exploited the favourable circumstances of its good port position and rich maritime history. They also had excellent trade and mercantile links with the Americas and Africa, and concentrated on specific markets such as supplying slaves to Jamaica, St Kitts and Virginia. Ironically, as the ban on the transatlantic slave trade neared in 1807, slave trading grew, particularly for Liverpool which increased its voyages and overtook Bristol, and then Rio de Janeiro, Brazil, as the largest slaving port in the world.

In 1795, though, Liverpool had sixty-three per cent of the British market, and forty-three per cent of the entire European slave trade.[9] Liverpool's rise in the latter half of the eighteenth century can be partially explained by its more northerly location, advances in ship-building specifically for slavery, financial systems and, ultimately, more efficient crews, who could cut days off sailing times on each leg of each journey.

Other English cities, such as Birmingham, supplied armaments to Africa which were used in tribal wars. Manchester's cotton textile industry boomed, while investors from northern England were also attracted to the growth in slave revenues from Liverpool. It is incredible to think today that before the American Revolution of 1776, the small islands of the West Indies were far more valuable to the varied British business interests than the American colonies. This was especially so as 'sugar overtook grain to become the world's most valuable commodity by the mid-century, accounting for one-fifth of all European imports'.[4]

The returns made from the slave trade are subject to fierce debate, ranging from five per cent to nearly forty per cent, but it is widely felt that the transatlantic slave trade made a major contribution to Britain's industrial development. Historian and former Trinidad premier Eric Williams states in his essential book *Capitalism and Slavery*, written in Washington DC in 1942, that:

> The West Indian islands became the hub of the British Empire, of immense importance to the grandeur and prosperity of England.

It was the Negro slaves who made these sugar colonies the most precious colonies ever recorded in the whole annals of imperialism.[10]

With sugar imports revenue doubling between 1748 and 1776, even taking a modest average of ten per cent would still have been a very good economic return for investors, financiers and merchants.

Bristol and the Transatlantic Slave Trade

During its growing role in the slave trade, Bristol enjoyed the prominence of being the second-largest city in England, behind London. One of its local citizens, an economic writer of the time named John Cary, declared in 1696 that slavery was:

> A trade of the most advantage to this kingdom of any we drive, and as it were all Profit [the traffic in negroes] being indeed the best Traffick the Kingdom hath as it doth occasionally give so vast and Imployment to our People both by Sea and Land.[11]

Bristol merchants had not only mounted a successful campaign to end the Royal African Company's monopoly in 1698, but also been involved in illegal private ventures before this. Edward Colston (1636–1721) owned shares in Bristol's oldest sugar refinery, St Peter's Sugar House, and worked with the hugely influential Society of Bristol Merchant Venturers, still going today. They helped increase the number of slaves taken from Africa, and also directly boosted their own wealth and prominence. These Bristol merchants were involved in all the complexities of the slave trade well into the nineteenth century. This is not disputed by the Society of Merchant Venturers itself, whose membership today is still shrouded in secrecy, but creditably it provides a substantial amount of money in charitable donations to projects in Bristol. On its website it says, 'At its peak during the middle decades of the eighteenth century, it is estimated that sixty per cent of Bristolians, including a number of Merchant Venturers, were directly or indirectly associated with this dreadful trade'.[12]

According to Professor Kenneth Morgan in his insightful

dissection of Britain's role in the transatlantic slave trade, *Slavery and the British Empire*, 'The leading slave traders at Bristol in the eighteenth century included: Sir James Laroche, Isaac Hobhouse, James Jones, John Anderson, James Day, Thomas Deane, Richard Farr Senior and Junior, and James Rogers.' Among the sugar merchants who gained their products from the slave plantations, he lists 'Michael Atkins, Mark Davis, William Miles, Evan Baillie, John Curtis, Richard Bright and Protheroe & Claxton'.[13] Also heavily involved in the slave trade was Henry Bright, a Bristol-born Jamaican plantation owner who said in September 1750 that slavery was 'The chief motive of people venturing their fortunes abroad'.[14] In one example, Professor Morgan cites Thomas (Daniel) Jr, who spent his apprenticeship doing business in Barbados before moving to Bristol as a sugar merchant and becoming a philanthropist. These men were mostly drawn from the wealthy and powerful business and ship-owning communities of their fathers, and they would turn their attention to positions of politics and influence. Professor Morgan also states that 'in Bristol between 1670 and 1750 all of the city's parliamentary members had a strong connection with the Caribbean'.[15]

Those profits made from slavery not only enhanced Bristol's standing as a major maritime trade port, but also brought wealth to the region. You can still see the lavish opulence in buildings in the city such as those in Queens Square, which was then one of the finest addresses in the country. The bountiful lifestyles enjoyed by these men, who lived and invested heavily in Bristol, included the use of slaves as pageboys and servants, though this practice was not widescale in Britain during the transatlantic slave trade. Indirectly, these men became patrons of the city and donated money to a number of Bristol's institutions and buildings. Streets such as Guinea Street, Princes Square and Farr Street – named after the Farr family – all housed prominent slave trading families. Several Society of Merchant Venturers members, who had links to slavery, lived in Clifton. Their slave-derived wealth is seen in stately homes in and around Bristol at Arnos Vale, Blaise Castle, Kings Weston House, and Ashton Court, mentioned in Madge Dresser's book *Slavery*

Obscured – The Social History of the Slave Trade in Bristol.[16] Their real-estate portfolio extended throughout the South-West, including ownership of property in the beautiful Georgian city of Bath.

Further evidence of Bristol's prominent role in the slave trade can be found courtesy of my former employers, Bristol City Council, which in a report to the House of Commons in 1713 stated, 'Bristolians depended for their subsistence on their West Indies and Africa Trade which employed greater numbers of people in shipyards and in the manufacture of wool, iron, tin, copper, brass etc, a considerable part is exported to Africa for the buying of Negroes'.[17]

The 100-Year Battle for the Abolition of Slavery and Global Emancipation

So slavery was entrenched into British society through its sanction by the Crown and legislation by government. It was also supported by prominent institutions and individuals, and condoned by an ambivalent general public. Due to Britain's laissez-faire attitude to slavery, the colonies had been left to their own devices and had introduced their own slave codes, making clear distinctions between those who were free and those who were enslaved. These codes sanctioned murder and torture, banned relationships between the races, and gave the slaves little or no rights.

In the middle of the eighteenth century, few major figures had spoken out against slavery. In fact, several people spoke in its favour, often using quotes from the Bible. The philosopher John Locke, who was born in Wrington near Bristol, was a renowned defender of liberty, but excluded African slaves from this tolerant thinking and was an investor in the slave trade. He was also an early founder in the formation of South Carolina, which heralded the rise of the slave plantations on a grand scale.

The Abolitionists' Coalition in Britain and America
In response to the institution of slavery, an alliance of philosophers, politicians, social activists, religious movements and people who had

suffered the injustice of inequality, such as female rights campaigners and ex-slaves, joined together to begin the fight for the abolition of slavery. The dawning of the Age of Western Enlightenment made those societies question the accepted beliefs, values and customs of the day. Several texts and books from ex-slaves and European, British and American authors provided a literary context, a commentary and a philosophy that influenced the artisans and chattering classes, who came into frequent contact with the emerging coalition of abolitionists.

US Abolitionists in the Eighteenth Century

Petitions had been received in Britain from its Northern American colonies to remove them from the slave trade. This prompted King George III in 1770 to make a proclamation that slavery was not to be removed in America. George III was subject to great criticism, ironically from Thomas Jefferson who blamed the British for 'the institution of slavery' during the drafting of the Declaration of Independence.[18] The pacifist Religious Society of Friends, known as the Quakers, had been making incremental bans on slavery and disapproving of the ownership of slaves by its members since a Quaker in Germantown, Philadelphia, first publicly spoke out against it in 1688.[19] Pioneering individual campaigns from Quakers such as John Woolman, who believed slavery to be contrary to their Christian doctrine, also helped to make inroads for the cause. At the 1772 annual meeting of the Quakers, Anthony Benezet was heard to give such an impassioned speech that the Quakers became one of the first public organisations to formally ban its members from participating in the slave trade. Benezet became a fierce advocate of abolitionism and wrote several anti-slavery books. His works came to the attention of several prominent people, such as Benjamin Franklin, who told Benezet that he himself 'frowned on the iniquitous trade in humans, and wanted nothing better than to hasten its end'.[20] Benezet's work became widely read in Britain by several abolitionists, including Thomas Clarkson, and influenced the founder of the Methodist movement John Wesley.

Meanwhile, in 1772 a young Londoner named Granville Sharp brought a landmark test case through the British judicial system. Sharp successfully argued that, as there was no law allowing slavery in England, James Somerset, a slave, could not be returned to Virginia. The case resulted in an estimated 15,000 slaves in Britain being freed.

In 1786, a major turn of events occurred when the unassuming academic Thomas Clarkson won a prize from Cambridge University for his groundbreaking work written in Latin, entitled *Essay on the Slavery and Commerce of the Human Species*. Researching and compiling the material for his thesis was to transform Clarkson's life, and he became a lifelong abolitionist.

James Ramsay was a former Scottish naval doctor who had toured the West Indies and tended to sick slaves on-board an intercepted slave ship. The conditions he'd witnessed had made a profound impact on his life, leading to him becoming a reverend. Reverend Ramsay made one of the boldest statements of the time, saying that there was 'no difference between European and African mental powers' at a time when the African race was largely considered inferior.[21]

Clarkson, Ramsay and Sharp, along with several prominent Quakers, founded the Society for the Abolition of the Slave Trade in 1787. Their poignant and historic emblem of a manacled slave – though in a stereotypical kneeled and bowed poise – praying for freedom with the words 'Am I Not A Man And A Brother?' was made into a Wedgwood seal by the famed potter and abolitionist, Josiah Wedgwood. Clarkson was a shy, diligent academic, and Quakers were banned from holding public office, so what the abolitionists required was a charismatic spokesman. This came in the guise of William Wilberforce.

Wilberforce was already an MP for Hull at the age of twenty-one, and was a charming orator who had close connections throughout high society to both the Crown and the then prime minister, William Pitt the Younger. Wilberforce had converted to Christianity, and together with a group of evangelicals had formed the Clapham Sect. The abolitionists gathered compelling evidence against the trade, with

Clarkson touring Bristol and Liverpool to collect an armoury of data through over 20,000 interviews with guinea men – the name given to sailors involved in the slave trade.[22] These exposed the appalling conditions aboard the ships, and discovered a mortality rate among the guinea men of one in five, as well as high number of disabling injuries.[23] This data was to be used as a key strategic point by the abolitionists to arouse the greatest concern and garner the support of Britons domestically against the slave trade.

The abolitionists enlisted the help of freed slaves, such as Olaudah Equiano and Ottobah Cugoano, who could articulate the horrors of slavery through their own first-hand experiences, and who had become authors. By his own account, Equiano had had an extraordinary life. After being transported to America during the 1750s, Equiano had become the personal servant of a British naval lieutenant, with whom he toured the world in various battles before he was sold to a slave-holding Quaker, Robert King. Due to Equiano's excellent capacity for education and learning, he worked as a mercantile clerk and courier inspecting some of his master's plantations.

Upon hearing that King was due to free him, Equiano wrote:

> These words of my master were like a voice from heaven to me: in an instant all my trepidation was turned into unattainable bliss...My imagination was all rapture as I flew to the Register Office [to have the manumission document drawn up].[24]

Equiano paid for his freedom by serving on ships, and his naval prowess led to him being employed by Dr Charles Irving, whom he witnessed discovering the process of desalination and converting salt water into drinking water. Equiano sailed on various global expeditions which included seeing Mount Vesuvius erupt, witnessing battles between French and English warships, going to the opera in Italy, and visiting the North Pole where he saw snow for the first time.[25] Equiano was courted, and toured Britain to read extracts of his 1789 autobiography, aptly titled *The Interesting Narrative of the Life of Olaudah Equiano or Gustavus Vassa, An African*, to audiences who would not have seen a Black man before, let alone think an African would be literate. In fact, Equiano was one of the earliest Africans to both live and document life in Africa, America, the West Indies and Britain.

The founder of the Methodist Church, John Wesley, who had visited the cotton fields of Georgia to see the appalling conditions for himself during the 1730s and had provided vital transatlantic links between the abolitionists, was a regular visitor to Bristol. In 1788, his anti-slavery sermon there was interrupted as the pews in the altar split. Wesley himself described it as a supernatural occurrence: that 'Satan fought lest his kingdom should be delivered up'.[26]

The abolitionists were highly organised, with talks around the country in front of huge audiences, and their zeal and fervour produced thousands of pamphlets and books. They also delivered countless speeches and years of lobbying and petitioning, all of which made inroads into the consciousness of millions of Britons. For example, the Bristolian social reformer and playwright Hannah More and other local female campaigners played prominent roles in the Bristol boycott of slave-produced sugar in 1792.

The Wedgwood seal began to appear on 'snuff boxes, bracelets and combs'[27] as the plight of the slaves became the cause célèbre of its day. The abolitionists used campaigns to bring attention to the cruelty of the slave trade and gain public sympathy. They became adept at exploiting injustices in slavery and utilising PR campaigns to highlight their cause. Following its 1783 trial they fully publicised the case of the slave vessel the *Zong* to great effect.

During a Middle Passage voyage, approximately 170 sick slaves had been mercilessly thrown overboard by the *Zong*'s crew in a bid to gain compensation for the ship owners. The owners claimed insurance on the condition that their human cargo had been lost at sea, and not due to the conditions on-board which would have invalidated their claim. The *Zong* judgement, and the ruling of 1772 that chattel slavery was not supported by law in Britain (a law not applied elsewhere in the British Empire) were both made by the most prominent law-maker of his day, Lord Mansfield, who had a mixed-heritage niece, Dido Elizabeth Belle. These were landmark victories in the century-

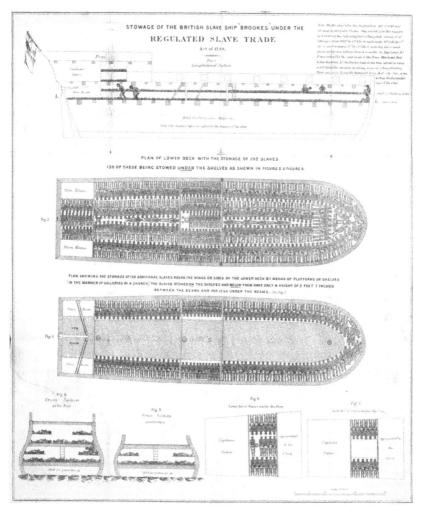

long battle against slavery, and the 1772 ruling immediately set free up to 15,000 former slaves in Britain.

The illustration of the Liverpool slave ship *Brookes,* with its top deck removed to reveal slaves packed together like congealed pasta, was also widely publicised, and is still one of the most evocative and widely seen images of the slave trade. Both these examples shocked the public and were influential in changing national opinion. They also led to an Act of Parliament called the Dolben Act (1788), which legislated for better conditions in the way the slaves were transported across the Atlantic. The gains towards abolition, however, were incremental where it mattered most: in parliament. Although the abolitionists had turned the tide, gaining public and social momentum, they were not garnering enough political and legal support.

The Delay in Abolition – West India Interest and Pro-slavery Supporters

The chief opponents of abolition were naturally those with the most to lose from it. These formed the powerful cabal of plantation owners and merchants who had links to the Caribbean, known as the West India Interest. Among their ranks was the richest of the Jamaican absentee planter dynasties, the Beckfords, three of whom served as MPs in Westminster. Through their clubs and associations they lobbied favourable MPs, including those in Bristol, encouraging them to vote against abolition bills in 1788 and 1789 to further delay abolition. The West India Interest successfully blocked Wilberforce's petitions a further five times in eight years, between 1797 and 1805, by arguing that conditions had improved for slaves and that abolition would make the British economy suffer.

The death toll for the first Haitian Uprising in 1791 reached over 10,000, and alarmed the American and European powers. They feared further revolts, and so became even more cautious in freeing the slaves toiling on the plantations. At the beginning of the nineteenth century, talk within Whitehall about abolitionism cooled due to war with Napoleon's France. The abolitionists persevered, however, and with brilliant political manoeuvring made a bold case that slavery was not in Britain's best interests, with thousands of slaves being sold to

Britain's European rivals who were helping its enemies' economies and war efforts. This, along with changing economic factors, resulted in a law enacted on 1 March 1807 that finally abolished the transatlantic slave trade from Britain's ports, and stipulated that no slave could be landed within its colonies after 1 March 1808.

US Abolitionism in the Nineteenth Century

At around the same period, President Jefferson signed a bill to end the importation of slaves, which came into effect on 1 January 1808. The plantocracy, however, turned to the flourishing internal market which was spreading throughout the Deep South, mainly due to one of the world's greatest technological advances in 1793, Eli Whitney's cotton gin. The cotton gin ('gin' was short for engine) was a machine which changed the production of cotton from hand-picked to a mechanical process. It removed all the seeds and pulp from the crop, vastly increasing the amount of cotton that was manufactured. Production went from thousands to millions of bales a day worldwide, and its influences can be seen in textiles and modern fashion today. Where sugar had proved king in the Caribbean plantations, cotton became the world's latest, biggest slave-reared commodity, with increasing profits fuelling 'the growth of slavery [in the South]'.[28]

While three of the original thirteen American colonies – Virginia and both Carolinas – had slave populations of over 100,000 in the 1790 census the production of cotton on the plantations fuelled the growth of three new states in the South: Georgia, Mississippi and Alabama. By the 1860 census, these southern states were growing in number, and were nearing half a million slaves in each state. Just ahead of the Civil War, the total number of slaves now in the Deep South had reached over four million.

Freed slaves, known as 'freedmen', such as anti-slavery campaigners Frederick Douglass and Sojourner Truth, joined the abolitionists in America. Douglass was described as 'an articulate, handsome, witty and charismatic escaped slave, who quickly became a star-turn of the abolitionist lecture circuit and was constantly threatened with recapture and physical assault'.[29] His account of slavery in *The Life and Times of Frederick Douglass*, published in 1845, helped to transform views of slavery in America.

Harriet Beecher Stowe's 1852 novel *Uncle Tom's Cabin*, which told the story of a slave in America and sold millions of copies, helped to strengthen the abolitionist cause further. Female campaigners had yet to receive the vote, and were virtually invisible in political life and citizenship. Many women, such as abolitionist and suffragette Angelina Grimké who had moved from South Carolina because of her distaste of slavery, learned a great deal that would prove valuable in the campaign for women's equality, the suffragette movement, and contribute to the push for abolition. Emily Winslow and Elizabeth Cady Stanton used the Declaration of Independence to point to the inequity within the Constitution, rewriting the eternal phrase from the Founding Fathers to read 'All men *and women* are created equal'.[30]

The Aftermath of the Abolition of the Transatlantic Slave Trade

While the transatlantic slave trade had been stopped in Britain and America, this only applied to the curtailment of the shipping of human beings across continents. The trading of Africans had been nurtured and developed over centuries throughout Europe, and would not be eradicated so easily. A number of British interests and individuals continued to use slavery, and its produce from the plantations where slavery remained legal. It would take another three decades before slavery was officially abolished in the British colonies. Even then, this was tempered by a twelve-year period of apprenticeship for slaves, with only those under six being exempt. This was designed to protect the slave owners' interests, although they also managed to exact £20 million in compensation from the British government.

In the last decade of the transatlantic slave trade, 'Liverpool sent 135 ships a year to Africa between 1798 and 1802, carrying an average of 37,086 slaves per year, and 103 between 1803 and 1807 carrying 25,953; compared with London's mere 18 [ships] and 13, and Bristol's mere 4 and 1 respectively'.[31]

After the abolition of the transatlantic slave trade, the ports of Bristol and Liverpool continued to trade in the products of slavery.

Sugar was still a major global commodity, and West Indian produced sugar continued to be central to both cities' economies. By exploiting the numerous contacts they had made from the slave trade in West Africa, Liverpool's merchants turned to the lucrative palm oil, widely used as a lubricant for machinery and a component in soap and detergents during the nineteenth century.[32]

After both the 1807 and 1808 abolition bills had been passed into law, the British turned from being one of the major traders in human traffic into a self-appointed global police force against the trade. In what would be a classic case of poacher-turned-gamekeeper, Britain coerced the other European powers to bring global slavery to an end, but once again progress would be a long, protracted battle.

*

Growing calls for emancipation in America had led to its northern states passing emancipation acts between 1780 and 1804. America's ban on the import of slaves to its shores in 1808 was the earliest it could impose the ban constitutionally. The Founding Fathers had decreed that slave trading would continue for twenty-five years to assuage the southerners' concerns. As had occurred in the West Indies, legislation banning slaves as imports did not end slavery in America. By now, millions of slaves had not only been transported from Africa, but had been born in America.

To meet the growing global demand for cotton, hundreds of thousands of slaves were marched thousands of miles across the Deep South, in what historian Ira Berlin terms the 'Second Middle Passage'. The new slave states of Mississippi, Kentucky, Louisiana, Tennessee, Alabama and Arkansas helped to form a southern alliance that was to lead to the Confederacy. A reliance on the internal slave markets developed new inhumane practices. Slaves were now bred, reared and sold like cattle, and names such as 'breeding wenches' for women and 'bucks' for men were adopted. This internal slave market and plantation life helped entrench slavery into the Deep South, until Abraham Lincoln intervened with his Emancipation Proclamation during the American Civil War to begin the end of slavery in America.

The Haitian Uprising and abolition laws in Britain and America had added to a sense of change and given slaves hope for emancipation. While previous plots had been brutally quelled since the end of the transatlantic slave trade, there had been further revolts against slavery on the plantations. This was one of the key factors in favour of full-scale emancipation, but not before more blood was spilt on both sides of the colour line.

Each of the decades between the turn of the century and the colonial repeal of the trade during the 1830s was marked by a major revolt in the Caribbean, the only region outside Africa where Blacks formed the majority of the population, but were ruled by a white elite. Guyana was subject to major unrest in 1808, and in 1823 the slave Quamina led 12,000 slaves to demand unconditional emancipation. 250 slaves were executed in reprisals.[33] Even in relatively conservative Barbados, an African-born slave known as Bussa led an uprising that saw hundreds killed and a quarter of the entire sugar harvest for 1816 destroyed.[34]

The island with the greatest history of turbulence and uprising was Jamaica, a source of slave power since the Maroon wars began in 1731. The most famous insurrection post-transatlantic slave trade abolition saw slave and Baptist preacher Samuel Sharpe organise an uprising that led to Jamaica's largest rebellion in 1831–32.

Though all of these ringleaders were executed and therefore none survived their rebellions, they played a prominent role in the abolition of slavery in the Caribbean. All three have statues, monuments and streets named after them in their respective countries, to commemorate them as national heroes.

The British abolitionists had always favoured a 'gradual' approach to ending slavery. For Wilberforce and the Clapham Sect their primary goal had been achieved. They naively believed slavery would come to an end, overlooking the hundreds of thousands that were still being reared in repressive surroundings. Sir Thomas Fowell Buxton, who took over the leadership of the British Abolition Movement in 1822, articulated the abolitionists' feelings thus:

'Slavery will subside; it will decline; it will expire; it will, as it were, burn itself into its socket and go out.'[35] In addition, Wilberforce and many benevolent abolitionists, including President Lincoln, thought outright and immediate emancipation would be dangerous to someone who had only known a life in bondage. They favoured gradual incremental emancipation, known as apprenticeship, which would prepare the freed slaves for a life after slavery by spending a number of years working for their former masters for paid wages. The naivety of the abolitionists was exploited by the greed of those with the most to lose. On the plantations, arguments ensued as the former owners – now turned employers – tried to exact as much labour as possible before parting with any wages. In some cases, they made their former slaves work a full forty-hour week before qualifying for remuneration. The slaves grew discontented and could see no improvement in their conditions. They wanted, as they termed it, 'full-free'.[36]

With war between European powers becoming less frequent, the cost of maintaining an armed presence in the colonies simply to guard against a slave rebellion did not make economic sense. So with the system of apprenticeship in tatters, the threat of bloodshed a constant concern, and the growing acceptance that waged labour would bring better economic value than that the slave model, full emancipation was granted within the British colonies on 1 August 1838.

With a healthy sum exacted from Haiti, France abolished slavery in 1848, giving full French citizenship to Martinique, Guadeloupe and French Guyana, which is still observed with full benefits today. Across Europe, Denmark abolished slavery by royal decree in its islands of St Croix, St Thomas and St John in 1859, as did Sweden with its tiny island of St Barts in 1856. Holland freed its slaves in 1863 in Surinam, Aruba, Bonaire, Curaçao, St Maarten, Saba and Sint Eustatius.

The Iberian joint superpowers of their day, who were responsible for the initial raids into Africa, had both continued to plunder its people and resources across the Atlantic. Between 1551 and 1810, Spain had imported nearly a million slaves to Latin America, while

Portugal, with its sugar and coffee plantations, had imported over 2.5 million to Brazil alone.[37] The spread of independence throughout Latin America from the beginning of the nineteenth century brought an end to slavery under Spanish rule in South America. However, the Iberian nations continued to trade slaves illegally well into the nineteenth century, assisted by individual British merchants. The global demand for sugar had seen thousands of slaves continue to be transported into the Spanish Caribbean. Santo Domingo, which had been caught up in the violence of its northern Hispaniola neighbour Haiti, had now been renamed the Dominican Republic by nationalists.

By harnessing new technology in steam-powered mills, railway systems and better refining methods, Cuba had taken over from Haiti as the biggest producer of sugar in the region, making a quarter of the world's sugar and easily surpassing the archaic methods of the British colonies.[38] Cuba finally freed the last of its slaves in 1886.

Although Brazil had gained its independence from Portugal in 1822, it continued to use slavery on its sugar and growing-coffee plantations. Unlike in Latin America and across the British and French colonies, it actually increased the numbers of slaves imported, violating global agreements championed by the British government. To stop the loopholes that saw illegal slave traders continue to flourish, in 1811 Britain made slave trading a felony that would mean banishment to a penal colony, and in 1827 gave it the same terms as piracy, which was a capital offence.

Frederick Douglass travelled to Britain in 1846, where he witnessed Britain's remarkable semi-transformation from its past at first hand. Like Equiano before him, Douglass toured the country with his book, giving talks. He visited Bristol, and after being introduced by the Lord Mayor, gave a speech which was noted by observers for its 'powerful reasoning, keen sarcasm, with facts impressively brought out' while also branding Bristol's slave owners 'vagabonds and villains'.[39] Douglass wrote of the experience in Britain: 'I came a slave; I go back a free man. I came here as a thing, I go back as a human being.' Those were not mere words either: £700 was raised in donations from members of the public during his

British tour to buy his freedom from his American master.[40]

With Wilberforce's death in 1833, a month before King William IV signed the full emancipation bill into law, Clarkson took on the grand statesman role of the abolitionists, becoming the president of the first World Anti-Slavery Convention in 1840. In May 1846, he met Douglass and William Lloyd Garrison, who had published Douglass's bestselling auto-biography, *Narrative of the Life of Frederick Douglass* (1845). An eighty-year-old Clarkson greeted Douglass by saying, 'God bless you, Frederick Douglass. I have given sixty years of my life to the emancipation of your people, and had I sixty years more they should all be given to the same cause.'[41] Clarkson died that year, and fought slavery until his last breath. Alongside Wilberforce, he became one of the key campaigners in the struggle for human rights in British history. Douglass himself would become a leading civil rights campaigner, visiting President Lincoln in the White House on numerous occasions to advise him on the recruitment of Black slaves, who would gain their freedom by fighting for the Yankee Army during the American Civil War.

Britain's diplomatic skill, allied with the force of its Royal Navy – who had stop-and-search powers even back then for suspected slave ships – plus support from the US Navy, eventually saw Brazil become the last nation to abolish slavery in 1888. Just like the other regions throughout the Americas that had participated in the transatlantic slave trade and imported slaves on a mass scale – the West Indies, United States and Latin America – Brazil would be visually and culturally changed forever.

An Alternative View of Abolition: The Five Rs of Insurrection

It would be easy to assume, with the range of such powerful vested interests to keep them in perpetual bondage, that the slaves were totally subservient and accepting of their fate. Despite the vast odds stacked against them, and with severe punishments meted out for any acts of insubordination, defiance was rife and ranged from simple disobedience to armed insurgency.

In his 1956 book *The Peculiar Institution,* which became central to the study of American slavery, American historian Kenneth Stampp championed this view, and countered the then commonly held view of the paternalistic ruler who treated his slaves benignly, which had gained credence among slavery apologists. Stampp felt that in these acts of insurrection, however small, slaves had exerted some control over their lives, and were not animals to be whipped into submission. He later summarised that the civil rights campaigners, who successfully began to exert their rights in the same decade that he wrote his book, built on this with their proud acts of civil disobedience while maintaining their dignity. The uprisings against the inhumane treatment the slaves received can be categorised into five areas: *Resistance, Runaways, Rebellion, Revolt* and *Retribution.*

Resistance

Resistance in the form of disobeying orders was the most common form of challenging authority, as it could be carried out on a daily basis. There were several ways to resist, such as malingering, or go-slows to give it a modern nickname; a slave could feign misunderstanding instructions for a task; openly refusing to comply with a command; responding with verbal abuse; undertaking a hunger strike. Sabotage was common, and could be used to hang tobacco leaves incorrectly, or flood the rice paddy fields which could ruin a planter's harvest, or by setting fire to the sugar cane fields.

Resistance during the torturous Middle Passage involved many mutinous plots to overthrow the ship's crew, which were generally unsuccessful given the thousands of voyages that successfully crossed the Atlantic. With numerous fatal diseases rife on-board the slave ships, the crew had far more to fear than life-threatening plots. Abolitionist Thomas Clarkson was able to prove that the *guinea men* – the name given to sailors involved in the slave trade – suffered a higher mortality rate than the average sailor. With millions of slaves dying due to the torturous conditions during the Middle Passage, a final act of resistance was to refuse to live a life in bondage and take your own life, by jumping overboard into the ocean.

Runaways

Escaping slavery by running away from the harsh life that existed on a plantation was seen as the best way to a semblance of freedom, but the threat of recapture was never far away and life as a fugitive was not to be romanticised. Runaways in Jamaica were given the term *Maroons,* taken from the French *maronage,* meaning literally to run away. Small Maroon communities existed throughout the West Indian colonies within the rugged forests and dense terrain where recapture was difficult. One of the most celebrated forms of slave insurrection took place in Jamaica. The Maroons of Jamaica waged a guerrilla war against the British Army – predating that of George Washington and his patriots – and forced a peace treaty to be signed in 1739 for the right of the Maroons to live peacefully on 1,500 acres of designated land. Other Jamaican Maroon communities waged war against the British during the eighteenth century, and the Maroons became a symbol of hope for other slaves in the West Indian colonies. The leaders of these uprisings, Nanny Maroon, Cudjoe and Tacky, are part of Jamaican and West Indian folklore, creating regional pride with ceremonies held each year to remember their achievements and sacrifice.

In America, a secret network known as the Underground Railroad was formed to send escaped slaves north to free states such as Pennsylvania, and free territories in Canada. One such network was famously led by Harriet Tubman, herself an escaped slave. Together with the help of many white abolitionists and freed Black ex-slaves, the Underground Railroad gave food and shelter to thousands who'd escaped to their freedom. Frederick Douglass named his anti-slavery newspaper *The North Star* after the star that slaves would follow to freedom.

Rebellion and Revolt

In the Caribbean and America over the centuries of slavery's existence, there were numerous official reports of mutinies, rebellions and armed struggles. The majority of these were small or merely plots, but some involved hundreds, and in some cases thousands, of slaves not prepared to accept their subjugation. With the growing clamour for abolition gaining momentum in Britain and the United States, and the successful overthrow of the French aristocracy following the French Revolution, the time was ripe for self-determination and independence from the European colonies, especially those in Latin and Central America. The French colony of Saint-Domingue had become the richest in the region, dwarfing the incomes gained from the British colonies. In 1797, the ex-slave Toussaint L'Ouverture, dubbed the Black Napoleon for his warfare skills, led over 400,000 Blacks to rebellion and expelled France from the country, the first and only such defeat of a European power. The slaves renamed the country Haiti, and the rebellion struck fear into the slavery elite. It was responsible for a lot of policy relating to later treatment of the slaves.

The Stono Rebellion, which happened near Charleston, South Carolina, was the largest American uprising. On 9 September 1739, a group of slaves escaped, beheaded two white men and attempted to flee to Spanish Florida. They gathered more runaways until they numbered approximately 100, before they were hunted down and their leaders executed. Though small in number, the Stono Rebellion was significant as it struck fear into the southern plantocracy, and brought harsher punishments and regulations written into slave codes in the southern states. Slave revolts were regularly planned, but in almost every instance uprisings were brutally ended.

Retribution

The common factor in all of these acts of insurrection was not their modest gains or successes, but the severity of punishments meted out to offenders in retribution. Penalties on the plantation could be public whippings until blood was drawn and a criss-cross of scars left behind. Absconding slaves were commonly placed in iron-collars, leg-irons and shackles, while hanging of slaves was also used as a visible deterrent to others. Mutilations of bodyparts, such as brutally demonstrated in Roots to Kunta Kinte who had his foot chopped off for his constant escaping, were used as punishments, as were castrations. Recapturing of slaves was turned into a business, with advertisements for missing slaves placed in newspapers offering rewards for their return. The Jamaican Maroon war of 1760 was notable for other Maroons siding with the British in order to remain free, which led to the capture and execution of the Maroon leader Tacky, a hero in parts of Jamaica. The leaders of the Stono Rebellion were not only decapitated, but their heads were put on poles. Mental cruelty was also used, with recaptured slaves sold and sent away from their family and the social circles they had built.

The power of these acts of reprisal could last for decades. Napoleon ordered the might of the French Army to recapture Haiti in 1802, and Toussaint L'Ouverture was captured and died imprisoned in a French garrison. However, led by the brutal Jean-Jacques Dessalines, the Haitians once again repelled the French Army, this time banishing them forever in 1803. After Nelson's victory at the Battle of Trafalgar in 1805, the French were never to regain the powerful foothold they'd once held in the region, only retaining a scattering of islands such as Guadeloupe and Martinique. Long after global emancipation had been gained, France's response to Haiti's declared independence was to demand millions of francs as severance pay. It also discontinued relations with Haiti, ignoring the colonial chaos that it had begun and plunging the country into political misrule and decline for decades. Only the massive earthquake in Haiti in January 2010, and the global humanitarian appeal that followed, would finally bring a French president – Nicolas Sarkozy – to visit the French-speaking former colony.

Millions of Black people in the Americas had been uprooted from Africa, and had little economic, political, military or social power. On both sides of the Atlantic, it would take a white liberal religious movement to help begin the process of slave emancipation, and it would take over a century before it was outlawed globally.

After Abolition

British and American Repatriation Schemes

Encouraged by Granville Sharp and a number of abolitionists, the British government began a programme of repatriating destitute former slaves from England to West Africa. Sharpe provided a picture of a utopian future where the ex-slaves would be able to flourish in their 'natural' environment of Africa, despite the fact that many ex-slaves had not been taken from the continent. The government initially provided three Royal Navy ships, and the ex-slaves were joined by a number of white men and women, some of whom had married ex-slaves in Britain.

In May 1787, they landed in West Africa and founded the colony of Sierra Leone, naming its capital Freetown. Olaudah Equiano, who had initially been sent by the government as a consort to the group, complained bitterly about the treatment of the Africans. He was effectively sacked before the ships had left port in Plymouth. Although assisted by donations from British abolitionists, this 'Province of Freedom'[42] was nothing like Sharp's vision, with Black and white slavers patrolling the West African coast in large numbers. Thousands of Black people were sent to Sierra Leone, but many went of their own accord from Canada, America and even Jamaica. Although conditions were dangerous, with illness and starvation rife, many felt that at least they could live a life free from bondage.

A wealthy freed American ex-slave, Paul Cuffee, had financed and captained several successful repatriation voyages to Sierra Leone. Although Cuffee died in 1817, his work had influenced leaders of the American Colonization Society, including their leader, American abolitionist Henry Clay, who helped to repatriate thousands of American ex-slaves to form the new nation of Liberia in 1821. They named its capital Monrovia after the American president of the day James Monroe, and adopted a similar Stars and Stripes flag. The American Liberian colony differed from the British Sierra Leone colony. This was mainly due to the support of several American slave owners who, fearing the growing presence of freed slaves would cause a rebellion, gave financial assistance to repatriate ex-slaves. The author Charles Stuart summed up the difference, stating, 'In the British case, settlement was the harbinger of abolition; in the American case it was a pernicious alternative to it'.[43]

The two colonies, however, had identical principles at their cores: to provide ex-slaves with an option to live in relative freedom and equality, and, in the words of Paul Cuffee, 'To rise to be a people.' This philosophy has continued, and is still being explored today throughout the Black diaspora. Many people have left the lands of their birth, both Britain and America, where they believe the indignities of slavery have been replaced by the intolerance of racism, to return to what they consider to be their home and mother country, Africa. These people included my sister Marilyn who, conscious of her faith as a Rastafarian, lived in Ghana for many years.

The Heritage of Slavery in West Africa

There are many reminders of Africa's past situated on the shores of its west coast which hold a sinister as well as a spiritual element for its descendants. The commercial forts, such as Cape Coast Castle and Elmina Castle in Ghana, were holding camps for the slaves. Today these former forts-turned-museums are sensitively trying to straddle the balance between restoration and memorials.

Dr King and his wife Coretta in 1958, and the Obama family in July 2009, are just some of thousands of visitors who have looked at what is termed 'The Final Gate' or 'Door of No Return'. This would have been an African's last view of their homeland before being inhumanely shipped across the vast expanse of the Atlantic Ocean. Tinubu Square, a main thoroughfare in Lagos, Nigeria, is controversially named after an African female slave-trader, Madam Tinubu, while Bunce Island in Sierra Leone, Gorée Island in Senegal and James Island in Gambia also provide glimpses of Africa's slave trading past.

The Role of Africans in the Transatlantic Slave Trade

This examination of the transatlantic slave trade began with my earliest memory of slavery: Kunta Kinte's capture in *Roots*. The capture of Africans by Africans and their role in the despicable trade is something of which I am often reminded by my white friends. It is a valid point, and as anyone of African descent knows, it can only be answered after a painful voyage of discovery and understanding ourselves in our own time. Only by laying out the story of the transatlantic slave trade, stretching across five centuries, on these pages have I been able to put it into any kind of context.

My response begins by drawing from my latent thirst for the historical stories that the past has given us to teach us lessons for the future, and uses the French collaborators with Nazi Germany as an example. That Faustian partnership did not determine the outcome of World War II. It was part of the story, and has had a social and cultural impact that is deeply painful to its descendants, but it does not tell the whole story. The world of commerce exists only if there are commodities that people want to trade, and if there are no buyers there can never be any sellers. For all the slave-owning ancient and mediaeval societies that dealt their fair share of cruelty, none matched the inhumanity of the transatlantic slave trade that lasted for centuries.

The eminent historian Professor CM MacInnes sums up my feelings, putting the transatlantic slave trade in its rightful context as one of the worst periods in history. He states:

> In spite of all that has been written, the Middle Passage still remains one of the blackest spots on Britain's escutcheon. It is impossible now to picture the terrifying state of mind of helpless savages, torn from their native surroundings, forced by long marches to the coast along paths strewn with the bones of earlier victims, subjected to all the indecencies of the slave market and the barbarity of the brand and then driven like beasts, frequently naked into horrible ships. To these inland peoples the ocean was a strange forbidding monster, and the vessels in which they were compelled to sail something worse than the blackest hell imagined by man.[44]

After slavery, colonialism and imperialism played significant roles in Africa's history, and the list of its problems has continued to grow. AIDS, famine, drought, debt burdens and poverty are among them, and it will take longer than three generations of independence to change and improve. Africa's many natural resources, such as gold, diamonds, oil, minerals, artefacts and even its animals, have been exploited, in part facilitated by a series of corrupt regimes and strongman dictatorships who have managed to fill their Swiss bank accounts. Oil spills, the likes of which hit the Gulf Coast of America in April 2010, have been regular occurrences in the Niger Delta thanks to Shell. However, they have gone without any government challenges such as the one President Obama heaped on BP, forcing it to carry out a $20 billion clean-up campaign with further billions to be paid in fines and compensation. West Africa has seen nothing like this.

West Africa has produced the Benin Bronzes, diamonds from Sierra Leone and oil throughout the Niger Delta; now the continent's scarce resources of land and water are being exploited. Away from the multiple stories about Africa's poverty and famine, a major issue facing Africa is that of land tracts, some the size of European countries, being sold to foreign corporations for farming to export produce. These corporations are mostly from the Middle East, with seven countries leasing land in Ghana alone. A report in *The Observer* newspaper in 2010 warned of scarce resources that have belonged to African communities for centuries being taken, while Africans continue to go hungry. The counterargument states, however, that jobs are being created, and some of the foreign national companies are involved in sustainable community projects.[45]

So the controversies and debates about the world's second-largest continent continue, but how did slavery affect Africa and its people, who have now dispersed throughout the world?

5

Personal Reflections
of the Transatlantic Slave Trade

Legacies of the Transatlantic Slave Trade

During the centuries of slavery the vast majority of Black people were in bondage. They were kept illiterate, and feared acts of violence, rape or separation from their family ties by being banished to another plantation. After the transatlantic slave trade had ended, even though there were barriers and limitations to their emancipation, for many this was the first time they had the power and freedom to determine their own futures.

The enlightened men and women who'd helped to abolish slavery had had the best of intentions for post-slavery race relations, but many policies and attitudes still remained which were to determine the future for Black people post-transatlantic slave trade across the world. Whether these policies and attitudes were kept in place through fear, ignorance or loathing is a matter for debate; however, several myths have helped to perpetuate the legacy of subjugation and inferiority, and some still remain.

Some of these myths even predate slavery. The stereotypical images of Africans as heathens, or to patronising abolitionists as noble savages in need of salvation, were still the prevalent views of the day. They have led me to wonder, given the ways the Europeans treated Africans during the transatlantic slave trade, just who indeed were the savages. Evidence of African culture and knowledge has existed in Britain, most notably with the Benin Bronzes being displayed prominently in the British Museum. These artefacts were looted from West Africa in 1897, and date back to the fifteenth century. Before the Europeans arrived, cities flourished across the so-called Dark Continent, with educators, religions, craftsmen, kings and queens creating empires that stretched across Africa. The brilliance of the ancient Egyptians is well documented, but less well known are the empires such as Kush and Nubia that followed them. Other empires included the Ashanti, Igbo and Yoruba in the west, and the Berbers in the north who assimilated cultures from Asia.

Africa has some of the world's most valuable resources in danger of being stolen from the continent, including gold, diamonds, oil, precious minerals and exotic animals, all of which are a far cry from the famine or flood images I grew up being taught about at school or watching on television.

Legacies in America

In America, according to the acclaimed historian Ira Berlin, 'Blackness and whiteness were redefined...confining people of African descent to a place of permanent inferiority.'[46] Back in the Deep South, this ushered in the era of Jim Crow laws, which replaced the slave codes that had been enacted to prevent any uprisings. Jim Crow prevented Black people from participating in civil life and society, making them in effect non-persons. One of the few places where Black people could be found in large numbers was prison, due to a lack of income, education or mistreatment, and there is still a disproportionate amount of Black people within the judicial system and in prison today. This would lead to the fight for civil rights and a new battle to gain respect through non-violent insurrections. Dr King said of slavery, 'The whole dirty business existed on the basis that the Negro was a thing to be used not a person to be respected.'[47] Former Trinidad premier Eric Williams adds that the transatlantic slave trade 'Left mental and subconscious images that Black people were seen as inferior, or something less than human.'[48] Even enlightened men such as Wilberforce and Lincoln thought that people from Africa were naturally inferior to those who were white. However, their perspective was that of paternalistic benefactors rather than the white supremacists' viewpoint that has influenced latter beliefs. Tracts and passages from the Bible, fatuous scientific studies and unfounded biased findings have been used to promote this myth.

Actions based on prejudicial views against people of a different skin colour or race became racism, and the policies created became institutional racism. Dr Stephen Small stated:

> From the de facto subordination of Africans across European colonies and Apartheid in South Africa, to legal segregation in the United States and discrimination across Europe, institutional racist practices have been central to the creation of modern states (both inside and outside Europe) and current conflict in Africa, South America and the Caribbean. Racist practices also shaped the realities of citizenship and non-citizenship, and the extension of denial of the inalienable right to life, liberty and the pursuit of happiness.[49]

The four million African-Americans that remained on the American continent after the Civil War ended slavery in 1865 meant that the issues surrounding slavery are far more complex in the US and are under constant examination. I vividly recall watching, from the comfort of my Atlanta hotel room, an emotional Spike Lee featuring in an American episode of *Who Do You Think You Are?*[50] Lee, himself an acclaimed film and documentary maker, discovered that his four times removed grandfather had made weapons for the Confederate Army during the American Civil War in his owner's armament factory in Georgia. Ironically these guns were to be used against the very Yankee soldiers who had come to liberate his great-grandfather. To view the painful look of bewilderment and disgust on Spike Lee's face as he held one of those weapons was to watch a dark cloud of history colliding head-on with the present.

Legacies in the Caribbean

Plantation houses, like Jefferson's Monticello in Virginia, still stand today throughout the chain of Caribbean islands. In Barbados, Bristolians helped establish the Great House, with surrounding lands that made slave-reared goods and produce, which became known as plantation houses. Some of these plantation houses are in ruins, but some remain and have been restored as museums or hotels. My mother lived in Barbados for ten years, and on my first trips to the Caribbean to visit her in the 1990s, I found the plantation houses foreboding places. Initially I would not go inside them. For a long while I refused to acknowledge this uncomfortable part of my ancestry, but eventually I reasoned that my history and heritage are entwined and interwoven in places like this, whether they are in the United States, the Caribbean or South America. I still find them emotionally disturbing once I'm inside, and while my logical mind roves over the walls filled with pictures, paintings and portraits of the landed gentry of the day, my insides churn. There they stand or sit, proudly presenting their ill-gotten artefacts of wealth alongside their instruments of torture or labour, or both. My soul and spirit are in turmoil as I glimpse an image of someone who looks like me staring back at me, silent to the horrors they, and those who went before them, have witnessed.

The transformation from slavery to self-rule continued slowly in the Caribbean, and a further century elapsed before independence and self-determination occurred in the former colonial empires. A series of social and political reforms swept through the region, inspired by the place where it had all begun – West Africa. In 1957, led by its first prime minister and president Kwame Nkrumah, Ghana became the first African former British colonial society to gain independence. This raised hopes of a pan-African movement of unity, influenced by the works and writing of Jamaican Marcus Garvey and African-American scholar WEB Du Bois.

Sugar's prominence in the Caribbean severely damaged the soil and led to the rise of a single-crop culture in each island, which was unsustainable as the world's economies expanded. Other countries around the world diversified into a range of markets, causing economic decline in the region summarised aptly by author James Ferguson as 'Creating the paradox which has plagued the Caribbean ever since [slavery] that it produces what it does not consume and consumes what it does not produce.'[51] Against this background, many like my parents seized the opportunity to leave the West Indies voluntarily for new, far-off lands and the promise of a better life. Their passage had already been paid in full by their ancestors, and the only reparation that was considered back then was access to the labour markets. Reparations remain a complex issue for all concerned, however.

Bristol – Now and Then

Depending on your viewpoint, Britain's entry into the slave trade enabled either the advancement of modern society through the technological advances of the day, or the accruement of territories and wealth from this global industry. Alternatively, you may believe the slave trade exploited other civilisations, disrupted cultures that had existed for centuries, and ruined the lives of millions of people. One place where the impact of all these viewpoints can be seen is Bristol.

The impact of slavery on Bristol has been quietly debated within the city's boundaries for centuries, and for a number of years the debate's central target has been the legacy of Edward Colston. A concerted campaign has been mounted to rename one of the city's many landmarks that bear his name, the performance music centre Colston Hall, especially with Bristol's most famous band, the trip-hop underground sound of Massive Attack, refusing to perform there. Over the years several celebrated Black artists have performed at the Colston Hall, including Otis Redding, Paul Robeson, Ray Charles, Ella Fitzgerald, Duke Ellington, and the politically conscious Bob Marley in 1976. I have danced the night away there to the likes of UB40 and RnB band Cameo, and laughed aloud at Lenny Henry and various Black comedy nights since its multimillion-pound refurbishment by Bristol City Council.

A number of eminent historians and academics have provided a welter of evidence of Bristol's role in the slave trade, and argument and counterargument continue regarding that role and the city's prosperity and wealth. Peter Borsay puts Bristol's rise down to the English Urban Renaissance in the eighteenth century, which saw a surge in 'democratic growth, prosperity and refinement'.[52] This included town squares, paved streets, theatres and spas. Respected Bristol-based historian Madge Dresser offers an alternative summary, stating that when Bristol was the biggest slaving port in the country in 1729, this coincided with the urban renaissance, and that some of the wealth derived from slavery was recycled into the city's infrastructure in the form of new housing, buildings and civic squares.[53]

The issues of slavery and forgiveness are deeply personal and individual choices. Nelson Mandela was a man who, in order to move forward, never looked back. His foresight and forgiveness are depicted in the 2010 film *Invictus*: after his incarceration for twenty-four years, he wore the emblem and shirt of his captors' favourite team, the South African Springboks, who were a predominately white Rugby Union team. Mandela used this powerful image to propel the Rainbow Nation to victory and unity. Without his forgiveness, one can only speculate about how long it would have taken for reconciliation, or even if reconciliation could have been achieved, let alone South Africa being selected to host Africa's first football World Cup.

As we are about to explore, whenever President Obama looks out of his window he, too, sees monuments to famous slave owners from the place he now calls home, the White House – itself built by slaves. While being sympathetic to any renaming of the building, I am more concerned with what happens inside and that its projects give an equal opportunity to people of all backgrounds. Several independent tour guides of Bristol, including Pirate Pete and Mike Campbell, remain true to the city's rebellious past. They recount Bristol's hidden history by taking tourists to Edward Colston's bust and explaining his dark deeds alongside his philanthropist efforts. 'Remove the history, remove the story,' they caution me.

The 2007 Bicentennial Commemorations of the Abolition of the Transatlantic Slave Trade

The bicentenary of the abolition of the transatlantic slave trade was marked with ceremonies all over Britain. The Archbishop of Canterbury held a service at St Paul's Cathedral attended by The Queen, and the then prime minister, Tony Blair, who apologised for Britain's role in the slave trade, saying, 'It is an opportunity for the United Kingdom to express our deep sorrow and regret for our nation's role.'[54] I attended a commemoration service at Bristol Cathedral, beamed to my seat in the historic main hall of the then Council House. Several protesters demonstrated outside about the prominence given to William Wilberforce and the abolitionists. In London, Toyin Agbetu confronted The Queen and Tony Blair inside St Paul's Cathedral before being ejected. He termed these ceremonies 'Wilberfest', and felt they 'eradicated any mention of resistance, rebellion and revolution instigated by millions of African people.'[55] William Wilberforce's body rests across the Thames from Sir Christopher Wren's resplendent dome at Westminster Abbey. At his feet is a monument to the end of the transatlantic slave trade, as well as monuments and exhibitions in his home city of Hull.

It has fallen to Britain's museums to provide a way forward, sensitively depicting the horrors of Britain's heritage in a story which will not alienate white people or disappoint Britain's Black communities. The International Slavery Museum, located within the Merseyside Maritime Museum in the Royal Albert Dock of Liverpool, was opened by Maya Angelou in 1994. Extended in 2007, it is Britain's longest permanent major exhibition of its size. It was built following collaboration between Liverpool's disenfranchised Black community, the art world and politicians, and displays a range of artefacts, videos and illustrations providing vital social, educational and cultural connections to the past. Among its artefacts is the depiction of the Liverpool slave ship *Brookes*, which is one of the most enduring images synonymous with the slave trade, and has been viewed by millions around the world. *London, Sugar & Slavery* became a permanent exhibition at the Museum of London Docklands, East London, having transferred many artefacts from an exhibition at the Empire and Commonwealth Museum in Bristol, which closed due to financial reasons. Bristol chose to channel its resources into a three-year programme called the Legacy Commission, which progresses areas in cultural representation, health, education and young people, in response to a lengthy communication with its Black community, who wanted to change the continual shadow of Black children's poor educational attainment.

Sadly, the spectre of slavery still exists today as slave merchants and traders ply this wicked trade for profit, despite gallant work undertaken by modern-day abolitionists in gaining new global human rights decrees. The Anti-Slavery Movement's definition of a slave in the twenty-first century is someone who is:

> Forced to work through mental or physical threat, owned or controlled by an employer; usually through mental or physical abuse or threatened abuse, dehumanised, treated as a commodity or bought and sold as property, physically constrained or has restrictions placed on his/her freedom of movement.[56]

Amnesty International states many millions of people, including children, are enslaved into forced labour and trafficked into the sex trade, or smuggled into countries as illegal immigrants against their will.

On the Trail of the Transatlantic Slave Trade in South Carolina

America's legacy from the Civil War was four million emancipated ex-slaves. Many of them wanted to leave the South immediately and, like the Native Americans and settlers before them, they made another epic trek across America. Without the vote and disenfranchised due to Jim Crow, millions of Blacks voted with their feet and took part in the Great Migration to cities in the North such as Chicago and Philadelphia, dubbed The Freedom City, and to Los Angeles in the west. They also migrated north to New York, which would become home to one of the biggest Black communities in any city in the world, and would attract uncles and aunts from both sides of my family. Many Blacks, however, decided to stay in the South as the former slave and Confederate states consolidated into the Deep South. This established a way of life that would not only be etched into consciousness and culture around the world, but also be very distinct from the rest of America.

The former slaves were enjoying their first taste of freedom, and large numbers of them remained in South Carolina. After making their fortune in the West Indies in 1670, three ships with connections to Bristol set sail from Barbados to found the colony of Carolina. 'The wealth of Barbados derived from the production of sugar cane using slave labour from West Africa, a pattern already established from the Portuguese in Brazil.'[57] Thanks to the granting of generous land rights and religious tolerance, plenty of settlers expanded the colony, and in 1712 Carolina was divided into North and South, which remains today. Such was the growth of plantocracy that 'by 1740 slaves outnumbered free whites by two to one, making it the only American colony with an African majority.'[58]

Some of the earliest and most brutal plantations that existed were run by wealthy Bristolian brewers, the Yeamans, who were among the earliest settlers in Barbados before founding South Carolina.[59] John Yeamans became a knight, and was governor of the new colony of Carolina from 1672 to 1674. His brother was a sheriff and Mayor of Bristol during the 1640s. 'Such people helped to shape South Carolina into a slave-based society, closer in character to the West Indian sugar islands than any other mainland colony.'[59] The Yeamanses' slave trading preceded Bristol's boom period in the trade, which did not occur until the next century. By then the Yeamans family had sold its brewery, which evolved into Courage's Brewery. Like the Wills tobacco factory, it was another former major employer in Bristol during the twentieth century.

The Gullah Community – A Piece of Africa in America

On the coast of South Carolina, with the Atlantic Ocean that brought slaves and settlers from Africa and the West Indies surrounding its shores, is a chain of islands called the Sea Islands. I am driving across one of the bridges that link the three islands of Beaufort, St Helena and Hilton Head together. This region, also known as the low country, is virtually flat, and full of creeks, marshes and wetlands. It is also home to one of the most established Black communities in America, to which the term 'African-American' is fully appropriate. The *Gullah* community was originally drawn from a community of freed slaves who had been taken from various regions of West Africa, and stayed to build their own rural community, keeping their language and traditions. One of the reasons the African slaves flourished in these Sea Islands was due to the similarity in climate and vegetation to Africa, and much of its appearance and stillness reminds me of the West Indies. Its remoteness to the mainland meant that the only way of gaining access was by boat until the mid-twentieth century, and in many respects this has helped to preserve the Gullah traditions. It was here that, before cotton, rice was harvested using the skills that had first been gained in Africa. At the Penn Cultural Heritage Center, which showcases the Gullah culture, I view how this self-contained community has kept strong links to its heritage via oral traditions passed down by *griots*, or African storytellers. Wherever I hear the Gullah language spoken or written it reminds me of the West Indian patois, whether from Jamaican, Bajan or my own Guyanese dialect. The slaves mixed the various African mother tongues of Wolof, Vai, Twi, Ewe, Yoruba and Mandinka with English to form a language so that they could communicate with each other. After slavery had ended, they survived independently with the help of some benevolent whites by establishing educational facilities that taught industrial skills as well as academic programmes. Dr King and his Southern Christian Leadership Conference members often came to the Sea Islands to plan during the civil rights campaign, as this was one of the few places Black and white people could mix together in the South. The Gullah community marks the social transitions in African-American life from slavery to emancipation, and from segregation to social change. Today their main battle is with property speculators who greedily view their beautiful lowland environment as waterfront real estate.

Sixty miles along the Atlantic Coast I visit Charleston Harbor, and feel surrounded by history as the bonds of my past from Africa and the Caribbean, and my present in America and Britain, become more transparent. I walk past a replica of one of the cannon that fired the first shots of the Civil War, when the Confederates captured Fort Sumner here in Charleston Harbor. That declaration of war on the government would lead to the bloodiest war in America's history, which ended with the emancipation of the slaves. It was here, too, that Bristolians first set ashore after they had established their plantations in the Caribbean. They brought their African slaves with them, and helped to found the plantocracy practices of owners, grand homes, slaves and crops which spread throughout the South. African slaves would have arrived in chains, and would have taken their first steps on American soil where I am standing. Charleston was one of the busiest American slave trading ports, and was the centre of the internal slave trade market long after Britain had abolished slavery. Slaves were first sold openly on the harbour, and then, when it was thought the selling of human beings was harming the genteel image of Charleston, sales were held at the Old Slave Mart. I walk into charming Charleston town centre, stopping to admire the sweet-grass baskets on sale by members of the Gullah community near the Old Slave Mart, which is now a museum. There I understand how the slaves were viewed as mere commodities. The price in 1860 of a twenty-year-old male slave (the prime age for sale), for instance, would be $1,500–$1,600 (approximately $42,000, or £28,000, in 2015 prices). The slaves would be asked questions based on their experience, such as how many rows of cotton they could pick in a day, or whether they had worked in a master's house. No consideration was given to the splitting of families or any ties that had been made. A range of instruments of torture are displayed on the museum wall to illustrate chillingly how the overseers kept order. The financial institutions in Charleston were heavily involved, as they were across the world, while the state of South Carolina collected taxes on the sale of each slave. The slave trade contributed greatly to the grand infrastructure of Charleston (just as it had done in my adopted home of Bristol) on which its wealth, fortune and fame capitalised, and still does capitalise.

The former high sheriff of Bristol, Peaches Golding OBE, has family who can trace their roots back to slavery in the Carolinas. She was born in Winston-Salem, North Carolina, and she can vividly recall being told about slavery, as well as enduring segregation and the menacing presence of the Ku Klux Klan. Her role as high sheriff of Bristol as The Queen's representative involved working with young people to promote the benefits of education and opportunity, which she believes will lead to social mobility and break down barriers across all boundaries, a major change from her humble transatlantic beginnings.

Driving away from the South Carolina Sea Islands, I pass over the waters of the Savannah River which separates South Carolina from Georgia. The two states are spanned by the Talmadge Memorial cable bridge, which is akin to a rollercoaster ride for motor vehicles as it loops and spins me around its concrete walls before I enter The Gateway to the South – Georgia. I admire the natural unspoilt beauty that surrounds me, and it is easy to marvel as the mystical Deep South comes alive. Acres of beautiful savannah prairies, blooming magnolia trees, hot sultry days of sunshine, calorie-busting rib-sticking food and enough musical variations for every palate, from blues, jazz and gospel to bluegrass and country and western, all lay ahead. I am told to expect it all served with the trademark Southern charm and hospitality. We shall see.

I play Nina Simone's 'Summertime', and her voice floats above the purr of the engine as I hum along to the chorus which is evocative of the South with its lyrics of reaping cotton and easy living. The song is from George Gershwin's opera *Porgy and Bess* which is set in 1930s South Carolina. My next selection is Ray Charles's 'Georgia', which I play to herald my arrival into the state as it is the official song of Georgia. These records are some of the signature tunes of the South, but none is as powerful as the Billie Holiday 1939 classic 'Strange Fruit', also covered by Nina Simone.[60]

This song never fails to bring a chill to my bones. The strange fruit of the southern trees bears testament to the many lynchings that took place here in the South. As I travel through the rural hinterland of Georgia, I catch glimpses of the great crop of the South, cotton, rustling in the fields. I stop the car for a closer inspection of the miniature white candyfloss balls amid the tangle of twigs and leaves upon which they grow, and find it hard to believe these fluffy-shaped plants have not just shaped America but also influenced modern history and fashion. America remains the world's largest exporter of cotton, thanks largely to the billions of dollars it pays its farmers in subsidies which deny small African cotton producers valuable access to American trade.

Just inland from the South Sea Islands, and fed by the same Atlantic sea, is one of the great American historical cities, Savannah. Its celebrated town centre is based on a grid system linked by twenty-four enchantingly kept squares, to which the locals refer as their outdoor living rooms. Savannah is one of America's oldest cities, and like its twin sister Charleston, from which I have just driven a hundred miles south, it enchants you with its beauty. Savannah is a lovely 'chocolate box' city, which is appropriate, for this is where *Forrest Gump* was filmed. It is full of southern charm, and some of its town houses appear as if still wrapped in cellophane to best preserve its former glories. Beautiful, large, tall, skinny town houses with sweeping balconies and balustrades are more European than the brownstones of Brooklyn. This romantic view of the South had its first widespread appeal with the 1939 film *Gone with the Wind*, which referenced General William Tecumseh Sherman's infamous 1864 *March to the Sea*. During the Civil War, General Sherman's troops operated behind enemy lines, living off the land and destroying everything in their path, severely damaging the Confederate Army's ability to wage war. In Atlanta he ordered his troops to spare only the churches and hospitals, burning the city to the ground and only stopping scorching the earth when his troops reached the Atlantic Coast here in Savannah. The idyllic view of the Deep South as depicted in *Gone with the Wind* is one that holds its appeal in places like Savannah. The grand houses and the city itself are reminders of that past, and are a living, breathing modern-day advert. Most of the older houses have their living spaces above ground on the first floor to prevent the dirt from the roads coming directly into the homes. If I close my eyes, I can almost hear the horse-drawn carriages pulling up to load their wagons with supplies, and imagine well-mannered gentlemen bowing to fragrant Southern belles as they swish along in their long dresses with petticoats, fanning themselves vigorously under the hot sun. The locals will tell you, however, that it is not your imagination but just a ghostly visitation, as Savannah revels in the title of America's most haunted city.

A contrasting view of the South, however, is held by those who lived a different southern life and therefore have a different perspective. Alice Randall's *The Wind Done Gone* best tells of these parallel lives with the story of Cynara, the slave half-sister of the pampered Scarlett O'Hara from *Gone with the Wind*. Whichever view you hold, though, Savannah is a beautiful city, best viewed on foot. I end my visit on the river front, which was once home to one of the busiest ports in the world. On Factors Walk the tramlines still remain among the cobblestones, and I imagine the trams trundling up to the bonded multi-storeyed warehouses that stored and despatched King Cotton across the world from the Savannah River, yards to my left. Among the cobbled streets on River Street, I view the African-American monument, with its moving dedication by the recently deceased writer and civil rights campaigner Dr Maya Angelou, encompassing the horrors of slavery and celebrating the rise of the Black family. It reads:

We were stolen, sold and bought together from the African continent. We got on the slave ships together. We lay back to belly in the holds of the slave ships in each other's excrement and urine together, sometimes died together, and our lifeless bodies thrown overboard together. Today, we are standing up together, with faith and even some joy.

Born in Guyana, Living in America, Visiting Bristol My Grandfather's Odyssey

Nearly a decade after *Roots* first aired, I came face to face with my history when I met my maternal grandfather, Charles Coleridge, for the first time. He had flown to Britain from New Jersey, where he had moved after leaving Guyana in his senior years to be cared for by my aunts.

On his one and only visit to Bristol in 1985, he asked me to take him to a local monument which was near to one of my former playing haunts at Blaise Castle, Henbury, in Bristol. My grandfather wanted to see the grave of Scipio Africanus, a slave who had been buried in 1719 at the adjoining church, and whose headstone is marked with this epitaph from his owner:

I was Born a PAGAN and a SLAVE
Now sweetly sleep a CHRISTIAN in my Grave.
Wath tho' my hue was dark my SAVIOUR'S Sight
Shall change this darkness into radiant Light.
Such grace to me my Lord on earth has given.
To recommend me to my Lord in heaven
Whose glorious second coming here I wait
With Saints and Angels Him to celebrate.[61]

I never knew how my grandfather had discovered Scipio's grave, as it was years before the age of the Internet. Sadly, he was the only surviving grandparent I ever met, and he died in 1990. Scipio's grave was a mile from my school and three miles from my home, yet I'd never visited it before. My grandfather's influence helped me discover this piece of shared heritage.

Bristol has always obscured its history with the slave trade, and its only prominent landmark relating to the slave trade is Pero's Bridge situated near the point at which the Avon and Frome rivers meet. This was where the slave ships departed. A barely noticeable plaque, falling in between respectful and hidden, is placed on the ground just before you cross the footbridge to the vibrant waterfront and Millennium Square, and says much about Bristol's uneasy relationship with its past. Twenty miles away in rural Stroud an arch was erected to mark the end of slavery in the Caribbean in 1834, the only memorial of its type in Britain. I can't help feeling that if a rural town with no significant Black population can manage a fitting tribute, surely Bristol could do so more publicly, especially with its history of slavery, including both slavers and abolitionists, and vibrant West Indian and African populations that have contributed much to its recent history, including music and night-time economy.

In June 2011 I attended the opening of the M Shed museum at the old industrial wharf which focuses on all things Bristol. Inside there is an impressive interactive exhibit which depicts some of Bristol's history and its role in the transatlantic slave trade. This helps to educate Bristol's citizens and visitors on some of the city's inglorious past. In addition there are artefacts from Africa, including copies of the famed Benin Bronzes. The display, curated by author Dr Madge Dresser, takes an admirable neutral role by posing key questions of the visitor as they assimilate the facts for themselves.

From there I begin a quick journey around Bristol's city centre to discover some of the city's hidden history. Just behind my old offices in the Council House is the Georgian House Museum in Great George Street, just off Park Street. The house belonged to sugar merchant John Pinney, who owned the slave Pero to whom the bridge on the harbour side is dedicated. Saint Stephen's Church, just off the city centre, is hosting an art project, Reconciliation Reredos, by acclaimed artist Graham Evelyn, which examines some of the legacies of the slave trade. Crossing the busy Colston Avenue, I pass by the prominent statue of Edward Colston, reaching the Lewins Mead area which houses several charming historic buildings and offers some of the best fish and chips in the vicinity among its cobbled streets. A pub called Three Sugar Loaves at the bottom of Christmas Steps is just one of several inns that bear the name of trade in its title. Next door, situated in a former sugar refinery, is the award-winning Hotel Du Vin and Bistro, which acts as a fine footnote to my mini-tour. Their website once stated, 'Throughout the eighteenth and into the nineteenth century sugar and tobacco became two of the principle commodities traded through Bristol.'[62] I relax in the cool elegance of the hotel's interior at The Sugar Bar, which has a fine collection of rum and tobacco from the Americas. Quite what my father or my grandfathers would have said about a 25ml shot of 1971 Demerara rum costing £28 I can only imagine, and I wince as I ignore their astonished voices in my head. Back in their native Georgetown, I could buy a case of rum for that price, offer a shot for any passing patron, as is the custom in Guyana and throughout the numerous West Indian rum shacks, and have plenty left in the bottle to enjoy on my next visit.

Ten minutes from The Sugar Bar, adjacent to the Broadmead Shopping Centre, is a £500 million shopping mall, Cabot Circus, named after the explorer John Cabot, who departed from Bristol to become the first European to 'discover' Newfoundland in 1497.

Before it opened, its owners, the Bristol Alliance, wanted to call it Merchants Quarters in a bid to keep with the city's seafaring history, and it was only changed after a successful campaign led by Bristol's Black community.[63]

'It is only a name, why the fuss?' a Bristol businessman asked me during a meeting a few months after Cabot Circus had opened in 2008. My first thought was to ask him how he would have reacted if a German conglomerate had bought the shopping centre and wanted to rename it the Luftwaffe Mall in remembrance of those who had levelled Bristol during World War II. I can only wish that in the future, after understanding how prominent Bristol's merchants were during the expansion of the transatlantic slave trade, questions such as his will become redundant for future generations.

The reason why this question provoked such an immediate reaction was because it reminded me of the day I visited the first Nazi concentration camp built at Dachau, Germany, a metro ride away from the Munich hotel in which I stayed during the 2006 World Cup. I squirmed as I stood underneath showers that once spewed poison gas instead of cleansing water onto their unsuspecting victims. The only water that was spilt that day was through my own tears, and those of hundreds of visitors. The thoughts of utter revulsion that overwhelmed me will live with me forever. There have been so many taken and wasted lives in various global concentration camps; people tortured, shackled and bound together, with some of the victims' bones piled high into the air or buried into the African soil. Today we recognise these as acts of genocide, and they should always be renounced with the words that stand tall on the wall at Dachau: 'Never Again'.

Personal Reflections of the Transatlantic Slave Trade

This personal review of the transatlantic slave trade is by no means an exhaustive study, to which I acknowledge I could have easily devoted an entire book. I have tried to reflect its various elements that elapsed over seven centuries. Those requiring a deeper knowledge may wish to read works by two fine historians: Simon Schama's *Rough Crossings*, or Ira Berlin's *Many Thousands Gone,* a study into the first two centuries of North American slavery. Former Trinidad prime minister Eric Williams's *Capitalism and Slavery* provides an Afrocentric view from someone who lived and governed with the after-effects of colonial rule. James Ferguson's *A Traveller's History of the Caribbean* is an excellent historical companion if you find yourself exploring the region. Those with Bristol in their blood, or those who are just visiting the city, will find Bristol's Central Library reference section an illuminating experience. Particular praise goes to David Richardson's chronicles listing ship after ship that left Bristol as part of the triangular trade, as well as his many informative books on the subject, and Dr Madge Dresser's varied and informative works. In 2010 Bristol City Council supported the Bristol Race Forum to produce an excellent booklet entitled *Myths, Facts, Feelings: Bristol & Transatlantic Slavery* by Rob Mitchell and Edson Burton. A more thorough walk around Bristol's history can be found at *Sweet History?* (www.sweethistory. org/about/triangular-trade-Bristol). A full reference list is found in the bibliography.

The 2006 film *Amazing Grace* portrays Wilberforce's worthy efforts to abolish slavery in Britain, and *Amistad* tells the extraordinary story of a slave revolt aboard the ship of the same name in 1836. Following an uprising the slaves ordered that the ship set sail for Africa, but ended up in America. There they were the subject of an extraordinary legal case, and were represented by former president John Quincy Adams, who secured their release and passage to Sierra Leone. The director of *Amistad,* Steven Spielberg, won several awards for *Schindler's List,* which details the horror of the Holocaust. Several other films about the Holocaust, such as *The Reader, The Pianist* and *Sophie's Choice,* have been correctly critically acclaimed and awarded several Oscars. However, Spielberg's depiction of Alice Walker's novel *The Color Purple,* set in post-slavery southern America, failed to win a single Oscar despite eleven nominations. The stunning film *12 Years a Slave* by Black British director Steve McQueen did gain that coveted Oscar, and I will reflect on that, as well as new moves for reparations from the Caribbean countries, when I visit New Orleans where the film was set. In the Smithsonian Libraries in Washington, there are recordings of slave experiences from an oral history project called *Remembering Slavery – African-Americans talk about their personal experience of slavery and emancipation*. Bristol playwright Edson Burton's play *Seasoned*, which premiered at Bristol's Tobacco Factory, examines the process of breaking newly arrived slaves to the Caribbean. Lastly, of course, don't forget the book that started all of this for me, the TV depiction of which has yet to be repeated on terrestrial television despite the record audiences on both sides of the Atlantic when it first aired in 1977: Alex Haley's *Roots*.

*

Numerous legacies, myths, stereotypes and scars have remained over the two centuries that have followed the abolition of slavery and the harvest of the African continent of its people and resources. A sample list of the issues that always spark controversy includes: Black [dis]-unity, family breakdown, mixed relationships, poverty, wealth distribution, skin pigmentation, educational attainment and Black self-esteem. Even the word 'Black' is a subject for debate. It's seen as a source of pride for many about their race, but is watered down by the mainstream into 'urban' in popular culture. In 1964 Dr King examined the subtext 'that makes Black seem ugly and degrading'. In Roget's Thesaurus Dr King found '120 synonyms for blackness, and at least sixty of them are offensive.' He also found '134 synonyms for whiteness, and all of them are favorable'.[64] Just how much slavery and racism are the causes, or even relevant to these issues, continues to be a subject of fierce debate. At this point in time when we have a Black man seen as the world's leader, perhaps we can finally have a mature debate and further exploration.

From The *Windrush* to the White House

During his trip to Italy for a G8 summit on 10 July 2009, President Obama and his wife Michelle were in Rome visiting the Vatican. Purely coincidently, I was downstairs with my mother and sister

Laurice waiting for his private viewing of the Sistine Chapel to end. The crowds stood patiently, eager to admire the Renaissance artists and Michelangelo's wonderful celestial fresco.

Later, on a balmy Italian evening still warmed by the fiery Mediterranean sun, I stand on the banks of the River Tiber at Ponte Cestio bridge, watching it foam not with blood, as prophesied by Enoch Powell, but with the perpetually bubbling current. Laughter and bohemian music spin into the air from the banks of the numerous open-air riverside bars and cafés, as Rome cavorts as it has done for centuries, led by examples from its emperors.

Alongside the splendours of the Vatican, Coliseum, the Trevi Fountain and Pantheon are elements of African culture from the Egyptians. After conquering a civilisation, the Romans would allow those they had captured to keep their own language and culture. In return they borrowed, learned and assimilated those cultures into their own, including in Roman Britain. Egyptian architecture can be found around Rome, and seen in hieroglyphics on the remnants of the great emperors' palaces on the Palatine Hill overlooking the imposing Coliseum. The Palatine Hill was a Roman prototype of Beverly Hills as it was home to ancient Rome's rich and famous, where great feasts and fun would last for days. There are also Egyptian obelisks in London, Paris and President Obama's home, Washington DC.

During our family break I admired all these sights and now join Rome's revelry still contemplating the legacy that has been passed to me from the *Windrush* Generation. Their stoicism, courage, dignity, self-belief and ability to overcome adversity to create a new way of life from virtually nothing have been largely ignored until recently. In 1998, the fiftieth anniversary of the *Empire Windrush's* arrival was celebrated to honour that generation's contributions to modern British society in helping to create multiracial Britain. This long-overdue recognition caused both Black and white societies to consider and appreciate fully these pioneers' struggles and achievements, and hopefully provided a legacy for future generations to give them a sense of personal pride and strength. Seeing as my parents had guarded their past like secrets handed to them from the Mafia, the recognition of this period was a revelation and uncovered many stories. Among those stories were many like my own: of men reunited with wives, and with children they hadn't seen grow while they gained a footing in the 'Promised Land'.

With the Obamas dining across town, while I was in Rome my thoughts turned to America and the exchange of people who had been taken to the Americas as slaves, becoming the first Africans in the United States, and now the self-titled African-Americans. I think of the uprisings on both sides of the Atlantic during the 1950s and 60s; the fighting to gain civil rights and respect. These are the stories that triggered my own personal odyssey and search for identity, meaning, purpose and understanding of who and what I was, and from where I had come. America had been at the heart of my discovery and identity, through the African-American struggles for equality that I had found intriguing yet shocking, inspiring yet horrifying.

Once I'd traced my ancestral journey through my parents, I found a shared history that had rarely been explored. One story in particular compelled me: that of Dr Martin Luther King Jr, the struggle for civil rights and how he'd led ordinary people to create extraordinary things that would change the face of history. I wanted to understand why the Deep South in America had become a battlefront for the struggle for social justice, how heroic achievements had overcome state-sponsored violence and racism, and how that had influenced my life and those of many others who recognised this struggle. Their story became our shared story: a part of the Black diaspora that begins and stretches from Africa, throughout the Caribbean islands and around the world.

The story became an inspiration to millions of others throughout the world, including the man I would cross the Atlantic to watch historically enter the White House in January 2009. The stories and links were fascinating to me as I added depth to my knowledge and discovered new stories. Some came as a total surprise, one example being that days before my birth on 6 August 1965, President Lyndon Johnson had signed the Voting Rights Act in Washington, with Dr King and Rosa Parks among the audience. This significant legislation meant that for the duration of my life, African-Americans had gone from being without the right to vote to helping install Barack Obama as President of the United States of America.

My soul was on fire. Words and pictures were no longer enough. I wanted to bring these issues into living colour and undertake a personal pilgrimage by travelling and documenting the mythical American Deep South during Obama's presidency. I wanted to examine, learn and understand how this story had become a cause to overcome oppression and deliver a dream; how this message of hope and unity had inspired many. Most of all I needed to examine whether the Civil Rights Movement and the *Windrush* Generation, with their shared themes and stories of sacrifice and resilience, were still relevant today.

6

The Power of the Presidency
Washington DC and Virginia

Return to the National Mall, Washington DC, Spring 2010

Returning to Washington DC, and the steps of Capitol Hill, just over a year after President Obama's inauguration, I am overwhelmed by emotion. Memories of 2009 criss-cross through my mind as I view the great expanse of Washington's National Mall around me. As befits America's capital city, Washington DC is home to the nation's grandest monuments, housed within the great expanse of a national park. Walking down the steps of the resplendent Capitol Building, I recall the sight of over a million people huddled together in sub-zero temperatures on that momentous day of 20 January 2009. We all became individual colourful cheerleaders to the occasion, standing side-by-side, bedecked in flags and banners, loudly cheering, whooping and singing. We crowded onto the grassy Mall and packed the side roads and avenues, craning our necks for a better view of the occasion on the jumbo-size screens. Often we would stare open-mouthed and ask each other, 'Can this be true? Are we really going to see a Black president?' Not a single person departed without a ray of hope for the future, and not a single individual left without putting this piece of history into their collection of personal stories to be relived on countless occasions in front of families and friends all over the world, beginning with the words 'I was there...'

Obama's Tough Time

The nature of change, be it moving to a new country or adapting to a new career, can be exacting, and since becoming President, Obama's life has certainly been challenging. It is surprising to me, however, to view how he and his achievements are now perceived by his friends and supporters, or by his enemies and detractors. Obama has had to make the adjustment from the idealist visions of a candidate, detailed in his book *The Audacity of Hope,* to the reality of the daily decision-making of presidency. His insights within *Dreams from My Father,* documenting his touching but often difficult relationship with his own dearly departed father, are a support to me, but, in reality, there is no room for sentiment within the White House.

Once the music of Etta James's 'At Last' – controversially sung at his inauguration ball by Beyoncé – had drifted away into the night, the President woke up the next day to face as tough a set of challenges as any of his predecessors have encountered in their rookie year. Obama's first twelve months saw him commit more troops in Afghanistan than the previous incumbent, George W Bush, in what became America's war, as support from its European allies dwindled away. He began to reduce the military presence in Iraq, and introduced a $787 billion dollar economic stimulus package to bail out the banks and financiers of Wall Street, who had sent the world's economy into financial meltdown. He disappointed his more liberal supporters by failing to meet his pre-election pledge to close Guantánamo Bay. During America's 2009 *fall,* Obama's personality ratings tumbled dramatically as he and his adopted city, Chicago, lost an Olympic bid to Rio de Janeiro. His presence in the White House had given hope to parts of the developing world, which led to him being prematurely awarded the Nobel Peace Prize, joining illustrious recipients such as Dr Martin Luther King Jr and Mahatma Gandhi, from whom Obama had gained inspiration. However, the fog of Middle Eastern politics has drifted over his presidency, and gaining an Arab-Israeli peace agreement has proved as elusive as ever.

Enemies and Frenemies

In what has become an increasingly polarised and angry country, Obama's plans to support the poor through healthcare reforms and assist Wall Street bankers with a stimulus package have proved most controversial. His critics have been drawn together in an unholy alliance, with a welter of personal attacks coming from America's conservative right and his supporters on the liberal left subjecting him to stern criticism. His efforts to bring healthcare reform to America's disadvantaged (dubbed Obamacare) crept through Congress. The debate had already sparked more dissent and protest than the Iraq War, before the whole shouting match began again in the Supreme Court, and still continues.

There were farcical attacks from a group of people, including Donald Trump, calling themselves Birthers, who questioned Obama's legitimacy to the presidency. Despite validation of his birth certificate from officials in his birthplace of Hawaii, they believed Obama's birth certificate to be false and that he was, in fact, born in his father's country of Kenya. This would have made his election null and void, as the US Constitution clearly states that if someone was not born in the United States of America they cannot become president. This clause would prevent a Hollywood-style ending for former Governor of California Arnold Schwarzenegger, who is among the millions making up the self-proclaimed 'nation of immigrants'. Like my American family members, Schwarzenegger was born overseas but has made America his home.

The right-wing media, led by Rupert Murdoch's Fox News, has stoked up the opposition against Obama to unprecedented levels. According to the left-wing satirical pundit Jon Stewart and the programme he fronts, called *The Daily Show*, Fox News has repeatedly falsified accounts and news stories to discredit Obama's presidency. Former President Jimmy Carter has stated there is a racial element to the personal attacks, and to add insult to injury, monkey images appeared of Michelle Obama on Internet search engines. These attacks put into question the whole ideology of a post-racial America, and the new beginning in race relations across the globe that was trumpeted after Obama's inauguration. This new beginning seems to be no more than a myth to many in the Black communities I have since visited.

Arriving outside 1600 Pennsylvania Avenue, I stop to take the obligatory pictures of the White House, home to the Obama family. I imagine Malia and Sasha as they roam the White House, exploring its history, watched by their mother Michelle, whose popularity has overtaken that of her husband. The images of the Obama family at work, rest and play present a very different image to that of the previous forty-three presidents. A sense of disbelief still envelops me that Barack Obama is actually the President of the United States of America, and I wonder, in his early days, if a similar sense of awe was felt by him. As I stare at the gleaming ivory façade of the building built by slaves, I picture Obama having a quiet moment of contemplation; looking out of his window from behind the curtains; looking over my shoulder at the powerful landmarks of the National Mall. In his Oval Office, he will be surrounded by a sense of history and, as former President Lyndon Johnson claimed, 'ghosts of past presidents'.

America reveres its presidents like no other country in the world. In part, this is based on the theatrical title of 'the most powerful man in the world' accompanying the reality of the person who holds the codes that could unleash Armageddon. The president holds a unique place in the psyche of America. As head of state he is part royalty, part statesman, part CEO and, since the 1960s, part showbiz and scandal; both celebrated and despised in equal measure. Mount Rushmore in South Dakota, in the heart of America's Midwest, shows the heads of four of the greatest American presidents: Abraham Lincoln, Thomas Jefferson, George Washington and Theodore Roosevelt. Their images have been carved into the stone mountains, and thus into immortality in the hearts and minds of Americans. In Britain we do things slightly differently, giving our prime ministers an occasional bust or statue, while sometimes looking with British disdain at the prominence of some of America's 'rockstar politicians'. However, around the rest of the world, the President of the United States of America has one of the most recognisable profiles. He has made decisions that shape the world's future ever since the beginning of the twentieth century, when the United States overtook Britain to become the latest empire with massive global influence.

Washington DC (District of Columbia)

The United States of America's capital is an odd city, which exists simply for the purpose of accommodating the federal government. Washington, or 'DC' as the locals call it, was chosen as a compromise site between the northern and southern states in 1791, and is the neutral central point between those two factions. Along with slavery, this was one of several tensions between the North and South that would boil over during the following century. DC bears the name of its first president, George Washington, who, after defeating the British Army, declared independence from Britain on 4 July 1776. The National Mall is the capital's centre point, which hosts millions of visitors throughout the year.

Today, while tourists zip about the Mall on Segways (electric self-balancing scooters), I see many others throwing American footballs, baseballs or frisbees. Onlookers enjoy picnics on the grass during the Cherry Blossom Festival in the hot spring sunshine. During the sweltering summer they will be trying to find shelter from the blistering sunshine, and later in the year will stroll through the autumnal foliage as leaves fall to the ground, while kite-fliers tussle with the wind, and ever-watchful grey squirrels dart to and fro between the trees. And, of course, once every four winters on the third Tuesday in January, these visitors, onlookers and other park wildlife including many squirrels can see the ceremony inaugurating a newly elected president.

My first visit to the Washington National Mall was after I'd visited New York when I was sixteen, back in 1981. I have described it to friends as a huge, diamond-shaped park, with several grand monuments placed at various stages as you walk, glide, jog, cycle or, if you must, drive between the historical tributes. The National Mall sits on a gentle slope and is a real pleasure to explore, beginning at the steps of the Capitol Building on Capitol Hill. The Capitol Building and the nearby Supreme Court are neoclassical structures mostly influenced by the Romans and Greeks, but the Capitol's dome reminds me of St Paul's Cathedral, London. Washington owes its lack of American skyscrapers to a decree declaring that no building can be taller than the bronze Statue of Freedom that sits on top of the dome. Inside the Capitol, politicians debate various bills and legislation. Sadly, due to security, access to the Capitol has been restricted since I first marvelled at its paintings, friezes and sculptures as a teenager.

Moving down the Mall, the Smithsonian's complex of museums houses the nation's history in the form of over 138 million exhibits of paintings, books, sculptures and other artefacts. The Washington Monument is an Egyptian-style obelisk to honour George Washington which dominates the central esplanade. Crossing past Washington's Obelisk and walking to the eastern side, I arrive at Thomas Jefferson's Rotunda Memorial, surrounded on three sides by the Tidal Basin, fed by the expanse of the Potomac River. From there you can stroll to the Lincoln Memorial, where Lincoln sits imperiously on his presidential throne with the celebrated mural of him freeing the slaves carved into the stone wall behind him, along with references to Lincoln's 1863 Emancipation Proclamation.

These three memorials ensure Presidents Washington, Jefferson and Lincoln's lives are immortalised in history, all outside the current president's window. All three made huge contributions to create the foundations of modern America, and their accomplishments are rightly honoured. However, while reading the words of the Emancipation Proclamation at the Lincoln Memorial, a definite disquiet envelops me. I have been advised many times on my visits not to let the contradictions of America frustrate me. This is far easier said than done, as I have been raised on Guyanese straight talk and the British principle of fairness. On the one hand, these presidents seemed ignorant of the suffering of their countrymen – if, that is, they deemed African-Americans to be Americans. On the other hand, without their presidential interventions, which inspired people everywhere, life would have been even harsher for African-Americans.

Two of the Founding Fathers of America who were at the birth of the modern nation, George Washington and Thomas Jefferson, kept slaves during their lifetimes, and carried out their presidencies in acquiescence to slavery. Before the Civil War began, Lincoln stated that he had no interest in the plight of slaves, and he also favoured repatriation to Africa for freed slaves, ignorant that millions had been born in America. For Lincoln, however, the ends outweighed the principles, and if the only way to keep the union of the United States of America together was to free the slaves, then he would do so. Without Lincoln's Emancipation Proclamation that led to the Thirteenth Amendment to the American Constitution, the slaves would have remained in bondage. So it was that Lincoln reluctantly took his country into a bitter and savage Civil War to preserve the union and to end the chiefly southern institution of slavery.

Politicians, historians and socialists worldwide have acclaimed the words of these former presidents, and how they envisioned America by updating the principles of democracy passed to them by the Greek Empire. These principles are embodied within the documents of the Declaration of Independence (1776), the American Constitution and Bill of Rights (1787) and the Emancipation Proclamation (1863). These documents would not just change and eventually shape the rights of Americans, and not just free the slaves, but also provide a template for democratic rights, principles and freedoms for civil rights campaigners and countries around the world. Many have used their words to ensure that the famous pledge 'All men are created equal' is upheld and enshrined by governments for the good of their people. Ironically, before the Americans invaded Vietnam, Ho Chi Minh quoted the Declaration of Independence as he began to liberate his country from the occupying French in 1945.

Watching the icy-cold waters of the Potomac River, which was used by the first settlers to these lands thousands of years ago, surrounding Jefferson's Memorial, an uneasy feeling settles over me again, and questions arise. The United States of America's history officially began in 1776, but we know the Native Americans had founded a nation before the Europeans' arrival. Americans had been importing African slaves since their arrival in Virginia, and when South Carolina was founded in 1670, the settlers brought slaves from the then slave colony of Barbados. Once more, my soul stirs as I discover another connection from my past bridged by the Atlantic Ocean.

The Asian and African-Caribbean communities of Britain and other emerging societies across the world each chose how far to tread along the path towards either integration or isolation when they first migrated to new lands. For the Native Americans, however, this dilemma was reversed when they were confronted with new migrants to their country from Europe, and the outcome would push their culture to the brink of extinction. Before I can begin my journey into America's civil rights past, observe its present condition under Obama and draw a few comparisons and contradictions with my life in Britain, I need to go back to the beginning of America and its first inhabitants, to examine the very roots of its violent and bloody history.

The First Americans – Native Americans

While the first known Homo sapiens are acknowledged to have evolved out of Africa, there is no defined agreement of where prehistoric man first set foot in North America, or from where he came. Most research strongly suggests it was before the ice ages, around 20,000–30,000 years ago, when a nomadic tribe trekked across Asia and Siberia to reach what is now Alaska. Thus, one of the last states to be admitted to the union in 1959 – along with Obama's birth state of Hawaii – forged the beginning of America. This race of people evolved into what we know as the Native Americans. Their society expanded, incorporating many tribes, settlements and cultures across the vast North American continent. They were far from being savages; in fact, along with their Aboriginal cousins in Australasia, they were among the first eco-cultures, living and cultivating the land and respecting nature's wealth of resources.

Christopher Columbus and the Arrival of the Europeans, 1492

When the Europeans arrived to 'discover' America – arguably through the Italian explorer Christopher Columbus under the Spanish flag in 1492 – they found fully functioning communities, complete with various tribes such as the Cherokee, Seminole, Creek and Apache. These Native Americans had their own different languages and methods of communication, means of travel, religion, rituals, art, food and housing. Columbus thought he had landed in India and named these people *Indians*, as well as naming the Caribbean islands that he founded the West Indies. Both incorrect terms stuck, and later the foreign settlers expanded the Indian terminology to 'Red Indians' to differentiate between the races, thousands of miles and a world of difference apart. Columbus brought back to Spain new and exotic items that are still part of our lives today, such as corn, beans and sweet potato, turkey, pumpkin, peppers and tobacco.

In what would be a perennially unfair and unbalanced exchange between the two worlds, Europeans nearly wiped out an entire race across North and South America, with diseases that were fatal to the indigenous people, such as smallpox and measles, killing millions of the 'Amerindians'. Those who remained were put to work on the land as the first slaves of America, killed in wars, or subsequently pushed further and further to the margins of the country as their European controllers seized their lands.

Perhaps the best example of the mentality of the times, and a chilling portent for the Europeans' future intent, can be found in the way Columbus relayed news of the new world to the Spanish king and queen, who had sponsored his journey. His views set the tone for how the Europeans would view America's indigenous population:

> [They] have no arms and are without warlike instincts; they all go naked and are so timid that a thousand would not stand before three of our men. So they are good to be ordered about to work and sow, and do all that may be necessary and to build towns, and they should be taught to go about clothed and to adopt our customs.[65]

In such words, the template for European domination that led to colonisation, subjugation and – for better or worse – the movement of peoples and cultures across not only the Americas, but Africa, Asia and Australia, was established.

In the early seventeenth century, thousands of new settlers crossed the Atlantic from Britain to set up homes in the new frontier colony of America. These colonists left Britain to create new and different lives on foreign soil, and gain wealth across the Atlantic. Their backgrounds varied from landowners, granted land by the Crown and anxious to exploit the riches of new territories, to sharecroppers, which in America were barely a few rungs up from slavery on the scale of exploitation. Tenants rented land and animals, as well as their bed and board, from the landowner for a small share of the crop – all the work for little pay. Added to these frontier-folk were some 'ne'er-do-wells' – criminals that Britain was fond of exporting abroad to help expand its new colonies, as in places such as Australia. The settlers set up homes in Virginia and Maryland, known as the Chesapeake area after an estuary in the region.

The Deep South began with the formation of North and South Carolina and Georgia. Settlers here became the merchants and planters of the South by trading off the land in tobacco, indigo, rice and cotton, but they needed labour to assist them cultivate the land and enhance their growing riches.

In the east and north of the country, religious groups had migrated from Britain, among them the *Mayflower* Generation of pilgrims, Puritans and Quakers, to settle along the eastern seaboard and found states such as New England, New Hampshire, Pennsylvania, Massachusetts and Rhode Island. America became their home as the colonists found wealth, fame and fortune that had been denied to them in Britain due to its class and money structures. Their colonies were bordered by the vast range of Appalachian Mountains, stretching down from Maryland and Virginia to Georgia, and acting as a natural barrier from the rest of the vast country, where the British had decreed the Native Americans could roam. Instead, that was where other European settlements began.

In the two distinct groups of colonists America's history and culture can be traced. The northern, more religious, groups split into their various doctrines, whose laws, cultures and religions would shape the nation. In the South, the methods that were used to help its principal trade of slavery flourish would be integral to its way of life, and its perceived right to use slavery as a method of commerce.

The European Battle for Control of America

North America is a vast mass of land, which was divided up between constantly feuding European nations, whose legendary battles over the centuries included Waterloo, Trafalgar, Agincourt and the rise and fall of the Spanish Armada. A map of 1756 shows that the French controlled the northern lands of America, most of which would become Canada, and, helped by an alliance with the Native Americans from that region, they travelled south along the St Lawrence River through Detroit and St Louis to establish Louisiana, named after King Louis XIV. The Dutch controlled the Hudson area of New Amsterdam, later renamed New York by the British after its patron of the battle, the Duke of York. The British established modern-day New England, and their Puritans and pilgrims created Pennsylvania and Massachusetts, as well as the areas along the north-east coast of America. Due to the warmer tropical climate and agricultural conditions in the South, they established very different colonies in Virginia, North and South Carolina and Georgia which were to change the face and fate of a nation.

The biggest power already in the region at this time was the Spanish who, emboldened by their capture and overthrow of the Aztecs in Mexico, the Incas in Peru and Mayans in Columbia, ruled most of Central and South America. When compared with Spanish colonisation over the same period, the British colonies were modest. During the 1740s, the biggest city in an English colony was Boston, named by English pilgrims from Lincoln, with a population of 16,000. In Spanish America, several cities had already been established with populations in excess of 100,000, including Mexico City. The Spanish also controlled vast areas within North America, which became the states of New Mexico, Texas and Florida. The Spanish/Latin influence completely dominates Central and South America in language and culture today, and, to an increasing extent, in the United

States, especially in California, Arizona and Florida.

Global warfare was waged during the eighteenth century among the Europeans, and included wars in Asia and Africa as well as the Americas. Each of the respective European countries deemed wars on foreign soil vital for the establishment and maintenance of their empires, but they were costly in terms of resources used, and some wars dragged on for years. Just as with the modern-day conflicts in Iraq and Afghanistan, soldiers and their welfare, equipment, wages and deployment in wars came at a hefty cost to the various Crowns, costs covered by ever-increasing taxes.

Meanwhile, as the Europeans battled for control of their lands, the Native Americans worked for or against various European warlords. Without the advanced might of weaponry, and weakened from illness and infighting, they sought the best deal for themselves, tribe by tribe or region by region. With outbreaks of war occurring across the globe, pressing domestic issues, resources dwindling and the costs of war rising, European rule in North and South America was to come to an end ironically instigated by the very same people who had been sent there to establish European empires.

The American Revolution and the Declaration of Independence, 1776

The British wrestled control of most of North America, establishing a dominion of thirteen territories, and drafted treaties with the Native Americans, declaring the rest of the country as wilderness designated for their remaining tribes. Thousands of new colonists had now settled in America and felt firmly established on the new land, with fewer ties to the motherland and its entwined aristocracy, class structures and allegiance to the Crown. The ruling British levied a series of taxes and laws which the colonists thought was unfair, especially as they were denied any representation in Westminster. Eventually they rebelled from the tyranny of Britain with far-reaching consequences. The colonists wanted not only freedom, but also new values to be at the core of the new country.

John Adams, one of the Founding Fathers of America, described these values as 'More equal liberty than has prevailed in other parts of earth must be established in America'. To further establish their claims to be self-governing, after months of debate the Founding Fathers drafted the document the Declaration of Independence. It began: 'We hold these truths to be self-evident; that all men are created equal, that they are endowed by their creator with certain unalienable rights; that among these are life, liberty and the pursuit of happiness'. With these prophetic words, war was declared on American soil.

Twenty years after fighting with the British to defeat the French, George Washington fought and defeated his former imperial masters – ironically with the help of the French, who were more than happy to give secret assistance against their long-standing enemies. The war did not begin and end in 1776; it raged on and off for over fifty years, with Washington DC being burned to the ground by British soldiers in 1814. The bases for this continued hostility between Britain and America were trade, American alliances with the French and Spanish, and sheer revenge for past atrocities in the original War of Independence (1776–1783).

In addition, with the abolitionist movement gaining strength, Britain eventually banned slavery on home soil in 1807. Britain had growing concerns over the Americans' expansion of the transatlantic slave trade in the South, concerns that were shared in the northern states of America.

Role of the Founding Fathers

With independence gained, George Washington became the first leader of the new republic of the United States of America. He nobly stood down after two terms, setting a precedent that exists today to guard against corruption and the inertia of long-governing presidencies. His tenure gave birth to his iconic stature alongside his revered colleagues, known as the Founding Fathers of America. They included Thomas Jefferson, the equally multi-talented Benjamin Franklin, who during his life was an author, scientist, inventor, publisher and philosopher, and future presidents John Adams and James Madison. After the Declaration of Independence, they gathered the separate territories into unified states to form the nation by crafting the ideas, principles and powers of the country relating to trade, taxes, finance, law and governance. The nation was to be controlled by the federal government, which defined its relations with the states. This became the Constitution and the Bill of Rights, on which America's values and ideology are built today. Crucially, this birth of a new nation included a deal to appease those in the northern states, who wanted free labour to prevail and to end slavery there, and in the southern states, whose commerce depended on slave labour. This deal meant that the importation of slaves was not to be repealed until 1808.

The period between 1776 and 1851 is known as the *antebellum* period, from its Latin translation meaning before (ante) and war (bellum), and marks the period between independence and the beginning of the Civil War. This defining period in America's history would lead to the growth, in the words of third president Thomas Jefferson, of 'Empire and Liberty'. This proved to be one of several contradictions in terms of words and philosophy from the Founding Fathers and the new republic. However, their new values and principled concepts would mean a departure from the past ways of the 'olde world'. Empire for Britain and British subjects meant the imperial ruling of Westminster and the Crown, with the curtailment of liberties across the globe. The Founding Fathers had an alternative vision of a utopian land, where one day all of its citizens could be free and equal. A democratic set of principles enshrined within the Constitution, called the Bill of Rights, among other things gave its citizens the right to think and speak freely. In order to achieve this idealistic vision, given the dirty nature of politics and threats to break away from the union, deals had to be made. President Jefferson thus tolerated the chiefly southern practice of slavery, but he saw to it that it was not extended to emerging states in the Midwest of America. However, he could not stop the growth of slavery in the rapidly expanding South, where the southerners were becoming as powerful as they were agitated, fearing curbs on their dependence on slavery and the commercial prosperousness and political advantages it gave them.

In 1820, a line was drawn across the country from east to

west and the *Missouri Compromise* was drafted, named thus due to Missouri being roughly in the middle of the country. The states north of the line were to abolish slavery. Those below the line in the South would not abolish slavery, and would become de facto slave states.

Gradually, more new states became part of the United States of America. Some were bought, like Louisiana, from France as Napoleon needed to fund his quest for world domination. From the old European colonial world the first tide of self-rule, self-determination and democracy was emerging. The empires of Britain and Spain began to crumble, and in France *la guillotine* had cut its way through French aristocracy to forge a new republic of liberty, equality and fraternity, influenced by the Americans.

America grew rapidly, and the states were bound together by the Constitution and Bill of Rights. However, in the Deep South the prospects of equality and liberty were a distant dream for the millions of slaves who toiled the land.

Opening up the Midwest of America

Meanwhile, the original inhabitants of the land tried vainly to protect their rights and way of life. They had supported Britain in the War of Independence, as the British had protected Native American rights during their rule by preventing expansion to the great West. With the British defeated, however, the Native Americans were a conquered people as the victorious former colonists forged a new country. Several treaties and alliances were made with the new Americans as the Native Americans fought to stave off their inevitable subjugation and enforced removal from prime land. These paved the way for the next stage in the development of the country, and millions of Americans poured west over the Appalachians. America's expansion was assisted by the new technologies of the day, including the railroad, the telegraph and the newspaper, which gave fresh information on the hottest spots in the new frontier, a method the *Windrush* Generation would use ably in the next century.

People were urged to 'Go West!' There was a scramble for the best places to settle and discover new riches. Although today some people in Britain criticise the high percentage of Americans who don't own a passport, their ancestors had travelled in great numbers to reach America, and then had undertaken a second migration across its vast continent westward to conquer new frontiers. The states in the middle of the country, such as Illinois, Ohio and Iowa, began to form the mythical Midwest, also known as The Wild West due to its rapid expansion and unruliness. The abundance of land came with plentiful natural resources, such as coal, oil, gas, wood, and water from several fresh rivers. Millions more people migrated beyond the Midwest in the gold rush to just inland from the Pacific Ocean in California. As they laid down their roots, and tamed the harsh but fertile land, they built churches, schools, universities and many other social institutions that helped the expanding towns grow into the vast cities of today.

By using first negotiation and then force, the new Americans displaced the Native Americans, then wrested control of Texas and other territories in a war with Mexico, adding these to their portfolio of states. The country doubled in size between 1820 and 1840 to seventeen million, including migrants from Ireland, southern Germany and Italy desperate to escape the economic harshness at home. They brought with them Catholicism, to the angst of many ex-colonists who had left Europe to escape papist practices. Catholicism now added to the heady mix of fervent religion that was, and still is, central to the nation's fabric. The Protestant Church fragmented into Baptists, Methodists and other branches of faith as religious revivals attracted huge numbers, firmly bedding religion into secular America.

The country was becoming increasingly fragmented and less governable from Washington DC. The clamour to join the union of the United States was driving a wider crack along the fault line of simmering differences between the factions of North and South. Chief among these grievances was slavery. While there were those who opposed the practice of slavery on moral and religious grounds, the majority that opposed slavery did so on the grounds of commerce. In business terms: if the new states in the west introduced slavery they would gain an unfair advantage, as the cost of a free man's wages was more expensive than that of a bonded slave and his family on a plantation. Also, with the slave commercial links firmly established in the South, the slave states would have more power in Congress. The southern slave states therefore needed the institution of slavery – for that was what it had become – to maintain their income, commerce, lifestyles and power. Freeing Blacks through emancipation was a price that they were not prepared to pay, no matter what the cost. However, in the North the right to free trade was at the centre of the Constitution and the union of the United States of America.

The country could no longer, as Lincoln powerfully stated, be divided into 'half slave and half free'. It had to be one or the other. The issue of slavery would cause the country to implode into America's most bitter and violent period, seeing more American casualties than occurred through both world wars of the twentieth century combined, and the destruction of America on an unimagined scale. The American Civil War, 1861–1865, was when America finally began to acknowledge the existence of the hitherto exploited and ignored slaves. This would become the catalyst for civil rights, and examine where the slaves stood within the American Constitution. However, the answers would come at a huge cost.

The American Civil War, 1861–1865

When he arrived at the Oval Office, the newly elected President Lincoln was determined the differences that had split the country would not turn into the killing fields they were, in fact, to become, with American fighting American. In his inauguration address on 4 March 1861, with the country on the brink of civil war, Lincoln declared that his primary concern was to keep the union of the United States together, stating, 'I have no purpose, directly or indirectly, to interfere with the institution of slavery in the states where it exists'. This was his last desperate bid to placate the southern states and stop them from breaking away in secession, and also placate a large minority in the North who thought war was too big a price to pay for freeing the slaves. However, the South would not be appeased and formed the Confederate States of America.

This new Confederate Army of Southern States declared their

intentions by seizing government property the following month at Fort Sumner, near Charleston, South Carolina, in what had become Confederate heartland. They celebrated by raising their own flag, the Stars and Bars, or Dixie Flag as we know it today, to replace the Star-Spangled Banner. Soldiers and weapons were mobilised on both sides, and the bloody war began. In the grey corner (the colours the soldiers wore), with their newly installed rebel President Jefferson Davis, stood the Confederate Army, determined to preserve slavery and break away from the new tyranny imposed from Washington. Their aims were to hold their territory of eleven states and, if they could, capture the capital, Washington DC, which stood just twenty-five miles away from the Confederate capital in Richmond, Virginia and would provide a symbolic totem of victory. In the navy blue corner was the Union Yankee Army, determined to protect the Founding Fathers' dream of one nation. They knew outright occupation of the southern states would be the only way the South would capitulate, and thus secure the Union and end slavery in America.

Lincoln started the Civil War uncertainly, and the realisation gradually dawned on him that the Confederate Army wanted secession at any cost to life and property. Fighting during the American Civil War was bitter and fierce; its battles are etched into American folklore and battlefields remembered in national heritage sites. The bloody Battle of Gettysburg, Pennsylvania is one such battlefield, and resulted in thousands of casualties for the Confederate Army as they tried to advance upon northern ground. The North had a numerical fighting advantage and held all the infrastructure of government, including military superiority. Over a four-year period the battle raged, with both sides claiming notable victories but also many casualties.

On 1 January 1863, Lincoln carried out a masterstroke not by firing a weapon, but with the flourish of his pen. He announced, 'All persons held as within any part designated part of a state the people whereof shall then be in rebellion against the United States shall be then, thenceforward and forever free'. This was an opportunity for freedom for the slaves, and would turn the tide of both the war and history in Lincoln's favour, changing America forever.

The Emancipation Act was followed by the Thirteenth Amendment to the Constitution as Congress unequivocally put Lincoln's words into American law and statute. The Founding Fathers had deferred the issue of slavery, but had made sure future leaders, like Lincoln, would have to address it by decreeing that importing slaves would be abolished in 1808 – which it was, as a decree has to take place. Not only was freedom promised to America's four million slaves in the South, but Lincoln also gave them the right to bear arms and fight against their former masters, causing consternation among his own supporters. Though the institution of slavery had been discredited on financial and moral grounds, the thought of Black people being equal citizens of America – despite the grand words from the Founding Fathers in the Constitution – was still a step too far for many, whether North or South, Confederate or Yankee. Through Lincoln's stewardship, however, the Constitution was ratified, and the Thirteenth Amendment read:

> Neither slavery nor involuntary servitude, except as a punishment for crime where of the party shall have been duly convicted, shall exist with the United States, or any place subject to their jurisdiction. Congress shall have the power to enforce this article by appropriate legislation.

The latter part was in reference to the role of future politicians in upholding this law, which would take another century to be enforced.

Eventually the South, blockaded by superior forces which had driven its army to the point of starvation, and after suffering appalling losses to life and property, surrendered. The brutality of the Civil War is illustrated in the story of the burning and looting of Atlanta, Georgia. The scorched earth policy of the Yankee Army would leave deep scars when Reconstruction (of the southern states) took place (1865–77).

Lincoln accepted the surrender of the Confederate Army and rode into Virginia to the adulation of the freed slaves. Ten days later a delighted Lincoln, jubilant that the country was united once more, was enjoying an evening at a Washington theatre when an actor shot him at point-blank range. The audience only realised it was not part of the play when they heard the screams of his wife, Mary. Apart from starting an annoying American trend for using assassins' middle names, as with Lee Harvey Oswald, who would allegedly kill President Kennedy, and James Earl Ray who murdered Martin Luther King Jr, John Wilkes Booth's shot was the final act of a savage Civil War, with its death toll of over 600,000 soldiers and many thousands of civilians. Lincoln's death would make him a hero and martyr for many, but even in death he remained a figure of hate among the vanquished southerners for ending their 'peculiar practice' of slavery.

The Great Emancipator, as Lincoln was named, died for his policies and what eventually became his principles: to free the slaves and unify America. With Booth's assassination of the president came a portent of how the southern states would continue to defy the federal government. During the next hundred years they turned the war between northern and southern states into another violent national argument. As in the Civil War, the rules of engagement remained the same: that of an individual state's right to rule over its own boundaries against the law of federal government. Although vanquished in the Civil War, the southern states would ignore the clamour for social justice to trample over the freedoms deemed sacred in the Constitution, and continue their subjugation of African-Americans.

Colonial Virginia

While Washington DC struggles with its dual roles of playing home to a grand array of government institutions and trying to manage the challenging social issues of a modern city, the surrounding area is bursting with acres of natural beauty. Virginia has vast woodlands with near cloud-touching trees, lush fertile farming lands, and the Laurel & Hardy favourite: the 'Blue Ridge Mountains of Virginia'.

Visiting in 2012, I find much of Virginia appears untouched by modern life. Its present-day inhabitants give the impression that is just the way they'd prefer things to remain, which would have met with the early English migrants' approval. Their successors, the rebellious Founding Fathers of America, produced an elite group of men who would control not only the region but also the nation, and influence the world. The Virginia Dynasty, as they became known, produced four of the first five US presidents: Thomas Jefferson, George Washington, James Madison and James Monroe. All had inherited plantations from their fathers, and all of them kept slaves.

I had been drawn to Monument Avenue in Virginia's state capital of Richmond by British author Gary Younge's riveting passage from his book *No Place Like Home*. Monument Avenue is a wide boulevard with a grand central esplanade dividing the opposing traffic shuttling in and out of the city, and there I came face to face with the battle for civic recognition in the imposing stone tributes chosen by the city's fathers.

The first monument I saw was of Richmond-born tennis player Arthur Ashe (1943–1993). Ashe overcame the authorities who were banning him from playing against white boys of his own age by leaving the city to gain a scholarship in California. He went on to become world number one and Wimbledon champion. Ashe was different to many of his sporting contemporaries and ensured his life continued to fulfil and challenge him. He summed this up by stating in his autobiography:

> My innermost stirrings inevitably have to do with trying to overcome racism and other forms of social injustice, with the search for dignity and power for blacks, in a world often so hostile to us. Not the tennis court, but the area of protest and politics, would be the single most significant testing ground for me in the middle years of my life.[66]

Ashe became a prominent civil rights campaigner. He argued for and won better wages for the then poorly paid tennis players, and also fought against Apartheid, which led to him being arrested for protesting in Washington DC. He died tragically of AIDS from a blood transfusion. The equivalent of Wimbledon's Centre Court at Flushing Meadows, New York, where Andy Murray became the

2012 US Open champion, proudly carries Arthur Ashe's name.

Moving further along Monument Avenue I was met by towering testaments to the Civil War. Stone edifices of General Robert E Lee, General Stonewall Jackson and Confederate President Jefferson Davis led me into the city. I had reread Gary Younge's book before I left home, and his words revisited me as I struggled to understand my emotions as a Black Briton in the South. Of his time here, Younge said: 'Monument Avenue felt like the cultural and political equivalent of putting a huge statue of Adolf Hitler and his sidekicks up on Kurfürstendamm Platz in Berlin – not as trite a comparison as it might appear, given the number of blacks who died in slavery.'[67]

Much of Monument Avenue today is based in a diverse multicultural neighbourhood, with many of its inhabitants passing beneath these monuments that declare adoration for men who would have kept their ancestors enslaved. Regardless of whether one's sympathies are with the Confederates or the Yankees, Richmond and the neighbouring colonial city Williamsburg represent a fascinating, if unnerving, glimpse into the colonial history of America.

Arlington National Cemetery, Virginia

Back in DC, I've taken a short journey on Washington's efficient Metro system to the Arlington National Cemetery in Virginia. The Metro transports thousands of people daily from the surrounding states of Virginia and Maryland to Washington DC, and the great monoliths of federal government that Washington is purpose-built to house, such as the Pentagon, CIA and FBI. Arlington Cemetery is home to America's soldiers killed in service. Thousands of graves surround me: some marked with a single name, others with full military title and place of birth. The cemetery's origins stretch back to the Civil War, when General Lee left his Virginia home to fight for the Confederate rebels. Yankee soldiers commandeered his home and made it a burial site for their war-dead. It is now sacred ground, as observed by the hushed reverential tones, subdued atmosphere and muffled sounds of grief.

The thousands of Americans buried in Arlington Cemetery

include those from World Wars I and II, Vietnam and even from the Space Shuttle disaster of 1986. Also buried here is President Kennedy, who along with his brother Bobby would play a key role in the federal government's ongoing battles to ensure the South adhered to the Constitution and upheld civil rights for all of its citizens. JFK qualified to be buried here as a former president and commander-in-chief, and alongside him his wife and First Lady, the glamorous Jacqueline Onassis Kennedy, now rests. Like Mary Lincoln before her, Jacqueline had to suffer the tragedy of watching her husband slain in front of her.

Sadly, more war-dead are being buried here today from the conflicts in Iraq and Afghanistan, with grieving families in attendance. During winter, every hour on the hour there is an elaborate ceremonial changing of the guards at the Tomb of the Unknown Soldier. A moving rendition of 'The Last Post' is played, and while I am among a 200-strong crowd of onlookers, a nearby family is lost in private sorrow. A discharge of ammunition to salute the anonymous soldier penetrates the air, and the Stars and Stripes is given to the family to end the sombre ceremony. Towering behind the Tomb of the Unknown Soldier is an impressive white-stoned amphitheatre that plays host to around 5,000 guests at national ceremonies on American public holidays, including Veterans and Memorial days.

From the amphitheatre, a clear blue day stretches across the Virginian sky and around the nation's capital. Gazing at Lincoln's memorial in the distance, my mind drifts back to black and white images of Martin Luther King Jr at the very peak of his career, delivering his famed 'I Have a Dream' speech. Following that, Washington DC would never be the same again, but DC had always had an impact on Dr King. In 1944 he worked as a manual labourer in Connecticut, in the unsegregated North, helping to fund his education. He was on his way home to Atlanta when he felt the stinging effect of the racist Jim Crow segregationist laws of the South, laws that would force him to change to a *coloured only* carriage to continue his train journey. This occurred at a time when America was joining Allied forces in Europe to rid the world of Fascism, yet was still unwilling to put its own house in order and extinguish the racist practices of the South. It was an experience Dr King would never forget, causing him to state in his autobiography, 'The very idea of separation did something to my sense of dignity and self-respect'.

When I returned in 2010, I saw notices for a long-overdue memorial to Dr King to be erected next to the Lincoln Memorial in tribute to that momentous day on 28 August 1963, and I vowed to return to see it. This I did in 2012 and staring at its chalky-white granite edifice, part in awe, and part in surprise at the rather harsh stare returning my gaze, and found solace that, in among the slave-owning presidents of the past and the current Black president, there is space for a true king.

Burdens of the Presidency

America's fascination with conquering new untamed lands, creating a utopian colony from nothing with people of similar attitudes, beliefs and values, but with an unknown hidden enemy lurking in the shadows, is inherent within its culture and psyche. You can see the influence of this fascination in its mission to conquer the galaxies of space, from Kennedy's space-race with the Soviet Union, culminating in Man landing on the moon, to Reagan's Star Wars defence shield against what he called the 'evil empire' of Russian forces. New frontiers and worlds are also portrayed in American popular culture, from James Kirk in *Star Trek* 'Boldly going where no man has gone before', to James Cameron's futuristic highest-grossing film of all time, *Avatar.*

Yet as the nation moved forward from its bloody Civil War, building new cities, forging new technologies and creating unparalleled wealth to lay the foundations of the superpower it would become, something, or more pertinently some*one*, was missing from this fable. If the indigenous people, the Native Americans, had been forcibly moved to the margins of the country, then what was to become of the people who had been brought there in chains from Africa? When lofty concepts of nationhood, equality and utopian societies based on freedom and liberty were being drafted, what would America do with the enslaved labour it had purchased? Those invisible hands had helped boost not only America's trade and commerce, but also the fortunes of those around the globe, and in particular Britain as it, too, enjoyed the riches and rewards of the transatlantic slave trade. For centuries, ships laden with goods had left British ports – including my two home cities of London and Bristol – bound for Africa to pick up exotic goods and millions of slaves, before heading to the Americas, establishing the West Indies. Then they would make the return journey back to Britain with the produce harvested by the slaves in the Americas.

George Washington, Thomas Jefferson and the rest of the Founding Fathers agreed, decreed and signed the Declaration of Independence and led the coalition of thirteen states, sowing the seeds for the birth of the United States of America. The Constitution, the Bill of Rights and the Emancipation Proclamation are revered as some of the finest documents to espouse the virtues of freedom and provide a framework for democracy, yet at the time of these momentous declarations of equality, slaves were toiling the land in bondage, the Native Americans were being driven off their lands, and women were denied the vote and treated as second-class citizens. George Washington kept slaves, and on the eve of war with Britain, he wrote, 'The Crisis has arrived when we must assert our Rights, or Submit to every Imposition that can be heap'd upon us till custom and use will make us as tame & abject Slaves as the Blacks we Rule over'.[68] He'd doubled the size of his sumptuous Mount Vernon plantation in Virginia and owned over 100 slaves before he set out to fight for freedom against Britain in 1775.

Thomas Jefferson, a libertarian and campaigner for civil rights for Blacks, women and Native Americans, wrote some of his speeches from the comfort of his Monticello plantation in Virginia, where he kept over 200 slaves and was alleged to take Black women as his lovers. These lovers included his long-term consort, Sally Hemings, with whom he fathered at least one mixed-race child. Controversy still rages around this today.

Abraham Lincoln, on the eve of Civil War, stated he had no

quarrel with the southern peculiarities of slavery, and for freed Blacks he favoured reparation to Africa.

The Trouble with America vs America the Beautiful

How then do I look upon these men as their stone statues, monuments and tributes to their accepted wisdom surround me? Do I brand them hypocrites, or do I accept their flaws and contradictions to consider them men of their time who drafted a template for a new nation that could be amended and updated as time and the country evolved? Did they plan that their successors would become enlightened regarding the injustice of slavery, as President Lincoln had done in the aftermath of the Battle of Gettysburg? On 19 November 1863, Lincoln recalled the ideals of his predecessors in a stirring address to the nation: 'Four score and seven years ago, our fathers brought forth on this continent a new nation conceived in liberty and dedicated to the proposition that all men are created equal.'

I confess I struggle with the conundrum of contradictions, and turn to the words and wisdom of Dr King for guidance. He termed man's perpetual struggle as between 'illusion and reality'. Creating new ideas for a nation to adhere to is never easy, and my criticism is tempered by events across the world. In the twentieth century, there were enough repressive governments in Germany, Italy, Spain and the Eastern bloc of Europe, where speaking one's mind would mean the loss of liberty, if not life. Oppression and repressive dictatorships have flourished in the Middle East, Africa, Asia and the Caribbean, while in Australia, Aboriginal children were taken and sent to live with white families without the consent of their mothers.

In the UK we have an implied sense of liberty, but nowhere is it written for new citizens to the country. I grew up hearing the street slang 'Taking the fifth' (the amendment relating to the right to remain silent) as an implied sense of personal rights when dealing with authorities.

The Founding Fathers gave us the principles behind that solemn phrase of almost Biblical proportions: 'All men are created equal'. From there we can draw, as others have done, the essence rather than the practice of their words. From George Washington, we have equality: freeing his nation from tyrannical British rule. From Thomas Jefferson, we draw the beginning of the American Dream: setting the ideas for his countrymen having 'certain unalienable rights, among them life, liberty and the pursuit of happiness'; and from Abraham Lincoln, we have the Emancipation Act to free the slaves, which became freedom for millions. Equality, liberty and freedom: these words became the bedrock of many social movements and civil rights campaigns that followed, including the suffragettes who used the flaws in the Constitution to successfully campaign for women's rights. These principles and contradictions have in equal measure fascinated and repelled me since I first clambered around the Statue of Liberty in 1981.

The Road South via the Civil Rights Movement

So, at the end of the Civil War the slaves were freed, America was united and everyone lived together in perfect harmony. Then, 150 years later, a Black man became the forty-fourth president and made the White House his crib. I'm joking about the harmony, of course, and this narrative tells a mere fraction of the story of the Civil Rights Movement that led to Obama becoming president.

Many in the South grew more determined to keep their iron grip on the throat of African-Americans. In fact, far from freedom leading to liberty and equality becoming a natural process, the men and women of the South would defy the spirit of the Constitution. They introduced state laws and created institutional barriers, or, when that failed, resorted to violence, introducing a new tyranny. From my initial US visits and navigating my way through American history, I have struggled to comprehend the cruel impact of the South's racism. I could not fully understand what life was like living under Jim Crow laws, or imagine the full impact of segregation or the separate but equal doctrine. All of these practices denied the African-Americans their civil rights, including the right to vote or gain an education, and thus kept them in poverty.

Despite being bored rigid by history at school, these new historical perspectives fascinated me. It was now that my personal quest to explore my heritage, through the prism of the Deep South and the story of the Civil Rights Movement, began to take a greater significance. I wanted to walk in the footsteps of one of the most inspirational figures of the twentieth century, Martin Luther King Jr, to access the images, sounds and tales of the Civil Rights Movement.

The Caribbean, Africa and Britain had given me history and heritage, but I wanted to gain a closer understanding of the principles of social justice that had helped carve out my own identity, values and beliefs. So many questions swirled in my mind that needed answering. What had made the American civil rights story so central to so many across the globe? How, after the Civil War had ended, did a new battle for civil rights begin? What inspired the Black seamstress Rosa Parks, from Montgomery, Alabama, to refuse to give up her seat for a white man and sit at the back of the bus? What would cause a young Muhammad Ali (then known as Cassius Clay) to claim he had thrown his Olympic gold medal into the Ohio River in disgust at racism in his home town of Louisville, Kentucky? Why would howling angry mobs greet schoolgirls a fraction of their size with violence and vitriol in Little Rock, Arkansas, or blow them to pieces in a church in Birmingham, Alabama, just because they wanted to attend school or church? And what caused thousands of ordinary Black and white people to protest, march and die for social justice?

I also wanted to assess the conditions of the South in the twenty-first century, under its first Black president. I wanted to visit the formerly segregated cities such as Atlanta, known as the Gateway to the South, birthplace of Dr King, now dubbed as the unofficial 'Black capital' of America and capable of hosting the Olympic Games in 1996, and view how the same economic conditions that had helped Atlanta flourish had left New Orleans floundering when Hurricane Katrina hit the Big Easy. I wanted to see how the 'invisible hands' that had developed America under slavery continued to provide major contributions to the country within institutional bastions from which they were previously excluded, such as politics, business, music, education and sport.

Like William Wilberforce had been in Britain, Dr King would become the eloquent faith-based orator and flag-bearer for civil rights, leading a vast array of coalitions. As with the abolitionists, Dr King's battles against inhumanity and for social justice would last for decades, and like the abolitionists they would espouse a moral and legal argument rather than violence to succeed, but on this occasion Black people would be central to their own destiny.

My story was gaining momentum and substance as my odyssey was taking the shape of a celebrated American road trip. The voices and spirits swirled within me once more, causing my very soul to vibrate and my fingertips to tingle. 'Tell their story. Your story. Our story,' their voices chanted. I felt the tide of history surging within me, and to paraphrase fictional southerner Rhett Butler, 'Frankly, I did give a damn!'

Both Dr King and President Lincoln had died for their beliefs, each leaving a lasting legacy. The Civil War had freed the slaves, but thousands of Americans had died in pursuit of a unified nation. Nearly a century later, Dr King was to wage a non-violent war on the South, and restore a sense of dignity and self-respect for millions of others around the world. It was clear to me that the injustices of the South had their most pernicious roots within the former slave states of this vast area. There I would see, hear, taste and feel what lessons from the Civil Rights Movement I could understand, and assess first-hand the impact of Obama's election.

7

In Search of a King

My First Black Cultural Icons

Shortly after I returned from my visit to New York during my formative teens, my brain overactive from the exposure to a newly discovered identity and family heritage, I read the powerful *Autobiography of Malcolm X* as told to the author of *Roots*, Alex Haley. Even without the aid of rose-tinted spectacles, I can look back over thirty years later and say it was one of the cultural reference points that changed my life. The book was so searingly painful, honest and evocative that it has stayed with me to this very day.

Malcolm X was born Malcolm Little in Omaha in the corn-belt of America, the fourth of eight children. His father, Earl Little, who had been born in the South, in Georgia, was an outspoken Baptist minister, an admirer of Black activist Marcus Garvey, and involved in Black self-reliance programmes. Because of this, he was constantly harassed and pursued by racists throughout his life. Malcolm believes his father was killed by the white supremacist group the Black Legion when Malcolm was just six years old. His mother, Louise Little of Grenadian and Scottish heritage, never recovered from the death of her husband. She suffered a nervous breakdown and was committed to a mental institution; her children were separated and sent to foster homes.

As a young firebrand, I viewed Malcolm X's life as closer to mine than Dr King's, which explains Malcolm X's enduring appeal in youth culture, particularly with young Black men. His early life travelled through violence, racism, family break-up, loss of a father figure, alcohol, women, drugs, flash clothes, petty crime and jail before his conversion to Islam while in jail; all of which resonates with many young Black men. His was a true-life tale of the perennial outsider or rebel which has always had mass appeal, from the Bible to Hollywood where Spike Lee told the story of Malcolm's life in the 1992 film starring Denzel Washington. Malcolm's conversion to education while in prison, including learning from history books to teach himself, was illuminating for me and showed that it is never too late to learn.

Malcolm found special resonance in Black history, feeling that Black people had been written out of the history books by white men. One of the biggest early influences in his re-education was Carter G Woodson (1875–1950), a Virginian son of former slaves who became one of the first African-Americans to gain a Harvard degree. Woodson would later redefine how Black people documented, raised awareness about and promoted their own history by creating Black History Week. This has subsequently become Black History Month, which is in February in the United States and in October in the UK, to celebrate, restore pride and bring together communities in a multicultural society.

In his autobiography, Malcolm X cites Woodson's *The Mis-Education of the Negro* as one of the most influential books that he ever read. He also praises WEB Du Bois's *The Souls of Black Folk*, and, interestingly, renowned English author HG Wells's *The Outline of History* for attacking the assumption that white people were superior. So inspired was I by Malcolm X's words 'Education is the passport to the future, for tomorrow belongs to those who prepare for it today'[69] that many years later I named my business, which is now a consultancy specialising in working with communities, 2morrow 2day.

As a naïve teenager, I was always amazed that Malcolm X and Dr King met only once, on 26 March 1964 in Washington DC. Though perceived as polar opposites – literally one for war and the other for peace – their views, at the time of their murders within three years of each other, were a lot closer than they are depicted. This misunderstood and demeaning portrayal of the two men is particularly rife within the Black community, and a subject of a wide body of work.

Yet, far from the enduring image of a rifle-toting Black Nationalist racist, Malcolm X had found peace within himself with 'blond-haired, blue-eyed men' who, after his pilgrimage to Mecca, he could now look upon as brothers. He came to understand the folly of judging someone by their race, gender, appearance, ability, religion or age, stating, 'Some white people are truly sincere...and a blanket indictment of all white people is as wrong as when whites make blanket indictments against blacks'.[70] To read Malcolm X change his previous unpalatable, yet unshakeable, belief that white people were devils was a revelation to me as someone who abhors discrimination of any kind.

And far from the image of a 'chicken' walking away from a fight, Dr King repeatedly put his life in danger to face down racists, and made fatal enemies in power by criticising President Johnson for escalating the war in Vietnam. Instead of celebrating two great leaders and unifying against racism under two differing viewpoints, Dr King and Malcolm X's pre- and post-death personas have been goaded into separate corners like prizefighters. To this day, you are either for one and against the other, never both. Sadly, when they conceivably could have watched the genesis of their efforts and dreams enter the White House together, we have neither.

These two men burned brightly within my developing consciousness. A contrasting far-from-perfect pair of icons, troubled by their internal demons and party factions, and hounded by the authorities, both were brutally slain in the prime of their lives, aged thirty-nine, during the turbulent decade of my birth, the 1960s. For all their very human frailties, they were my heroes; chosen by me, not something I was told to do or handed from a school curriculum. Finding out about these two contrasting beacons was, to paraphrase former Black Panther leader Eldridge Cleaver, 'like using fire and ice for my soul'. Both were very much at the heart of the re-education of Roger Griffith. They were my reference points to Black culture, and remain at the head of a now healthy list of heroes. If anything, their faults – the extramarital affairs of Dr King, or indefensible words about other races by Malcolm X – made them even more accessible, as opposed to some pious deity that I could never emulate. Then, as now, I found depth and strength in their words and achievements, rather than admonishing or, as some do, perversely celebrating their feet of clay. Neither converted me to Christianity or Islam, but I did take from them a sense that you could lead a life true to your own beliefs and values, if, however, you were prepared to make sacrifices.

Yet despite my affinity with Malcolm X as the archetypal angry young man, it was Dr King's life which became more intriguing to me. You see, I understood Malcolm X, and knew just how racism could colour your judgement and push you along a path to hate others, who hate you in return, leading to an endless spiral of hostility. Growing up, it was the non-violent approach, to turn the other cheek in the face of racist taunts and brutality, that I could not comprehend. I did, however, appreciate it. I also admired Dr King's ability to mobilise a coalition from different backgrounds to fight inequality which, added to the senseless injustices and enduring mysticism of the Deep South of America, gave me a sense of purpose to add to my adventure. It was this story of civil rights, of many thousands of individuals uniting to fight racism and inequality (a scene that was mirrored in celebrating Obama's inauguration day) in which I became absorbed as I travelled throughout the Deep South. Making pilgrimages to the places of Dr King's birth, death and famous speeches, I remembered all I had learned about the background to this icon's feats of history.

On 18 January 2009, I attended a special service at the Ebenezer Baptist Church in Atlanta, to celebrate what would have been Dr King's 80th birthday a few days earlier. I stopped overnight in Raleigh, North Carolina, en route to Washington DC. Much like the rest of America, Raleigh was celebrating a public holiday with a difference for the entire weekend. The third Monday of every January is Martin Luther King Jr Day, while every four years the third Tuesday in January sees the president's inauguration. This symbolic significance was widely talked about in America at the time, and I can remember people saying it was the end of racism, with post-racial America being the theme debated on the airwaves.

After Lincoln's assassination at the end of the Civil War, America selected a new president, Andrew Johnson, to carry out Lincoln's legacy and reunite the nation. The country had been divided by war, but the task was now to rebuild the South, with much of it, such as Atlanta, in ruins. 'Nearly a fifth of white southern males, aged between thirteen and forty-three, had been killed and many were left severely disabled.'[71] America entered a period called Reconstruction between 1865 and 1877, which put the Yankee Army in charge of rebuilding the vanquished *Old South* into a changed landscape to create a *New South*. As is its creed, America set about this challenge with great zeal and rebuilt its infrastructure quickly, helped by an influx of new immigrants from Europe. Buildings, railways and roads were one thing, but changing the hearts and minds of southern folk would prove a far more difficult task.

The victory for the North meant that four million slaves were now free in the South. Many travelled north to build new lives, but millions more stayed. Their circumstances could be compared to long-term prison inmates released into a world of open hostility. Civil rights activist Frederick Douglass described the ex-slaves' plight as:

> He [slave] had none of the conditions of self-preservation or self-protection. He was free from the individual master but the slave of society. He had neither money, property, nor friends. He was free from the old plantation, but was turned loose naked, hungry and destitute to the open sky.[72]

President Johnson welcomed the southern states back into the fold on the conditions of their sworn allegiance to the union of the United States of America and their acceptance of slavery's abolition. Crucially, though, he left the southern states the freedom to pass their own laws. These included laws such as whether to give the newly freed men and women the right to vote, and thus full liberty and equality as decreed in the Constitution. The southerners rebuilt their lives with the bitter taste of defeat in their mouths, and still hankered for the days of their economic and racial superiority. They had already proved they were prepared to spill their own blood to keep their power, and exploited the president's unwillingness to purge the southern plantocracy by passing several legal measures, known as Jim Crow laws, with the overall aim of keeping Black people in further subordination.

After Reconstruction, the southerners gradually gained control of their old powers, assisted by the terror of the Ku Klux Klan. The 'KKK' was formed in 1865 by former Confederate soldiers. They intimidated Blacks, and any white supporters who wanted to rebuild the South on the principles of equality for all. Although slavery had been outlawed and Reconstruction completed in 1876, the legacies and prejudices that had existed between white and Black were never addressed.

North or South, the concept of the Black race being equal was not an idea that America was going to embrace easily. Even at the birth of a new republic, Black slaves were recognised as being only three-fifths human. This figure was used to determine a state's representation in the US Congress based on the size of that state's population. With the northerners unable or unwilling to enforce full emancipation and equality on the southern states, a systematic process was instigated and designed to keep the races apart and limit the rights of the ex-slaves. These practices and laws originated as Black Codes before becoming known as Jim Crow laws, and were both local and state regulations that kept the races separate in public areas and institutions. This separation covered all areas of life, such as schools, hospitals, public transport, and a variety of social arenas including eating places, churches, dance halls, and even separate sporting leagues. As well as suffering this indignity, Black people found their facilities were substandard, continuing a legacy of inferiority. This left millions of African-Americans not only economically and socially disadvantaged, but spiritually at the very bottom of America's ladder of opportunity.

*

The Supreme Court is another of Washington's symbolic federal monuments that played a major role in the civil rights struggle. Since the middle of the nineteenth century, the Supreme Court has made a number of decisions which prevented the progress of civil rights. In the 1857 *Dred Scott* decision, the court ruled by a majority of seven to one that Black people could not become American citizens, and as such were deemed property to be moved around the country at the will of their master. This was another key issue in the build-up to the Civil War. With America's growing expansion westward, the eternal question of whether the new territories would be 'slave or free' would finally need to be answered.

After the Civil War, the Supreme Court did pass a raft of racial equality legislations. The Thirteenth Amendment (1865) abolished slavery. The Fourteenth Amendment (1868) gave full citizenship and equal protection to male Blacks. The Fifteenth Amendment (1870) gave Black people the right to vote. However, the southern states gradually eroded the law of the land, and it would take America another century to practise what it not only preached, but also decreed.

Several southern states put clauses specifically designed to keep Blacks – and poor whites – off the ballot into the three amendments mentioned. These included literacy and comprehension tests, and Grandfather Clauses which only gave the right to vote to those whose grandfather had had the right to vote. As slaves did not have this right before the Civil War, Black people were excluded from the process and thus denied any political power.

In 1896, an early prelude to Rosa Parks's refusal to move to the back of the bus occurred in Louisiana, when Homer Plessy, a light-skinned mixed-race man, was arrested aboard a train for sitting in an all-white carriage. Plessy's actions were designed to test the Fourteenth Amendment of 1868, which recognised the equality of all US citizens, against the segregation laws of Jim Crow. The final decision was made in the Supreme Court, and its 1896 judgement ruled that Jim Crow laws were constitutional and legal, as long as facilities were maintained as 'separate but equal'. It also ruled that this was a matter for the individual states, and not for the federal government to interfere. Equally important was its ruling that legislation could not be used to assist in overcoming social prejudice to improve race relations. These landmark decisions strengthened segregation in the southern states, and as Dr King (as he would be most commonly known) viewed it, only the 'separate' part of the law was enforced, with facilities remaining unequal. It would take Dr King to lead and the Civil Rights Army to finally break down the 'peculiar' bastion of southern superiority, which used subjugation that had evolved from slavery into segregation. Dr King attacked the 'evils' of the Jim Crow laws against the 'underlying philosophy' of democracy, denouncing the psychological impact of segregation. For Dr King, regardless of whether someone received the same services as another, being excluded left you with a feeling of bitterness and loss of dignity.

Faced with a lack of protection and assistance from federal government and the White House for the next half-century, despite a wealth of evidence of the abuses of their civil rights, it was left to the African-Americans themselves to fight and lay down their own bodies, using the tactics of non-violence as espoused by Dr King.

The Life of Martin Luther King Jr
15 January 1929 – 4 April 1968

Early Life

Dr King was just thirty-nine when he was assassinated in Memphis, Tennessee, but the legacy of his lifetime of achievement will last for generations. He was the third in a generation of male preachers, following his father who had changed his name from Mike to adopt the name of the founding father of the Protestants, Martin Luther.

In many ways, Dr King was the archetypal reluctant hero: happy to accept a life in the pulpit serving God, until destiny called. His role in the civil rights struggle would test not only his faith, but also his convictions and the very essence of his humanity. He was born in Atlanta on 15 January 1929, during the Great American Depression, into a stable middle-class family. The queues for bread and images of poverty that he witnessed would leave a lasting impression of the inequality and social issues facing America. His loving parents created a solid platform for him to achieve greatness, with his father a particularly strong guiding influence in his life.

Martin Luther King senior, or Daddy King as he was known, would educate his son about the indignities of segregation and Jim Crow. A large man in size and stature, he would never accept the status quo of a Black man in the South: of second-class citizenship. Daddy King could trace the roots of his grandfather's life as a slave, and had watched his own father suffer indignities in silence as a sharecropper on a Georgia plantation. He vowed to leave the plantation life behind him and moved to Atlanta, labouring by day and educating himself by night. He became an activist in the early civil rights era, and after receiving a degree in divinity, became a pastor on the street on which he lived, Sweet Auburn Avenue. The Ebenezer Baptist Church became his son's 'second home'.

His parents' love could not protect him from what Dr King termed the 'inexplicable and morally unjustifiable Jim Crow laws of the South', and for a while he struggled to reconcile himself with the direct racism he experienced before it consumed him with bitterness. Where the young Dr King went to school, where he played and with whom were all things determined by the Jim Crow laws, leaving him with a burning sense of injustice.

Daddy King helped to develop his son's public speaking skills by making him read extracts from the newspaper out loud after dinner. At the age of fourteen, Dr King delivered his first public address against racism at an oratory contest in Georgia, where he called for the Constitution, Bill of Rights and relevant Amendments Acts to be translated into reality, and attacked the discrepancy between those words and actions. This winning speech would mark the emergence of one of the finest orators in history. In addition, it would represent what Dr King would devote the rest of his life to achieving, and in so doing would change both America's and the world's perceptions of the Black man.

By his own description, Dr King had an unremarkable childhood. One of the more notable things about the segregated neighbourhood in which he was raised was that poor and middle-class families lived on the same street, rather than living in separate areas. No one around him accumulated great wealth. Poor families lived in one-tier shotgun houses – so named because a bullet could pass through the front wall, travel through the house, and come out through the rear wall – standing next to Dr King's modest two-storey family home, which still stands today in Atlanta.

Dr King undertook manual work to supplement the cost of his studies and, after leaving high school in 1944 at the age of fifteen, he enrolled at Morehouse College, Atlanta: a renowned historical all-Black college and university (HSBCU). This was two years earlier than most of his classmates, and he recalls working hard to catch up. He revelled in the spirited atmosphere at Morehouse, the heady mix of active social life and modern clothing was where he developed his 'Ivy League' dress sense. The political debates on race, together with the knowledge he gained on civil disobedience, stimulated his eager young mind. With his spiritual roots strong, he entered the ministry in 1948, and later that year passed his sociology degree.

He continued his scholarship, gaining a divinity degree at Crozer Theological Seminary, Pennsylvania, in 1951, and received his doctorate in theology in 1955. It was while undertaking his religious studies that he began reading some of the accepted great philosophers of the world, such as Friedrich Nietzsche and Karl Marx. At each place of learning he added layers of knowledge and wisdom while being heavily influenced and abetted by his peers, teachers and mentors, building on the foundations of his faith and family. However, it was when he discovered Gandhi's non-violence philosophy that he was able to combine his religious, social and moral convictions to tackle what he saw as the 'evils of the world' – which for Dr King meant racism.

In 1952, he met the love of his life, fellow student Coretta Scott, while they were both studying at Boston University. They married after less than eighteen months' dating, and Dr King considered Coretta's self-sacrifice and patience major sources of strength during his darkest hours. The spiritual and emotional support between the two enabled him to become the leader of a movement of tens of thousands, and an icon for millions around the world. Coretta was also a prime source of support for the movement: marching, campaigning and inspiring others, along with raising their four children, as Dr King was away frequently. Dr King also had the support of his confidant, The Reverend Ralph Abernathy, to assist him in formulating strategy and campaigns against the southern segregationists.

With their studies completed, the Kings moved to Montgomery, Alabama, in 1954, and Dr King became the pastor of the Dexter Avenue Baptist Church. Coretta had been born and raised in Alabama and, despite there being more glamorous or rewarding positions elsewhere in America, as native southerners they felt a 'moral obligation' to fight for social justice. They planned to enter a career in teaching, and for Dr King to further his studies later. The Kings had their first child, and life in Montgomery was relaxed compared to the challenges that were to follow.

As well as his pastoral role, Dr King took an interest in local activism, making important links with both the Black and white communities of Montgomery. Then, on 1 December 1955, a forty-two-year-old seamstress called Rosa Parks decided that she was tired of the continual injustices she faced on Montgomery's transportation system. Her symbolic decision to refuse to give up her seat for a white male passenger and move to the back of the bus – as was the Jim Crow law of Alabama – would change the course of history, and ensure Dr King's life would never be the same again.

The Reluctant Leader – The Birth of a Movement in Montgomery
Rosa Parks's subsequent arrest, conviction and $14 fine were the catalysts that galvanised Montgomery's Black community, and later, under Dr King's leadership, united all the disparate figures of the Civil Rights Movement into a coalition of action. After Rosa Parks had been marched from her bus seat to jail, a bus boycott, or 'acts of non-cooperation', as Dr King preferred to term it, began. This called for Blacks not to travel on the public city buses until colour restrictions governing where they could sit were removed. An organisation, the Montgomery Improvement Association (MIA), was formed to coordinate the protest, and elected Dr King as its leader. He was

surprised at his elevation, as he had not been in Montgomery that long and did not regard himself as one of the city's leaders, but the vote was unanimous – a resounding vote of confidence in his potential.

In his first major speech at the beginning of the boycott, Dr King had to mobilise the Montgomery community, and in his autobiography admits, 'Feeling obsessed by a feeling of inadequacy...for the most decisive speech of his life.'[73] He summoned up his years of learning, and borrowed from Gandhi to call for a campaign of social activism that would rouse the soul, repair and regain self-respect, within the spirit of their Christian faith, without violence.

Despite being small in stature at just under 1.70 metres (5.7 feet), Dr King rose to great heights, and without notes delivered what would become one of his trademark speeches. He received a standing ovation from the packed church hall, as well as achieving the desired effect of raising spirits ahead of the bus boycott. The MIA swung into action to organise the tasks of the boycott, such as arranging carpools and asking taxi drivers to reduce their fares to that of a bus journey. With the majority of the Black community working in manual or domestic roles, many simply walked for miles and miles, month after month. Montgomery's Black residents, like Rosa Parks, had had enough, and would never be a cowering community again. After a century of indignities they were prepared to suffer whatever it took to achieve desegregation.

The Montgomery city officials came under pressure from the business community, who were losing vast amounts of money, and used the weight of office to bend the rule of law in an attempt to break the boycott. Dr King's family, friends and colleagues were threatened on a daily basis. Numerous churches and civil rights campaigners' homes were firebombed by the KKK, including the King family home while his family slept. Dr King was arrested several times. When physical intimidation failed, other measures were used, such as getting insurance companies to cancel the car insurance of the pool drivers, or pressuring employers to sack the MIA ringleaders. Their resolve could not be broken, and is fondly recalled in Dr King's autobiography where he describes how a pool driver stopped to give a struggling elderly Black woman a lift home. She refused, and said: 'I'm not walking for myself. I'm walking for my children and grandchildren!'[74]

With the economic effects of the boycott proving successful, the city officials were forced to the negotiation table. Eventually the 381-day campaign resulted in victory, which we know today as 'first come, first seated'. The Montgomery Bus Boycott was not only a breakthrough for the civil rights campaign, but within this first tumultuous battle can be seen the parable that encapsulates the overall struggle for civil rights. From then on, when an issue concerning a Jim Crow law flared up, the community would be mobilised into an organised campaign. Physical abuse and intimidation inevitably followed, which would include bombings, beatings and mass arrests. Then a protracted legal process would take place while the local Black community continued their daily lives, enduring their own individual unheralded sacrifices. Each campaign would at first be met with an indifferent response from the federal government, and even criticism, before it belatedly enforced law and order. Finally the protracted struggle would lead to gradual concessions to end segregation in the target city. In this way, the movement incrementally gained first their dignity, and then their civil rights as they literally battled for equality.

Dr King's Pilgrimages to Africa and India, the 1950s Civil Rights Era

Before long, the question of civil rights was no longer just a local, city or state issue, but had gained a national platform and become an international story. In 1954, the Supreme Court members, who more than the politicians saw themselves as the moral guardians of the Constitution, made a landmark ruling in the case that became known as Brown v Board of Education. The Supreme Court ruled that separate educational facilities were unconstitutional, overturning the 1896 Plessy v Ferguson 'separate but equal' ruling of its predecessors.

Two years later, in Little Rock, Arkansas, this exploded into violence. The federal government ordered troops to protect nine Black children from an enraged local mob to enforce the bussing policy that followed the Brown v Board decision. Dr King applauded

163

the federal government's actions, sending a telegram of thanks to President Eisenhower, though he felt that the White House should have acted sooner. Crucially, the Supreme Court's caveat that the southern states were to integrate with 'all deliberate speed' allowed them to desegregate at their leisure, and by the end of 1956 not one school in the Deep South had been integrated. Dr King remarked that 'The federal government were more concerned about what happened in Budapest than what happened in Birmingham'.[75]

By now, Dr King's global profile was rising, and he embarked on several travels abroad to further his own personal knowledge. This included an enlightening journey to Africa, where he joined the celebrations at the independence of Ghana on 6 March 1957. He also undertook a personal pilgrimage to India to observe the civil disobedience teachings of Mahatma Gandhi, who had used non-violent techniques to propel India toward its own independence. Coretta and Dr King were warmly received and widely recognised, as the Montgomery bus boycott had made international headlines. Like his spiritual mentor, Dr King was not solely concerned with single issues such as race or colonialism. Gandhi had been appalled by the treatment of the *untouchables* in India, and had adopted an untouchable orphaned child. Gandhi also went on a hunger strike to highlight their plight, which brought an end to the practice of not touching thousands of people from India's poorest in society.

This focus on the plight of the poor was to mark Dr King's latter years as he campaigned for social reforms. At the time of his death, he was in Memphis attending a rally for striking sanitation workers. A fellow Hindu had killed Gandhi, and Dr King nearly suffered a similar fate when a Black woman stabbed him at a book signing in Harlem, New York, in 1958. The woman was categorised as clinically insane, and Dr King came so close to death: his surgeon informed him that had he sneezed he could have died. His travels around the world, especially to Africa and India, gave him the strength, conviction and determination to strive for social justice and equality. Finding out about them inspired me to travel the world, too. I was most impressed that, by adopting Gandhi's non-violent methods, Dr King expanded the civil rights campaign throughout the South and away from his parish in Montgomery, Alabama. The influence of Rosa Parks and Dr King inspired many others to take action. After students staged their sit-in at the Woolworth's food counter in Greensboro, North Carolina (a place I will visit and discuss later in this chapter), in February 1960, 'Over 70,000 Black students staged sit-ins around the country, which saw 3,600 jailed'.[76]

From Montgomery to National Leadership

In February 1957, Dr King became the head of the Southern Christian Leadership Conference (SCLC), a network drawn from scores of civil rights movements throughout the southern states. This role would prove vital in helping him coordinate the campaign across the South through the affiliate bodies of the SCLC. Dr King led the non-violent war on Jim Crow and southern segregationists, and such were his personal charm and magnetism, he could advise protesters and presidents with equal aplomb, and turn bigots into activists.

Dr King's leadership was pivotal in assisting to overthrow centuries of state-sponsored inequality. His strategy and planning of the civil rights struggle was as good as any high-ranking military general, allied with the management skills of a top chief executive.

One of the many great unheralded things we can learn from Dr King is the leadership quality that elevates great leaders from mere mortals. As one of the world's bestselling management books, Stephen Covey's *The 7 Habits of Highly Effective People*, says, Dr King 'began with the end in mind'.[77] He created a vision of a desegregated South, 'where little Black and white boys and girls could play together'. He led from the front, displaying his courage and integrity while being abused, beaten and jailed. He spent many days away from his family, with Coretta supporting his decisions to remain behind bars to highlight injustice.

Dr King would learn lessons from defeats, such as the painful unsuccessful year of struggle in Albany, Georgia, in 1961, which he evaluated to plan a successful campaign in Birmingham, Alabama. Each campaign was planned with a full strategy, and a target city selected. Teams of individuals were organised into committees to deliver thousands of tasks and actions to the army of foot soldiers who were ready to lay down their bodies to achieve the goal. Within the target city mass marches would be planned, followed by rousing speeches with the specific aim to empower and embolden the local community. Protesters would take part in acts of civil disobedience, staging sit-ins within cafés and restaurants, and even kneel-ins inside segregated churches. With the jail cells overflowing, the judicial system would be pushed to breaking point. Grandparents, students, teachers, labourers and many others flocked to the South to protest, and lawyers from the National Association for the Advancement of Colored People (NAACP) helped to defend them. Local, state and federal politicians and power brokers were lobbied to give political support. The power of the Black dollar was utilised by economic boycotts, which were used as sanctions against shops that had segregationist policies. Eventually, when combined to maximum effect, these collective actions would make the target city's business community beseech the city officials to negotiate a compromise.

Dr King evoked the embodiment of hope as a key message to disarm opponents and accomplish change. Andrew Young, who was standing next to Dr King on the balcony in Memphis when he was killed, recalls Dr King's leadership skills, saying he would be 'meeting Black business leaders in the morning to help them understand the process of non-violence, and in the evenings after school he would meet with the students from the high schools and colleges to encourage them to support the movement'.[78]

When he returned from India, Dr King was more convinced than ever before that his moral convictions of non-violence should be deployed to break the southern bastion of segregation. He ignored the growing calls for *Black Power* and separatism, as he did not believe that Black people could win an armed struggle in America. It was also morally repugnant for him to embrace Black separatism, as he viewed it as a similar system to the one he was fighting against.

The Birmingham Campaign, 1963

Dr King faced harsh criticism from all sides for his methods, and history has recalled his legacy far more kindly than people felt about it during his lifetime. Even in his dark moments, he remained true to his beliefs, and would often meet his detractors personally. Those who argued for him to stay within the rule of law would be met with determined resistance. Dr King opposed what he saw as unjust man-made doctrines, and drew strength from his theologian studies, stating:

> Any law that uplifts human personality is just. Any law that degrades the human personality is unjust. Thus it is that I can urge men to obey the 1954 Brown v Board decision of the Supreme Court, for it is morally right; and I can urge them to disobey segregation ordinances for they are morally wrong.[79]

So the stage was set for Dr King and the Civil Rights Movement to gain arguably their biggest and most controversial achievement in the form of Project C – C for Confrontation. They chose Birmingham, a city in the industrial heartland of Alabama, named after its English relative and a living example of the terror and injustices of Jim Crow in America.

The leader of the SCLC-affiliated Alabama Christian Movement for Human Rights, Reverend Fred Shuttlesworth, had invited Dr King to Birmingham, which had a population of over 350,000. Dr King made no secret of his disgust at the primitive conditions he encountered. The segregation and the way it was enforced exceeded anything he had endured in his life. Dr King wrote of a Black child being born in Birmingham, and the infant drawing its first breath in a segregated hospital. The baby would return home with its parents to a life of poverty, as well as being excluded from certain schools, restaurants, cinemas, churches and other social institutions, all based on the colour of his or her skin.

After receiving a federal order to desegregate its parks, the city closed them instead. When it was told it should integrate Black players into its baseball team, Birmingham disbanded it. If you wished to protest against these injustices by joining America's most predominant national civil rights organisation, the NAACP, you would find that they were banned in Birmingham. If you wanted to vote you would find yourself the subject of discriminatory literacy tests. These would help to ensure that in a city where forty per cent of the population was Black, only one in eight had the right to vote. This lack of voting power meant racist politicians and officials, such as the Governor of Alabama George Wallace and police commissioner Eugene 'Bull' Connor, would ensure the Black community lived with fear and terror as constant companions. Reverend Shuttlesworth himself had seen his home and church bombed and destroyed, and both he and his wife had been assaulted, but, undeterred, Shuttlesworth continued to protest. He was jailed on eight separate occasions.

In summary, should that child about whom Dr King wrote overcome adversity and reach maturity, it would grow up to raise the next generation in the most segregated city in America. Therefore, Birmingham would prove the ideal place to expose the brutality of racism and the moral corruption of its officials.

The date of 12 April 1963, Good Friday, was symbolically chosen for the mass protest to highlight the fact that Dr King was in prison. He announced defiantly, 'It's better to go to jail with dignity than accept humiliation in humility'.[80] Dr King was used to going to jail for his principles, although he hated being locked away from his family and society. On one occasion, he was falsely arrested for an alleged traffic violation by the Georgia state authorities. They bound his arms and legs in shackles, before driving him 220 miles without food, water, access to a phone call, or informing him of his alleged crime.

Dr King received public criticism concerning his breaking of the law, not from the segregationists, but from eight clergymen of mixed denominations who he felt should have been supporting him in his bid to tackle hate and inequality. In jail, on scraps of leftover paper, he wrote his polemic *Letter from Birmingham Jail*. He restated his unshakeable beliefs and principles, and denounced unjust laws as invalid, as Nelson Mandela had done before being sent to jail at Robben Island, before him. Dr King attacked the liberal critics who lamented that this was not the right time for civil disobedience and that patience was required. Dr King replied, stating that his people had been patiently waiting for over a century since slavery was abolished. They could not and would not wait any longer, and through thousands employing the tactics of non-violent direct action, they would find America's salvation and unity.

It was now that Dr King played his riskiest strategy in the civil rights campaign by deploying children. He believed that harnessing their natural energy and exuberance would give the movement fresh impetus. Dr King also wanted the children to be able to shape their own destiny, and involved them, 'to give our young a true sense of their own stake in freedom and justice'.[81]

The local community was trained and prepared for the extreme courage the people would need to display to live under fire. A number of entertainers, such as Harry Belafonte, raised money for legal funds for the thousands who were jailed or suspended from school. Project C would lead to some of the most disturbing and violent scenes in civil rights history, beamed into homes and reported in newspapers around the world. These were brutal and damaging images for America, and would remain in the world's conscience forever.

On 3 May 1963, hundreds of schoolchildren set out from the 16th Street Baptist Church, marching towards the Kelly Ingram Park across the road. Their mood was exuberant and their resolve strong as they defiantly sang, 'We want freedom now!' This enraged Sheriff Bull Connor, whose openly racist views were expertly exploited by the movement. He ordered the fire engines to turn on their high-pressure hoses, knocking children to the ground, and released police dogs onto them. This incensed many Black spectators, some of whom had not received the non-violent training required, and they retaliated only to be met by club-wielding policemen. When Bull Connor was told Fred Shuttlesworth was one of those injured by a fire hose, he said publicly, 'I wish he'd been carried away in a hearse'.[81]

With the world's media attention on Birmingham, the White House became involved. The Attorney General was Robert 'Bobby' Kennedy, who played a key role in civil rights negotiations both for his brother and later for President Johnson, before Bobby was also assassinated in the turbulent year of 1968. President Kennedy sent a special envoy to negotiate between the two sides, but violence flared throughout May 1963, and even a tank was deployed to patrol the streets. Dr King's brother, The Reverend AD King's home was bombed, and a device was placed near to a room at the Gaston Motel where Dr King often stayed in Birmingham. These acts were aimed to provoke the Black community into retaliatory acts of violence, and fighting between the police and Black community raged.

When the Supreme Court declared Birmingham's segregationist policies unconstitutional, the Governor of Alabama, George Wallace, stood in the doorway of the University of Alabama to prevent Black students from entering. President Kennedy had to send in the National Guard to remove him. Eventually, hostilities eased, and with the economic boycott hitting white businesses, an agreement to desegregate the city's facilities and improve employment equality practices was reached. Andrew Young summarised the success of Project C thus:

> Everybody looks at the Birmingham demonstration and thinks that there was some kind of miracle performed, but it was a lot of hard work. Birmingham was not a non-violent city. Birmingham was probably the most violent city in America, and every Black family had an arsenal. To talk in terms of non-violence…in Birmingham…Folks would look at you like you were crazy because they had been bombing Black homes. They had been beating up Black people and the blacks thought there was no alternative for them but to "kill or be killed". The achievements of Birmingham were historic; help and support came from across the country in the form of donations, including some from the entertainment field and sportspeople. Volunteers gave their time, and the NAACP legal defence fund carried out sterling work in releasing the jailed and getting the students reinstated. The community itself was galvanised into action, taking control of their own destiny to win the battle of Birmingham.[83]

For Dr King it provided proof to the hardcore southerners, 'That the walls of segregation could be broken down.'

March on Washington, 28 August 1963: 'I Have a Dream'

If Birmingham proved to be his most successful campaign, then there was no doubt that events in the nation's capital would prove to be Dr King's finest hour. The March on Washington for Jobs and Freedom, to give it its full and appropriate title, was proposed by union leader A Philip Randolph to keep the world's attention on the cause of civil rights.

President Kennedy, who before Project C in Birmingham had stated civil rights legislation would have to wait, hastily tabled a raft of new legislations. The campaigners had seen centuries of broken promises befall their people in the fight for equality, and were determined to keep the spotlight on their cause. Though relations within the Civil Rights Movement were often fractious, the march on Washington was a great display of unity by the Black leadership, and Dr King was invited as just one of many speakers.

In the shadow of Lincoln's memorial, with a quarter of a million people of all races, denominations and backgrounds packed into the National Mall, he delivered one of the most historic speeches of all time, fondly recalled as the *I Have a Dream* speech. To hear Dr King's sonorous voice booming with passion and prose brings goose pimples to the flesh. The tumultuous ending to the oratory is drawn from a Negro spiritual: 'Free at last! Free at last! Thank God Almighty we are free at last!' Dr King received praise and plaudits from around the world, and, with his stature growing, America finally seemed ready to fulfil Lincoln's legacy.

However, from this zenith of success the Civil Rights Movement would plunge into despair, and America, too, would be forced to examine itself as the dark hand of violence exploded.

A Tragic American Fall from Grace, Autumn 1963

On 22 November 1963, in Dallas, Texas, the 35th president, John Fitzgerald Kennedy, became the fourth president to be assassinated by a fellow American. Although he declared himself non-partisan in politics, Dr King was convinced that JFK had won a very close 1960 election against Richard Nixon due to the votes and respect that he had gained from the Black community. A key moment had been JFK's efforts to rescue Dr King from a Georgia jail for the false traffic violation. Dr King went so far as to call the then Senator Nixon, whom he knew personally at the time, a 'moral coward' in his autobiography because Nixon had stayed silent, fearing a backlash from southern segregationists.[84]

Dr King's response to the President's assassination was less reported than his counterpart Malcolm X's infamous comment that 'The chickens had come home to roost'. Malcolm X was censured for this by the Nation of Islam, beginning a chain of events that would lead to his own assassination in New York in 1965. Much as he lamented the death of a president and personal ally, Dr King wept more for an America that 'Could produce the climate where they [men] express their disagreement through violence and murder'.[85]

Dr King evoked the lives of millions of African-Americans when he said that they, too, had tragically known 'political assassins from the whine of a bullet or the roar of the bomb that had replaced lynchings as a political weapon'.[86] Those words were said because two months earlier, in the same Birmingham church from which thousands of children had set out to demand their equality, a bomb had been planted that killed four little girls attending Sunday school (see chapter 8). Dr King had been highly distressed by these brutal murders, and had delivered a moving and rousing eulogy. He'd called for the girls' deaths not to be in vain, and for renewed faith and courage in the doctrine of non-violence to prevail in the face of such a shocking atrocity.

The newly installed President Johnson was determined to push through a raft of civil rights legislations and social welfare reforms as a tribute to President Kennedy, who had initially introduced them. President Johnson termed this vision The Great Society, and as a southerner combined his forceful personality with his knowledge of Southland to get his legislation passed through the Congress and Senate. On 2 June 1964 he signed the Civil Rights Act, which would outlaw many segregationist practices in the South.

However, as we have discovered, those ingrained practices had survived the writing of the Constitution, war and much prior legislation. The segregationists continued to use violence and intimidation to maintain their rule. In 1965 in Selma, during a voter registration drive, over 3,800 were arrested, but the net result of three months of non-violent demonstrations was only fifty extra Black people eligible to vote. Many had been beaten and sent to hospital when state troopers had turned on demonstrators during Bloody Sunday (see chapter 8). Dr King lamented that yet more blood had been spilt, but his faith gave him the strength to continue.

The violent events of Selma, like those in Birmingham, would prove historic. A fitting tribute to the lost lives, and lasting proof that their deaths were not in vain, was the passing of the 1965 Voting Rights Act. This gave federal jurisdiction over any state which used discriminatory practices in the voting process, and gave African-Americans the power not only to vote, but also to elect whomever they choose.

War and Poverty

Two major issues, war and poverty, were splitting the fabric of American society in half, and also causing turmoil for Dr King. The Civil Rights Movement had been a predominately southern cause to end institutionalised segregation. Dr King, though, had always believed that poverty was also a major factor in causing inequality, so he turned his attention to the economic segregation that he felt was the source of great poverty in the so-called American ghettos. Race riots flared across the country, fuelled by anger from those with the least to lose. Dr King visited Watts, Los Angeles, to appeal to the rioters for calm after violent riots erupted in August 1965. In 1966, he and his family moved to a Chicago ghetto for several months to sample the conditions 'at the grass roots' and lead a campaign for desegregated housing. Though more extreme, in terms of the appalling deprivation in the slums these experiences mirrored those of the *Windrush* Generation since their arrival in Britain in 1948.

Decades come and go among epochs, but the one marked 'The 1960s' was a decade of great political, social and cultural change. Assassinations of great leaders, a peace movement to oppose the

Vietnam War, driven by a new youth culture fuelled by the rise of The Beatles, and the appeal of Motown and Black artists on both sides of the Atlantic sparked a series of cultural changes that would have repercussions for decades to come.

President Johnson felt he had not only completed Kennedy's legacy of social reforms, but that he had gone even further by supplying finances and policies to tackle America's poverty, enhance education, promote the arts and even environmental measures. He introduced two health reforms, Medicare for the elderly, and Medicaid for those on low incomes, which are still integral parts of the American healthcare system today. However, it was President Johnson's duplicitous statements over whether America had committed troops in a war with a tiny nation, thousands of miles away, that were to taint and dominate his presidency.

Dr King was not alone in noticing that America's poor were dying disproportionately in South-East Asia, or that monies President Johnson had allocated to the war on poverty were being siphoned off to fight Vietnam. Dr King had been awarded the Nobel Peace Prize in December 1964, and as its ambassador and advocate, with his religious beliefs and moral convictions, the Vietnam War weighed heavily on his conscience. 'Moved to break the betrayal of my own silences', he became a firm and vocal opponent to the war.[87] This took him into direct conflict with his former ally President Johnson, making Dr King an enemy of the state.

The FBI, under its notorious chief J Edgar Hoover, closely monitored Dr King, and spied on his life with official clearance from a compromised White House. Dr King was criticised for his anti-war stance not only by the state, but also by other campaigners for moving the message away from civil rights issues. Black segregationists attacked him for his continued belief in non-violence, and the mood within the Civil Rights Movement began to fragment. This was to assert itself in Black Power slogans, misunderstood by many, by more radical Blacks.

On the eve of his death, Dr King would not take the podium as the celebrated icon we remember today. Monitored by the FBI, J Edgar Hoover, who hated Dr King, had leaked allegations about his private life to discredit him. His colleagues had denounced his anti-war stance, and some were losing faith in his methods, while Black militants were eager to respond to violence with violence. On what was to be the last full day of Dr King's life, 3 April 1968, as he gave his *Mountain Top* speech in Memphis, Tennessee, several questions about his methods, and even his relevance, were being asked across America.

Visiting the Student Sit-ins at Greensboro, North Carolina

In a country where there is a Martin Luther King Boulevard in every state, it is not difficult to find symbolic, if token, gestures to one of its most revered leaders. However, to appreciate fully the legacy of Dr King and the effect of his non-violence philosophy, I visited the university town of Greensboro, North Carolina. There, on 1 February 1960, four students from the A&T University, Franklin McCain, Joseph McNeil, Ezell Blair Jr and David Richmond, fully embraced the non-violent strategy and marked their place in history. After much planning, they attempted to get served lunch at an all-white food counter of FW Woolworth's. When they were refused lunch, they refused to move and staged a sit-in, sparking a six-month protest that spread throughout America.

The Woolworth's building has since been lovingly restored and turned into the International Civil Rights Center. The Executive Director, Bamidele Demerson, gave me a personal guided tour around the first-class museum that doubles as an arts facility, when I visited in 2010. The room where the sit-in was staged is much larger than I'd imagined, and every detail has been painstakingly preserved. My footsteps echo on the marble floor as I walk towards the famous steel and chrome counter. The original alternate blue and pink stools still stand there around the lunch counter, their leather surfaces aged and split open like over-ripened tomatoes. Behind the lunch counter the menu of the day is displayed. Appropriately, as it's Thanksgiving the next day, a roast turkey dinner is advertised, costing sixty-five cents, and for dessert a cherry pie costs fifteen cents, washed down with a Pepsi-Cola for just five cents.

As America is now gripped by the ravages of a global recession, the absurdity of the moment hits me with stark reality. Those Black students would have had green dollars in their pockets, but the colour of their skin would have prevented them from making any purchase. However, on that day, over fifty years ago, those four students did not care about hunger or capitalism. They cared about equality. Their stance brought America's segregation laws to the world's attention, and inspired many to take action.

Atlanta, Georgia

Sweet Auburn Avenue, the Birthplace and Resting Place of Dr King
The area where Dr King was born, raised and now rests is known as the Sweet Auburn district. With its network of businesses, churches and entertainment, for many years this was the heart and soul of Black Atlanta. I'm a frequent visitor to Sweet Auburn as Dr King's resting place represents my own personal Mecca and sanctuary. I always feel a pleasant sense of serenity when I'm within its family of buildings, which includes the Martin Luther King, Jr. Center for Nonviolent Social Change, featuring excellent artefacts on Dr King's life, a theatre and an old preserved fire station. It also includes the historic Ebenezer Baptist Church (seemingly under perennial renovation) where both Dr King and his father preached. Dr King's home, at 501 Sweet Auburn Avenue, sits at the top of a gentle hill and is still beautifully preserved, with free guided tours given by National Park guides if booked in advance.

Dr King won numerous awards and acclaim, but most of all his achievements was the ability to inspire a movement against hate and inequality. He was not a consensus leader who based his decisions on populist views; he was a conviction leader who, in the face of violence and intimidation, never wavered in his beliefs to achieve change... and he won.

At Dr King's resting place I wipe a tear away, and at the eternal flame I say a prayer in remembrance of my own beloved family members who have passed away. Inspiration, however, is the main reason I've returned here, and as I look along the shimmering reflecting pool by his and Coretta's graveside, I find strength building in me once again. I bid them both farewell in the knowledge that I will return after examining more of the achievements of the Civil Rights Movement and Dr King's legacy. Though Jim Crow had been abolished, many, like Dr King, worried about the psychological impact those racist laws would leave behind. He said, 'All too few people would understand how slavery and racial segregation wounded the soul and scarred the spirit of the Black man'.[88]

Though the physical scars from the plantations had disappeared, they were soon replaced by the mental scars of racism in America's ghettos and in Britain's inner cities.

Jewel of the New South

In the state of Georgia, all roads literally lead to Atlanta. Previously, I have driven into Atlanta from its western neighbouring state of Alabama, or from the tropical climes of Florida. In January 2009, I drove twelve hours north from Atlanta to Washington DC, to watch President Obama's inauguration after taking part in Dr King's eightieth birthday commemorations. On this occasion, I had driven six hours from Savannah in the east. I usually enjoy driving in America, but I never quite get to grips with the stock-car race conditions on Atlanta's highways. The main artery in and out of the city is called Peachtree Street. It snakes through the city for miles and is home to many of Atlanta's main buildings, as well as providing the setting for a number of the city's annual parades.

When Dr King died, parts of his home city were still segregated. Now, Atlanta is the major economic city of the South, and, as such, provides its power base. Its gleaming skyscrapers can challenge most US cities outside of New York for a skyline sparkling with prosperity and glamour. Atlanta's business and commercial institutions, however, provide me with fresh insights into one of the most important changes in America's history in charting how Black people rose from slavery, oppression and servitude to become proud, successful African-Americans.

Although Frederick Douglass's words post-slavery drew

attention to the plight of four million Blacks in the South, words alone would not feed and clothe them. Many freedmen, as they were known, and their descendants, such as Dr King's father, set about educating themselves. With the Black Church a crucial bedrock of their economic and social lives, they grew into a burgeoning middle class of professionals, including doctors, lawyers and pastors. Other businesses grew around them, and they gradually began to accumulate wealth by serving their Black customers, thus giving them economic power and a stake in society. In addition, through leaders such as Douglass, WEB Du Bois, Booker T Washington and Marcus Garvey, they took the first steps towards Black political consciousness, providing continued opposition to racial discrimination.

It was former Mayor William B Hartsfield who rebranded Atlanta with the slogan 'The city too busy to hate' in the 1950s, successfully modernising the Old South into the New South, and positioning Atlanta as a city at one with the world of commerce and an important transport hub. It is now the largest city in the former Confederate states, with the population in the metropolitan area close to six million (the population of the city itself is just over half a million). It is home to hundreds of businesses, including the headquarters of Coca-Cola, Delta Airways and CNN, and relied heavily on the Atlanta business community to bankroll its successful 1996 Olympic bid. Those games were not judged a sporting success in terms of fulfilling the Olympic idealism, but that mattered little to Atlanta's leaders and businesses. As far as they were concerned they'd won gold in promoting Atlanta as one of the world's great cities, and the games were a commercial success. This remains Atlanta's insular commercial legacy, which is far removed from the successful London 2012 Olympics that provided many messages that lifted the human spirit.

Commerce and Black Businesses

Always attracting those with an entrepreneurial spirit, Atlanta grew rapidly with the boost of the railroad after Reconstruction and as a commercial centre for the cotton industry. Large numbers of African-Americans flocked to the city to find their version of the

American Dream, and since the turn of the century Atlanta has had over forty per cent of its population declaring themselves Black. Since the early twentieth century there has been a network of HSBCUs in Atlanta providing creative energy and a solid educational legacy, including Spelman (all female), and Morehouse College (all male) which was where Dr King studied.

More African-Americans moved to Atlanta during the 1990s than to any other city in America, a trend that has not slowed. William E Simms, president and CEO of 100 Black Men of America, summed up the mood by saying: 'This city is the birthplace of so many successful Black businesses that you can't help but be inspired by it'.[89] Andrew Young has stated a feeling exists 'that if you can't make it in Atlanta, you can't make it anywhere. That's what keeps people coming here, rich people, poor people. They come from all over because they believe that anything is possible in Atlanta.'[90] The 100 Black Men of America is an organisation which aims to educate and empower young African-Americans, and its national headquarters are located on the historic Sweet Auburn Avenue in the heart of Atlanta's Black business district.

After leading the march from Selma to Montgomery, Dr King delivered a speech entitled *How Long? Not Long* in March 1965. He said, 'Let us march on ballot boxes until we send to our city councils, state legislatures and the US Congress men who will not fear to do justice, love mercy, and walk humbly with their God'.[91]

These words were not only prescient when referenced to Barack Obama's presidency, but also proved to be true in Atlanta. The city has had several Black mayors since Dr King died, including his friend Andrew Young, and they have all played a major role in the modernisation and diversity of the city that has since been dubbed 'The Black capital of America'.[92]

Atlanta's first Black mayor, Maynard Jackson, was elected in 1973, and during his three terms he had the vision to revitalise Atlanta from a provincial city to 'The crown jewel of the New South'. Though the ideas had come from Presidents Kennedy and Johnson, it was actually President Nixon who introduced legislation to readdress the inequalities and injustices of the past. The Affirmative Action programmes reserved jobs and contracts for people from an ethnic minority background. Jackson used these affirmative action initiatives aggressively, and supervised an era in which the percentage of contracts Black businesses received from the city grew from miniscule to millions. This acted as a magnet for African-American professionals in America.

Mayor Jackson's programmes started at Atlanta's Hartsfield Airport, and today the airport boasts of being one of the busiest in the world. Mayor Jackson's achievements are now shared with another visionary and former Mayor of Atlanta, William B Hartsfield, as the airport has been renamed in their joint honour the Hartsfield-Jackson Airport. The first Black female mayor of the South, Shirley Franklin, also took a strong pro-business stance during her time from 2001 to 2010. Her policies also played a major part in building what *Ebony* magazine has referred to as the Black Mecca.[93]

From the outside looking in, Atlanta has plenty to offer African-Americans: excellent educational facilities; a range of churches; big city amenities; a first-class transport system with links to the airport – which is not always the case in America. Its communities have a palpable sense of identity, aided by a strong civil rights history, and opportunities appearing light years from its slave-holding and segregationist past. The founder of *Black Enterprise* magazine, Earl Graves, highlighted this in the July 2010 editorial, celebrating forty years of his magazine's success.

> It's impossible to write this, my 40th anniversary Publisher's Page column, and not think about the extraordinary journey African-Americans have travelled, from slavery to the White House. Even more remarkable to me is how much of that journey I've lived to witness. Just to be clear, I just turned 75 earlier this year. That's old enough to have made one of my earliest visits to the American South riding a segregated bus. Ironically, I was on my way to an airborne school to serve my country as a US soldier, a full decade before my country saw fit to afford me, or anyone who looked like me, the full freedoms

and privileges guaranteed by the Founding Fathers. But here's what moves me to my core: Having lived through that era, here I stand half a century later and Barack Obama is Commander-in-Chief. We began our 40th anniversary celebration in Atlanta, the flagship city of a New South – a South that is viewed by more and more African-Americans not as the home of Jim Crow and fire hoses and attack dogs, but as a place of renewal, opportunity, and advancement. During times when opportunities for African-Americans in business were limited by racist exclusion, Black entrepreneurs managed to carve out financial opportunities for themselves as much as anyone, these early entrepreneurs were the architects of the New South.[94]

Although it appears a haven of opportunity, during my visits I see plenty of evidence that Atlanta has more than its fair share of the crime, drug and poverty issues that affect many of America's Black and poor communities.

Losing a King, Finding a President

There are many tales of coincidences and funny occurrences that happened during my American travels that prompted me to write this book; so many that all my trips to the United States fell into place while I was thawing out in the Washington DC bar after Obama's inauguration. My trips were, in fact, field research. My history was no longer tapping me on the shoulder, but was shoving me to explore further. It was no longer whispering or hinting, but shouting and urging me forward, and now even President Obama was in on it.

My first historical collision with Barack Obama happened on my first trip to Memphis, Tennessee, in February 2007, when I visited the Lorraine Motel where Dr King had been assassinated. I had to change planes in Chicago, Illinois, and decided to stop over and see some American friends. I was greeted with snow piled high on the sidewalks, and sub-zero temperatures that had changed Chicago from the vibrant spring city it had been on my last visit into an urban South Pole.

As we sat down to breakfast at my friends' home shortly before my flight, a tall, handsome, light-skinned Black man with sticky-out ears and a smile that radiated the confidence of a man with a plan came on to the television screen. The news pictures were being shown from the state capital of Illinois, Springfield, where symbolically President Lincoln had called for a divided house to stand together in the fight against slavery that would eventually rip America into two sides.

'Who is that?' I asked casually.

'It's Barack Obama,' came the reply from my friend, Andrea. I remember staring back at her, vaguely recalling his unique sounding name, but I was not ashamed not to know the details behind the then Senator Obama. One of the enduring appeals of my travels to America is the prominence of its Black businessmen and women, mayors and senators. They, along with the ubiquitous celebrity figures, act as surrogate role models that if we British do not wish to mimic, we can certainly imbibe. Besides this, I had been absorbed in America's past before I got propelled into its present, and symbolically its future.

'What is he making a speech about?' I asked innocently.

'He's announcing his candidacy for president, Roger!' Andrea said.

'He's our Senator from Chicago and he is really good. You should look him up when you get home,' Andrea's mum added.

'Good luck with that!' I snorted rather derisorily, and in an instant all my previous respect for the figure on the screen disappeared. As soon as I heard the words 'presidential candidate' coming from an African-American, I dismissed his chances. I immediately bracketed the young senator as a self-serving publicist with my British cynicism rearing its head in the land of hope and dreams.

I'd had immense respect for Jesse Jackson, even before I met him in Selma, Alabama, in 2012, and his presidential campaigns in 1984 and 1988 certainly blazed a trail. However, back then in 2007 I could not conceive that America would elect a Black man, even with a mixed-heritage background, anytime soon. Certainly not in my lifetime. America wasn't ready for that kind of change yet, I surmised.

Yet it was. What followed was a bruising Democratic nomination tussle between Hillary Clinton and Obama – by which time I was up to speed, and still did not think he would win. This time it was Obama, not America, who was not ready, I thought. Wrong again! My blushes were spared as Obama – a huge underdog – proved seasoned political pundits wrong, too, and won over luminaries such as Oprah Winfrey, a former Hillary Clinton supporter before endorsing Obama. The defeat of the much-vaunted Hillary Clinton, herself touching history in a bid to become the first woman in the White House, was the *real* political fight to win.

After eight years of George W Bush, Republican candidate Senator John McCain and Governor Sarah Palin were no match (this one I got right) in the November 2008 elections. I celebrated Obama's victory well into the early hours at an Americans Abroad National Democratic party in the heart of London, along with hundreds of jubilant people from across the political spectrum. We watched his historic victory speech in awe, and shared Oprah's tears. I resolved there and then to witness the inauguration of the first Black president with my own eyes, even if it was just to offer a guilty, unheard apology for ever having doubted the man. Andrea's mum had been right, but he was better than good – he was President of the United States. All of these memories and thoughts came back to me as I attended Obama's public housewarming party on the National Mall, though there was nothing warm about that bitterly cold day.

*

Though not a politician, Dr King's leadership qualities and ability to be a statesman for the Civil Rights Movement paved the way for Barack Obama's entrance into the White House. The phrase used by Obama, 'Standing on the shoulders of giants', was never more poignant or apt. Though Obama has inspired many around the world, no one person could live up to the expectation or the weight of history. This has led to some harsh, if understandable, criticism of President Obama's first term. Travelling through America during this period, I saw that in barbers' shops, soul-food restaurants and Black-owned motels Obama's image remains on posters, walls and T-shirts everywhere. Sure, it's not the euphoria of January 2009, but it makes for a positive change to see a Black person's image outside of a music or sporting context. Very often these artistic creations are framed along with Dr King's image, as dreamer meets hope and change.

Along with female voters and young voters aged eighteen to twenty-nine, from whom Obama got a combined two-thirds of the vote, the demographic of the Black working class was largely responsible for Obama's victory. Not only with votes, where ninety-five per cent of African-Americans voted Obama,[95] but also with campaign organising, fundraising (from jumble sales to large celebrity endorsements) and voter registration campaigns. These skills were harnessed during the civil rights campaign of the 1960s, and had not been fully utilised on a national scale since then. This was largely due to the Black community feeling disenfranchised, or disillusioned with national politics while still engaging on a local level, as seen by the proportion of elected Black officials in the United States compared to the UK.

Sadly, the majority of people in the Black community have found life during Obama's presidency has changed... For the worse. Things have got harder economically, with reduced hours at work, lay-offs, fewer jobs and the cost of basic goods – and for southerners that means fuel, too – rising. Yet a far more logical observation prevails from this group than from the Black intelligentsia and white liberal media. Bar a few dissenters, the Black community tells me in casual conversations that Obama *is* doing a good job, faced with the level of opposition from politicians and right-wing media, such as Fox News, over issues like healthcare, which has helped Black communities, and with the weight of history lined up against him as a 'first'. He is *still* their president; they have not lost hope. They have seen, felt, heard and experienced just how America can find different ways to resist change, and they are acutely aware that not even the keys to the most prestigious office in the land, with its fancy job title, can protect someone from the racism they face every day of their working lives.

Stone Mountain and Road to the Bible Belt

Before leaving Atlanta, I travel to its outskirts. If business has changed the skyline of the metropolitan centre of downtown Atlanta with a variety of twinkling skyscrapers and labyrinth of highways, once I reach the suburbs a more tranquil feel envelops me. The one-storey homes and nature reclaim the land as I head out of the city to the historic 3,200-acre Stone Mountain Park. Stone Mountain is a huge volcanic eruption which dominates the park, and on the face of it is a carving larger than Mount Rushmore. It is a dedication to the Confederate Civil War heroes President Jefferson Davis, General Thomas 'Stonewall' Jackson and Robert E Lee. Stone Mountain is also where the Ku Klux Klan revived their activities in 1915, holding annual rallies there for over forty years on what they still consider to be sacred soil.

Although at times Stone Mountain Park reminds me of a Confederate Disneyland, it is very popular with Atlanta's multicultural residents, many of whom are relaxing in the spring sunshine. Cable cars can take visitors to the top of the 825-foot-high mountain, and the park has a railroad, plantation house and riverboat cruises among its amenities. I watch the past converge with the present as I see children of all backgrounds playing together beneath the huge stone carving – dedicated, as with the monuments in Richmond, Virginia, to the very men who would have kept some of them as slaves and others segregated. I ask a young man who is standing admiring the stone carving what he thinks of our surroundings. I discover he is newly arrived to America from Haiti, and is blissfully oblivious to the Confederate history, but when he reads the dedications to Civil War heroes he reminds me, 'History is important and should never be forgotten, no matter what its history is.'

I am bowled over by such significant words from a casual observer. In the shadow of the huge monolith, I pack up my picnic and ready myself for the next leg of my journey. My next stop would be Montgomery, Alabama, the former capital of both the Confederacy and the civil rights struggle. There I would gain a closer view of the source of Dr King's strength, and the one unifying factor that was, and still is, the bedrock of Black communities on both sides of the Atlantic – the Black Church.

8

The Foundation of Black America
The Black Church

Alabama – The Citadel of the Southern Bible Belt

Sweet Home Alabama! Just humming the chorus conjures up some of the most evocative images of the Deep South. Alabama is at the heart of the 'Black Belt', so named after the colour of the fertile topsoil that feeds thousands of rural farms across the state. It is also home to the 'Bible Belt', which stretches throughout the southern states.

I push the search button on my car radio, as I love to do while driving on America's highways and freeways, to seek a familiar record or new opinion. Here in the South, that opinion has a more fundamentalist religious tone. Back home in Bristol, I am a presenter and chair of a local community radio station, Ujima Radio CIC, so I have more than just a listener's passing interest in the radio pundits hosting their phone-ins. The airwaves are filled with praise for God and utterances for sinners to repent their ways. There are few pauses for breath before the invective is filled with comments about 'big' federal government and attacks on Obama's socialist policies, while heaping reverential praise on the ultra-Conservative Tea Party movement's increasingly anti-Obama solutions. Without changing gear, these fire and brimstone presenters/preachers heap their damnations during their radio sermons about America's declining morals, laced with homophobic and anti-abortion sentiments. With so many references to the 'end of the world' and the 'second coming' I'm left feeling as if my ears are bleeding, and retune the radio to more spiritual gospel music.

Alabama was the battleground for some of the most infamous and brutal passages during the civil rights struggle. After I had returned from my New York trip I grew to learn the names of faraway towns and cities in Alabama. Montgomery, Selma and Birmingham became etched into my consciousness in ways that Soweto, Sharpeville and Johannesburg in South Africa would become a decade later. Montgomery is Alabama state's capital, and was where Dr King had his first posting as a reverend. His work to support Rosa Parks's protest would turn their cause and their names into legends. His first church, the Dexter Avenue Baptist Church, sits in the centre of Montgomery near the state Capitol Building. In 1861, the Confederate President Jefferson Davis was inaugurated on its very steps as the southern states declared secession from the union, and the Confederacy was born.

The Dexter Avenue Baptist Church is part of a network of tens of thousands of Black churches that have provided more leadership, finance and support than any other institution for African-Americans. This network also gave the civil rights struggle its moral and structural foundation. Due to its close associations, the Anglican Church is predominately Christian, but many other religions share in its cultural and moral strength found in worshippers around the world.

Religion and American Politics

The very first Bill of Rights for some of America's newly enfranchised citizens related to religion and was drafted by a Christian, Thomas Jefferson. He ensured the United States would become a secular nation with what he termed 'A wall of separation between Church and State', ensuring people would have the freedom to worship the religion of their choice.[96] The lines between religion and politics have, however, been less easy to define in reality, giving religion a political edge that is unusual for a secular country.

America is a deeply religious place, grouped into various denominations of pious ordinances rather than a total religion enveloping a single country, such as Islam is in Saudi Arabia. Religion in America isn't just a pastime; it is a way of life that envelops society much more than in Britain, or even Catholic Europe. Alabama is one of America's most religious states, with more churches per square foot than in any other state. Though the Anglican and Protestant churches dominate, the large Catholic presence from the European migrants stretches back centuries. There has always been a small but influential Jewish presence in America, and, increasingly controversially, more Islamic mosques are being built. Over forty per cent of Americans say that they regularly attend a place of worship, compared to just ten per cent in Britain.[97] New places of worship emerge every week, and there are nearly a thousand religious TV stations.[98]

In comparison, British politics and religion are like oil and water: not to be mixed. Tony Blair's former press secretary, Alastair Campbell, was quoted as saying, 'We don't do God at Number 10,' when asked if Bush and Blair would be praying at their first transatlantic summit. It was only after Tony Blair's departure from Number 10 that he felt comfortable announcing his conversion to Catholicism to begin his Faith Foundation in May 2008. British Deputy Prime Minister Nick Clegg's announcement that he is an atheist did not raise a flicker of concern for British voters during the 2010 general election. Current leader of the Labour Party, Ed Miliband, was elected as party leader while being the expectant father of his unmarried partner's baby. Although he is Jewish by birth, in an interview on BBC Radio 5 Live he said, 'I don't believe in God personally, but I have a great respect for those people who do'.[99]

Conversely, any candidate looking to make the White House their new home would find an atheist ticket unelectable, or if they had children out of wedlock they would find their campaign starved of funds in a country where millions of dollars are required in order to be nominated. Americans see character and faith as intertwined when entering the ballot box, and expect their president to be a person of faith. President Kennedy, who was a Catholic, has been the only non-Anglican elected. Since Ronald Reagan's presidency the incumbents have literally had to wear the badge of the cloth alongside the seal of office. Reagan's religious revolution energised the white and powerful Protestant right, ironically known as Conservative Christians. The Red Southern States (named after the colour of the Republican Party) have kept the majority of votes rolling in for the Republican Party here in the South. Eight of the ten states I visit in the south voted Republican in the last four elections. Even during Obama's most popular periods feelings towards Obama and the Democrats are at best lukewarm. The only recent changes to this have been former Georgia governor Jimmy Carter, who was a Baptist preacher and managed to appeal successfully to the Black Church during his 1975 campaign. Another southern president was Bill Clinton whose early life was immersed in the Baptist church, and his wife Hillary – who became Obama's Secretary of State – was raised in a devout Methodist family.

George W Bush's popularity can be linked to America's favourite kind of religious archetype, the fallen hero. Bush was famously redeemed from the bottle – a hangover from his boisterous college days – by the love of a good woman, his wife Laura Bush, and God. The conservative right voted for him in even greater numbers for his second term. In thousands of these rural Red State communities the balance of power to the presidency lies. This area holds a mythical power for campaigners, who try to court the electorate much like middle-England voters are wooed in UK elections. In the run-up to Election Day, presidential candidates can be seen adding to their air miles, criss-crossing the country on the campaign trail in these unheralded rural communities. Even at the height of his popularity as a candidate in the November 2008 elections, Obama failed to win a single state in the Old South.

Despite a constant stream of insinuations from right-wing detractors, Obama is a committed Christian. His first presidential campaign was sent into crisis by the comments of his Chicago United Church of Christ minister, Reverend Jeremiah Wright. Wright's comments evoked memories of Black separatists from the Nation of Islam, Malcolm X and their present leader, also from Chicago, Louis Farrakhan, when he criticised the American government for its double standards of carrying out wars abroad while allowing racism at home. He ended his controversial sermon with the words 'Goddamn America, as long as she tries to act like she is God, and she is supreme. The United States government has failed the vast majority of her citizens of African descent.'[100]

Reverend Wright was known as Obama's pastor. His words were broadcast extensively by the media, and sent shock waves throughout the country, putting Obama in a comprising political situation. For the conservative white media, Wright's views were abhorrent. For many Black people and white liberals, however, Wright was voicing an opinion that reflected the truth. With the race for the White House intensifying, Obama had to respond. Many applauded his response, while others felt that Pastor Wright was sacrificed to the baying media and public. Obama's background as someone who is not only mixed-race, but born from a Muslim father, gave him the unique legitimacy to deliver a seminal speech entitled *A More Perfect Union*, which became a plea for racial unity and for the country to address its divided social problems.

Men from every denomination have used the Bible for their own deeds. The Catholic Church, for example, through its convents and priests, owned more slaves than any other institution, business or family across the Americas. Ironically, it used the profits from slavery to fund a number of educational and humanitarian activities.[101] In the United States of America, Protestants exploited the Bible in many teachings to the slaves to preach the doctrine of loyalty and obedience to one's master. This was hardly a subtle message to a captive audience on the plantations, but the slaves' collective souls did begin to stir with the messages of salvation and redemption.

Early Beginnings of the Black Church

Religion's prominent yet complex role in America was established right from the birth of the newly claimed lands, with the arrival of the puritanical Protestant pilgrims. Fearing religious persecution in Britain, in 1620 they sailed across the Atlantic on the *Mayflower*, naming their new home in the state of Massachusetts Plymouth after the city they had left behind in the West Country of England. The Great Awakening during the 1740s caused religious revivals, which captured popular imagination as its fervour swept through America and became a major turning point for both owners and slaves.

Two denominations in particular, the Baptists and Methodists, built on this religious expression to popularise religion. Evangelists and Quakers had been at the forefront of the anti-slavery movement, which had brought together a number of different faiths. The message of the evangelists, which included rebirth, salvation and emancipation, captured the imagination of the slaves.

John Wesley, the founder of Methodism, was a fervent campaigner against slavery. One of the first revivalists of the day, the charismatic George Whitefield attracted crowds of thousands of slaves to his open-air religious rallies at a time when most American cities were mere towns.[102] He, too, encouraged the slaves to find the power of the Gospel that still resonates within African-American society today. The former slave Olaudah Equiano witnessed a Whitefield revival at a 1776 Philadelphia rally, which he described in his autobiography:

When I got into the church, I saw this pious man exhorting the people with the greatest fervour and earnestness, and sweating as much as I ever did while in slavery.[103]

During the second Great Awakening of the 1830s and 1840s the evangelists were determined to reform what they perceived as society's ills, and created several movements for change. One such movement was the Abolitionists Society, which in Britain contained evangelists William Wilberforce and Thomas Clarkson. Missionaries had poured into Africa, and in the West Indies Lutheran and Moravian preachers worked tirelessly to improve the conditions for the slaves. American abolitionist William Lloyd Garrison was a Baptist preacher in the North, and also a mentor to ex-slave Frederick Douglass. At a time when Britain had abolished slavery, many religious men in America still kept slaves. Clarkson criticised them in his 1844 essay *The Ill Treatment of the People of Colour in the United States*, attacking what he considered the blasphemy of the Church in justifying the continued use of slavery in America.

Ever since the Black American-born slave and Baptist minister Nat Turner's 1831 rebellion, the slave masters of the South had been nervous about the threat of insurrection. They outlawed large gatherings of slaves, and introduced slave codes which included banning the education of slaves, but in some places where slave numbers far outnumbered whites this proved impossible. Nat Turner led the largest slave uprising in the Deep South, which claimed the lives of over fifty white people in Virginia, for which he and his small band of followers were hanged. In the aftermath of Turner's carnage, Virginia slaves were only allowed to hold a church service in the presence of a licensed white minister.

John Brown was an Old Testament firebrand and prominent white abolitionist who advocated violence to end slavery. In 1859, he led a small band of followers, which included slaves and his sons, to attempt to overthrow the government's Harpers Ferry armoury near Virginia in a bid to inspire other slaves to revolt. The uprising was abruptly ended, and Brown, like many leaders of violent struggles against slavery, was executed. The raid on Harpers Ferry armoury was greatly exaggerated by warmongers in the South, and formed another piece in the intricate jigsaw that began the American Civil War.

Today the Harpers Ferry site is located in West Virginia where the Shenandoah and Potomac rivers merge. In a country that can appear to be dominated by glitz, glamour and skyscrapers, it is a pleasure to view this lovingly preserved nineteenth-century national historic site. Due to John Brown's revolt and ultimate sacrifice, Harpers Ferry is a culturally significant place for African-Americans.

In 1906, WEB Du Bois held a meeting of prominent campaigners at Storer College, a Baptist mission school set up to educate former slaves. This meeting of the Niagara Movement became one of the key foundations for the modern civil rights era, leading to the formation of the Association for the National Association for the Advancement of Colored People (NAACP). Du Bois concluded five days of stirring speeches, memorials and plans that would help form civil rights strategy with his *Address to the Country*:

We will not be satisfied to take one jot or title less than our full manhood rights. We claim for ourselves every single right that belongs to a freeborn American, political, civil and social; and until we get these rights we will never cease to protest and assail the ears of America. The battle we wage is not for ourselves alone but for all true Americans.[104]

Over the next fifty years, Dr King and thousands of others would rally to Du Bois's battle cry as fervently as John Brown, but utilising Gandhi's non-violent methods.

The Influences of African Religion

Africans arrived in the Americas with their own religions, rituals, customs and heritage that had lasted centuries, but they had to keep them hidden away. Both master and slave found different interpretations in the Bible. The stories of redemption fitted well into white reformers' attitudes of saving the Black heathens from 'lives as savages'. Slaves found strength and a spiritual release in the scriptures, and were given time off from the rigours of fieldwork to attend church. Eventually they produced their own preachers, and later churches as the Anglican religion spread. Several great Black leaders began their lives as preachers, researching the Bible, delivering sermons before packed audiences and gaining vital presentation, debating and leadership skills.

The African traditions, however, never disappeared, and can still be seen today in various styles of preaching, hymns, songs, dance and musical instruments, such as the African drum. Hymns were often set to popular folk music of the day, with simple but powerful messages about Christ and redemption, which would provide the inspiration and joy of the Black Church through gospel music.

From the humble beginnings of singing and playing the music of gospel hymns in church, several vocalists, including Sam Cooke, Marvin Gaye, Aretha Franklin, Whitney Houston and Michael Jackson, plus numerous musicians, have become the biggest-selling artists of their generation. Modern-day megastars, such as Beyoncé and Usher, have continued this trend, using their religious beginnings to influence music and popular culture, from jazz music to Hip-Hop, across the world.

After slavery was abolished, the practice of separate congregations continued, and the Black Church became a more distinct entity in its own right. The chief reason for this was the educational programmes that were run for the former slaves, who had been kept illiterate. These were funded and run predominately from the foundation of the Church, which grew to become more than a mere place of worship, but a vital community and social institution. As the years evolved, it also became overtly political.

The American Missionary Association (AMA) began as a religious abolitionist group before the Civil War, with one of its primary aims being the education of the former slaves. After the Civil War, and with donations from a number of philanthropists, it established hundreds of new schools, some of which became Historical Black Colleges or Universities (HSBCUs). The first Black ordained priests, Absalom Jones and Richard Allen, founded a number of independent churches within existing Christian structures that grew out of the Free African Society they had begun in 1787.

The African Methodist Episcopal Church (AME) established one of the first Black churches in Philadelphia during the 1790s. Their network of churches and educational programmes would attract thousands of new members over the next century. The Baptist Church in America also grew rapidly, and is the largest denomination of Protestants in America. The Baptist and Methodist doctrines grew into independent, self-sufficient, empowering entities, and they not only encouraged their flock to fund and build educational facilities, but also developed vital programmes to tackle poverty and racism. This provided an essential link in the emerging American society, where little or no funding from either the state or the federal government existed for those who were disadvantaged from birth.

The continued appeal of redemption through Evangelicalism throughout the nineteenth century, and the rise of Pentecostal churches from the turn of the twentieth century, spread with the growth of religion. Other religious groups provided important support and advice for modern issues, such as tackling gang violence or drug addiction. The controversial Nation of Islam has unparalleled success rates in rehabilitating ex-offenders from the brutal American penitentiary system.

In Britain, these tasks are state functions that are supplemented by religious groups. In America, these religious organisations can be a person's only salvation where the state and federal government fail to intervene. When these organisations are coupled with large American philanthropic donations, they become the biggest providers for America's poor. In summary, religious institutions are integral to everyday life in parts of America, not just as places of worship, but as providers, fundraisers and suppliers of essential services for the poor, elderly and needy.

The Inspiration of the Black Church and the Civil Rights Struggle

As a political movement, the Black Church's role in the civil rights struggle is unsurpassed, providing shelter behind its doors and inspiration from its leaders. Though lawyers, students, business owners, entertainers and sporting figures have all played major roles, none match the spiritual and emotional base that the Church has provided.

Throughout his sermons and speeches, one of Dr King's favourite images was to cast himself as the Black Moses, leading his children out of the wilderness. Most famously he used this in his 1968 *Mountaintop Speech*, stating, 'I would watch God's children in the magnificent trek from the dark dungeons of Egypt across the Red Sea through the wilderness and to the promised land'.[105]

In Alabama, the civil rights struggle and the Black Church can be seen within four historic passages in America's past. Each one is accompanied by a dark stain of violence and tragedy.

The Birth of a Movement: Montgomery Bus Boycott, 1955–1956
As symbolic gestures go, Rosa Parks's decision on 1 December 1955 not to move to the back of the bus, as the Jim Crow laws decreed, was one of the most powerful during the twentieth century, and

a source of inspiration for many around the world. On the grounds of Troy University, in downtown Montgomery, is the Rosa Parks Library and Museum, dedicated to Ms Parks's achievements. A replica of the yellow bus that began the protest greets visitors at the entrance, transporting them back to the civil rights era.

After a long day working as a seamstress at a local department store, Ms Parks felt she'd had enough: enough of having to pay her money to the driver then walk off the bus and enter it at the back, and enough of standing over empty seats in the white section, enduring racist comments. When the bus driver, James F Blake, who had previously left her stranded in the rain after taking her fare, approached her to give up her seat, she knew her moment had come. She refused to move, and was jailed and fined, and eventually lost her job.

Already a member of the NAACP, she continued to play a role in civil rights throughout her life, though more as a figurehead in a symbolic role than an active member. The female rights movement had yet to emerge fully, and sexist practices, of which she became a victim, existed within the civil rights struggle. Her life was beset by personal tragedy, and she was forced to find employment away from the Deep South. In her latter years she belatedly received accolades from both her country and her own people. Ms Parks died on 24 October 2005, and was given a burial and acclaim usually afforded to presidents. Her body was visited by thousands at the prestigious Rotunda building in Washington DC, an honour bestowed upon President Reagan before and President Ford after her death.

Ms Parks's action led to a series of coordinated events that inspired people not only in America, but also around the globe, including influencing activists in Bristol. It sparked a campaign that became the Montgomery Bus Boycott. This campaign led to the emergence of the then Reverend King from the Dexter Avenue Baptist Church as the leader of the Montgomery Improvement Association.

The Freedom Riders in Alabama, 1961

One of the bravest acts during the civil rights story occurred when a group of Black and white activists, known as the Freedom Riders, began a historic journey to desegregate the transportation systems of the South. On 14 May 1961, they boarded a Greyhound bus from Washington DC and planned to travel to New Orleans. They rode through the Carolinas without incident, but as soon as they crossed the state line into Alabama their troubles began. At Anniston, Alabama, a gang of racists attacked their bus and set it on fire. As the Freedom Riders tried to escape, all of them were badly beaten, and many were sent to hospital where they were refused medical aid.

Undeterred, they continued to Birmingham where they were attacked again, with particular viciousness meted out to white activists who were taunted as 'nigger lovers'.[106] They abandoned their journey, but waves of new Freedom Riders swarmed into Alabama, determined to desegregate the transport system. The Freedom Riders were repeatedly met with organised violence led by the Ku Klux Klan, and in Birmingham Sheriff 'Bull' Connor jailed some of the activists. In Montgomery, some activists and Freedom Riders were forced to find shelter at the First Baptist Church of Reverend Ralph Abernathy, who was a close confidant of Dr King. A siege occurred outside the church, where a baying mob of over 1,000 racists, armed with clubs and rocks and hurling Molotov cocktails, prowled.[107] They were only kept at bay by the Alabama National Guard, who had received orders from a recently installed President Kennedy and his brother Robert, who was the Attorney General, to protect the activists. The Kennedys would become reluctantly drawn into a political battle between appeasing the powerful southern segregationists or 'Dixiecrats' within their own party, and upholding the law of the land. The Freedom Riders' story provided valuable publicity for the Civil Rights Movement, and the public transport systems were eventually desegregated.

The Murder of Four Little Girls at the 16th Street Baptist Church, Birmingham, September 1963

Named after its British counterpart, this city, in the industrial heartland of the South, was dubbed 'Bombing-ham' following a series of outrages by the Ku Klux Klan. The Project C campaign had brought some reforms, but, such was the grip of violence and segregation in

Birmingham, the city's power brokers were never easily going to relinquish full power.

On 15 September 1963, just eighteen days after Dr King's historic *I Have a Dream* speech, Addie Mae Collins, Denise McNair, Carole Robertson and Cynthia Wesley, all aged fourteen, were blown to pieces by a bomb planted in the basement of their church while they attended Sunday school. This heinous act of extreme violence illustrates just how far the Old South was prepared to go to prevent integration.

No one from the Kennedy administration or local state politician's office attended the girls' funerals. The story of the death of the *Four Little Girls* was told in a 1997 Spike Lee film of the same name. As well as making seminal films for eager Black audiences, such as *Do The Right Thing* (1989) and *Malcolm X* (1992), in 2006 he made an HBO documentary film, *When the Levees Broke,* about the response to Hurricane Katrina in New Orleans. It is among his finest work, and showcases his talents as an excellent filmmaker and historical storyteller. In addition, Lee exposed the continual moral corruption that existed in federal government with the inept response of President Bush and the Federal Emergency Management Agency known as FEMA.

Two months after the murder of the four little girls, President Kennedy was assassinated, becoming the most high-profile victim of the maelstrom of violence that swept through America during the 1960s. Southerner Lyndon Baines Johnson was installed as president, and vowed to implement civil rights reforms as a legacy to the slain JFK.

Sunday Bloody Sunday, Selma 1965

When Dr King met President Johnson at the White House in December 1964, the president told him that any new voter legislation to tackle Jim Crow would have to wait due to the Great Society reforms to tackle poverty. Dr King and his supporters, however, would not delay their plans and began another landmark campaign. Tough literacy tests that would baffle Mensa, along with violence and intimidation, were being used to ensure that only a fraction of the Black majority was registered to vote. Selma, a rural town within Dallas County, Alabama with a population of just 20,000, was chosen as a place to be at the forefront of the campaign to increase Black voter registration.

On 7 March 1965, thousands of demonstrators gathered to march the fifty miles from Selma to Montgomery. They left the Brown Chapel AME Church and walked up the incline of the Edmund Pettus Bridge, where their path was blocked by police cars and 150 armed state troopers; some on police horses, others wearing gas masks. A crowd of locals had gathered to watch what was, for them, akin to Christians being fed to the lions at the Coliseum in Roman times. When the demonstrators refused to disperse, tear gas canisters were released, and in the melee that ensued the state troopers beat the demonstrators mercilessly with their truncheons, billy clubs, electric cattle prods and rubber hoses, causing scores of injuries.

The leader of the march was John Lewis, who would become the Black Congressmen for Georgia, and would later be verbally abused by Tea Party demonstrators as he voted for Obama's healthcare reforms in March 2010. Lewis had been badly beaten as a Freedom Rider, and in Selma he received a fractured skull.

These shocking events made headlines across the world, and became known as Bloody Sunday. However, it took the subsequent death of a white Unitarian minister, Reverend James Reeb from Boston, to have the greatest ramifications in America. After dining at a Black soul-food restaurant, Reverend Reeb and two other white ministers got lost and found themselves near the notorious Silver Moon café in Selma, a favourite meeting place of Klan members. They were attacked, and Reeb suffered a fractured skull which caused a blood clot on his brain. He eventually lost a two-day battle for his life. His death caused shock waves in America, and President Johnson was moved to call the Reeb family personally to offer assistance for Reverend Reeb's father, including the use of a private jet. This was something President Johnson had not done when Black civil rights activist Jimmie Lee Jackson had been shot dead three weeks earlier in Perry County, Alabama, in the lead-up to the Selma campaign. Jackson had died trying to save his mother and father from assault by a state trooper, and the disparity in the establishment's response angered Dr King and many others.[108]

A white housewife from Michigan, Viola Liuzzo, was so enraged by the television pictures she watched of Bloody Sunday she left her home and children to assist in the civil rights struggle. She gave car rides to the marchers, until one night her Oldsmobile vehicle was run off the road, and she and her passenger were shot at point-blank range. The world's media covered these stories from Selma, and in American homes pictures of the police brutality were replayed constantly. Demonstrations occurred across the country, including a sit-in inside the White House.[109]

The deaths of Jimmie Lee Jackson, Viola Liuzzo and James Reeb heightened tensions within America and forced the nation to confront its own issues. Here in the self-proclaimed citadel of democracy, as its government was sending more troops to fight for freedom in Vietnam, its citizens now had concrete evidence that its religious leaders and housewives, as well as its Black citizens, were being murdered for standing up for the values of the American creed: equality, liberty and democracy.

Dr King had missed the march in Selma, but he and thousands of protesters decided to finish the march as it went the eighty miles along US Highway 80 as a tribute. They marched for a week, camping by the roadside by night and running the gauntlet of racists by day. Dr King ended the march where Rosa Parks had begun the protest: in Montgomery, and symbolically on the very same steps where the Confederacy had been founded, on steps of the State Capitol Building, Dr King gained the acclaim of over 50,000 supporters.

A Bridge Across History – Visit to Selma, Alabama

Each year, during the first weekend of March, a commemorative event takes place at the scene of Edmund Pettus Bridge, Selma, where protesters were savagely beaten in 1965 on Bloody Sunday. The Selma Bridge Crossing Jubilee, to give it its official title, attracts several high-profile participants, and the Olympic torch was symbolically carried across the bridge on its way to Atlanta in 1996.

On Sunday 4 March 2012, I take part to pay tribute to those who had bravely marched before me. I park near to the Brown AME Church, where Presidents Obama and Clinton have each given the keynote address at previous Jubilees, and walk towards the infamous towering metal struts of the bridge where thousands gather patiently in anticipation on the short incline. Like many southern monuments, the bridge is named after a Confederate hero and defender of a system that we would recognise today as *apartheid*. The mood is respectful yet jubilant, and I am warmed not only by the spring sunshine but also by the presence of many flags of the Caribbean carried by local school children. I'm informed it's part of a school project about the West Indies and I smile as I pick out the Guyanese flag fluttering proudly among them. A signal is given and we march forward, crossing over the flowing Alabama River.

Suddenly, the black and white images of the past once more become my present. I can see the hatred of the watching crowds and hear them braying savagely as the sickening sounds of billy clubs connect with flesh and bone. I can smell the acrid tear gas swirling in the air, and shudder as the protesters blindly attempt to seek sanctuary to avoid the onrushing charge of a state trooper's horse.

As we complete the bridge crossing, we embrace each other by a monument to those brave foot soldiers. Speeches by many prominent politicians rouse the crowds ahead of the eighty-mile, six-day commemorative march to Montgomery. Near the monument is the Selma National Museum for Civil Rights, where I witness Reverend Jesse Jackson unveil a bust of himself to honour his work. On display within the museum are Sheriff Jim Clark's billy clubs and his sheriff's shield. The 1965 march was well-publicised and staged in broad daylight, in the full glare of the world's media with thousands of eyewitnesses. Men, whose primary purpose was to uphold the law, had instead used violence to protect the southern way of life that had outlived a Civil War and 100 years of segregation.

Later that week I, along with thousands, welcome the Selma contingent to Montgomery. They include The Reverend Al Sharpton, and Dr King's son Martin Luther King III, as well as Jesse Jackson.

Once again on the very steps where the Confederacy had been proclaimed, and just yards from Dr King's old church, they implored the crowds to continue the fight for social and economic justice. I watched others speak out against the increasing number of Black males being jailed in America's war on drugs. This is what author Michelle Alexander calls 'The New Jim Crow' in her book subtitled *Mass Incarceration in the Age of Colorblindness*. Disturbingly, in America more Black men are in jail than attend college.

*

Eight months after telling Dr King that it was not the time for legislation for voter reform, President Johnson signed the Voting Rights Act in front of a smiling Dr King on 6 August 1965. This act ended the barriers implemented by southern states to prevent citizens from voting. The effects were felt across the globe, and Britain passed its first race equality laws three months later in November 1965.

The Black Church in African-Caribbean Communities in Britain

Africans secretly maintained their religions in rituals, not only at worship but also at births, deaths and marriages. Olaudah Equiano witnessed this while on a sailing voyage in the West Indies during December 1771, and captured it in his autobiography:

> When I came to Kingston [Jamaica], I was surprised to see the number of Africans, who were assembled together on Sundays; particularly at a large commodious place called Spring Path. Here each different nation of Africa meet and dance, after the manner of their own country. They still retain most of their native customs: they bury their dead, and put victuals, pipes and tobacco, and other things in the grave in the same manner as in Africa.[110]

In the UK, West Indian spiritualists and preachers, with the support of missionaries, were at the centre of a number of rebellions during the nineteenth century, after the abolition of the transatlantic slave trade. The Anglican Church in Britain has also played a significant role within Black culture, but in keeping with its profile in the wider society, its significance has been far more social than political. Like their American counterparts, the Protestant and Anglican Churches have the largest numbers of followers in the UK. These denominations branched out with evangelical fervour into various Pentecostal creeds, including the Seventh-day Adventists, who were founded in America and have many members in Britain.

Spreading the word of God with missionary zeal is still practised most famously by the Jehovah's Witnesses, who also have large numbers of followers on both sides of the Atlantic, including famous names such as tennis champions Venus and Serena Williams, and the music artist Prince.

Due to the Israelites' time in Egypt, Africa has a religious significance for many Jews, while in Africa itself both Catholicism and Islam have had a reported growth in their numbers. Some of the African-Caribbean community welcomed the Pope to the UK in September 2010. The prophet religion of Rastafarianism has proved popular as a movement of self-expression and identity. With its links to music and fashion, use of dreadlocked hair to signal their affinity with nature and powerful use of symbols from African culture, it has proved particularly popular for young Black males. Its spiritual leader, the late former Ethiopian Emperor Haile Selassie, holds the same religious significance for Rastas as the Pope assumes for Catholics. And several African religions, such as Akan, still practise the traditions of their worship and observe the rituals of their heritage.

The Church and My Family

My mum was a Sunday schoolteacher in Guyana, so, before I became a teenager, it was as natural for me to attend Sunday school as it was to play football in the street. At Sunday school the messages from my West Indian upbringing about right and wrong, helping others, good manners and humbleness were reinforced. In addition to joining sporting teams, and civil societies such as the Boy Scouts, I found Sunday school to be an essential building block in my development.

Within sporting, religious and social institutions I learned team-working, contribution and leadership skills. These were important lessons and remain valuable moral codes today, for all the advances of technology that have changed adolescence forever. While I am not a practising Christian, I recognise that the Church has had a big moral and spiritual influence on my life, as religion was a supporting influence for both my parents, and contribution remains high on the list of my values.

The primary reason for my 1981 trip to America was to witness my Uncle Clarence (Coleridge) become ordained as the Anglican Bishop of Connecticut. That the eldest of sixteen children, raised in poverty in Georgetown, Guyana, was to become the first Black bishop in one of the more conservative states in America was an impressive feat. However, the story of how he made that choice, told to me as he enjoyed a small glass of his favourite tipple, Harveys Bristol Cream sherry, while we celebrated his eightieth birthday at his home in Connecticut in November 2010, was even more remarkable.

From Georgetown, Guyana, to Connecticut's First Black Bishop
Uncle Clarence Coleridge

Uncle Clarence's life in the modest home he shared with my mother and their siblings in Guyana included daily prayer, and attendance of a packed 11am service at their local Ketley Congregational Church in Old Boys Town, Georgetown, a stone's throw from Grandfather's shop – or 'Shoe Establishment', as my grandfather preferred to call it. Uncle Clarence can trace the roots of the Anglican Church within our family to the work of the London Missionary Society, both before and after the abolition of slavery in the British Caribbean in 1833. The London Missionary Society was founded by Henry O Wills as part of the Bristolian tobacco-maker's philanthropic interests.

At first, Uncle Clarence ignored the callings from the Church to pursue a career as a doctor. He chose to study in America, and arrived in New York in 1949 before moving to study at Howard University in Washington DC. There was no scholarship available, but he is still proud that he never became a financial burden to his father, instead working after lessons from midnight to 8am. By his own honest admission, he found studies in medicine very taxing, but persevered.

He later moved to the famed Tuskegee Institute in Alabama to study as a vet, and remembers vividly hearing on the radio about the fifteen sticks of dynamite that had been placed under Dr King's home which failed to ignite. This was during the Montgomery Bus Boycott, and Uncle Clarence felt an innate need to support Dr King, so drove eighty miles to Montgomery. Dr King came out of his home and addressed the small crowd with a powerful fifteen-minute sermon. My uncle cannot explain why, but after he had finished speaking, while walking to his car, Dr King stopped to talk to my uncle. On hearing of his struggling medical career, Dr King advised him to 'Join the missionary'. That profound moment changed my uncle's life, and the next day he enrolled on a theology course and joined the Church.

Uncle Clarence participated in several civil rights campaigns for integration in his diocese of Connecticut, in north-eastern America. Although the tough segregation rules of the South were not in force, racism was rife along the north-eastern states. My uncle remains the only Black bishop in Connecticut's history.

I asked him what he would say to Dr King if the great man were alive today. He smiled warmly, and simply said, 'Thanks!'

My mother, father and sister are, or were, regular church attendees, with faith a strong source of support in their lives. My late sister Marilyn was a Rastafarian, and lived in Ghana for a number of years before dying there in February 2001 of pneumonia. I have redefined my own religious and spiritual beliefs as the value of contribution, or as Dr King would describe it, 'Helping to build the capacity for getting along with people'.[111]

American Philanthropy v British Charity

What we British broadly call 'charity' is known in America as philanthropy. After the Civil War ended, America's capitalist structure grew dynamically. A group of entrepreneurs exploited the lack of governance to create some of the richest dynasties of the modern world. Andrew Carnegie (steel), John D. Rockefeller (oil) and Cornelius Vanderbilt (railways) were self-made men who created their own economic revolution. Although they were known as Robber Barons for their unscrupulous business practices, they left legacies for the cities of America with their industries, and established several charitable foundations.

This new philanthropic zeal is credited as being started by a Scottish immigrant to America, Andrew Carnegie. He sold his empire to what became U.S. Steel in 1901 for over a $1 billion. Carnegie's 1889 essay *The Gospel of Wealth* became the template for wealthy Americans as he asserted that the wealthy should donate their fortunes to the needy 'to produce the most beneficial results'.[112] Carnegie gave away over a third of his fortune, setting up colleges, universities, libraries, concert halls and 7,000 church organs, not only in America but around the world, including in his homeland, Scotland.[113]

Today, two of the world's richest men, Bill Gates and Warren Buffett, continue Carnegie's legacy, pledging to donate billions of dollars through the Gates Foundation. Oprah Winfrey is part of that wealthy elite of American billionaires, and her patronage includes huge support of the arts, education, health and sporting institutions. On a smaller scale, the assistance of tax codes, ensuring donations are tax-deductible, means giving money is made easier than in Britain for those with wealthier wallets.

Large philanthropic donations are as much a part of wealthy American social circles as having an exclusive zip code or visits to the country club, while any British black-tie charity function does not raise anywhere near the same high levels of donations. The majority of British charitable donations come from year-round contributions to agencies such as Oxfam, which are decreasing, or from annual appeals such as Comic Relief. For Americans, philanthropy is a two-way exchange between benefactor and recipient, and builds on the Christian values of the country. The artistic director of the National Theatre in Britain, Nicholas Hytner, attacked the contributions of British multimillionaires.

If you made that kind of money in the US, you would have to start giving it away simply in order to live there – where the social life revolves around charity benefits. But here you can be rich and keep it all and you don't feel the pressure from your peers that you would in the US.[114]

A welfare system exists in both countries to assist the poor, with different systems of state distribution. In Britain, central government provides funds that are administered by a network of council departments. In America, welfare is a lifeline that only the very poor receive from the individual states, with many functions outsourced to the private sector, assisted by philanthropic organisations that can hire community organisers. The most famous of these is Barack Obama, whose meagre wages were funded by a collection of Catholic churches. He worked in Chicago's notorious Projects to establish employment initiatives and housing programmes.

Visit to 16th Street Baptist Church, Birmingham, Alabama

In Alabama, I visit Birmingham to pay my respects to some of the courageous men and women who had died in the battle for equality. I drive past the Birmingham-Shuttlesworth International Airport, which has been renamed after the brave and feisty Reverend Fred Shuttlesworth. My first stop is the scene of the murder of the Four Little Girls at the 16th Street Baptist Church. I step inside; it's cool with a beautifully preserved interior, and I attend Sunday service. Upstairs is a beautiful crystal-glass window depicting a Black Jesus, called The Wales Window. After its glass was shattered by the nine sticks of dynamite, the people of Wales responded to a campaign by the *Western Mail* newspaper and donated money to have the window rebuilt.[115]

The Birmingham bombers were Klansmen, and it took fourteen years before they even stood trial. The last of the four bombers involved in the murders, Thomas Blanton Jr, was only convicted in 2001, aged 63, and another, Robert 'Dynamite Bob' Chambliss, died in prison.[116] In the church basement is a moving tribute to the young girls' lives, tragically taken along with those of other local civil rights workers.

I cannot visit a place where I sense evil has had a deathly presence and not feel moved. I welcome the crisp spring freshness in the morning air as I stumble outside. Shielding my eyes from the bright sunlight, I notice the skyscrapers soaring into the crystal blue sky stretching across downtown Birmingham. I cross the road into Kelly Ingram Park, scene to one of the major turning points of the civil rights struggle. The Children's Crusade had set out from the 16th Street Baptist Church behind me, and they were in full song with the joys of youthful protest in their souls as they attempted to march the half-mile to downtown Birmingham. They only got a few hundred yards before being stopped by police with dogs, sticks and water-cannons. Many children were beaten, and thousands were arrested. In the park today there are stone statues depicting the brave children under attack from snarling dogs and water-cannons. A museum and civil rights complex stands nearby to convey their story to visitors.

A block away is the Gaston Motel where, in room number 30, Dr King finalised his plans and strategies during his many visits to the city. A place where Dr King used to speak was the former Masonic Hall, now a men's barber's shop and home to shapes, patterns and fades of the Black haircut. I negotiate the language barrier to find my style of haircut is translated as a 'low fade' (shaved sides, low amount of hair on top). As in the UK, and the world over, the barbers' and hairdressers' shops are not only Black community hubs, but also valuable places of information on politics, sport and local gossip.

In Praise at a Southern Black Church

A visit to a Black church in the South, regardless of your religious beliefs, is a must as part of your southern experience. In 2009 I had begun my journey to President Obama's inauguration in Atlanta, where I attended a special service at Dr King's former church, the Ebenezer Baptist Church. It was the weekend of what would have been Dr King's eightieth birthday, and with the nation celebrating a public holiday and the induction of a new president, it seemed like churchgoers were not the only ones who were rejoicing.

The service was a celebratory event, and the atmosphere more akin to a concert. A seven-piece band with a full choir was led by three preachers, who took turns to implore, cajole and sing to the packed congregation. We were royally entertained, and spent as much time dancing on our feet as we did in prayer. Although not as dramatic as the *Blues Brothers* scenes, I have returned to a Black church in the South for many an encore, and it certainly leaves me uplifted. So much so that at the point when I left Atlanta for my twelve-hour journey north to witness President Obama's swearing-in ceremony, I had no idea that, forty-eight hours later, I was to have what I describe as an epiphany: the idea to share my personal odyssey within this book.

Bombs, Bullets and the Bible

Religion, whichever faith a person may follow, is integral to the American way of life. As BBC reporter Matt Frei succinctly summarised: 'Americans believe, Europeans doubt'.[117] Yet America is a country riddled with contradictions (part of its attraction as well as what annoys me about it), slave owners becoming freedom fighters to overthrow the tyranny of British rule being just one such anomaly. Another is that the more overtly religious states of the South have a higher than average murder rate.[118]

Much as Americans treasure their Bibles, they also embrace their right to bear arms. The country's foreign policy seems to favour the Old Testament approach of an eye for an eye. When Japan attacked Pearl Harbor in 1941, the Americans joined World War II, and later responded by dropping atomic nuclear bombs on Hiroshima and Nagasaki. Planes flown into the World Trade Center and Pentagon by terrorists on 9/11 led the Americans to respond with the Afghanistan War which lasted over ten years, finally managing to track down and execute Saddam Hussein in Iraq and Osama bin Laden in Pakistan.

Since the beginning of the twentieth century, America has kept more than a watchful eye over foreign affairs, despite its reputation for insularity. This interest in foreign policy was promoted initially by President Woodrow Wilson, who was the first president to travel overseas to form an alliance, called the League of Nations, following

Germany's surrender after World War I. The League of Nations has since reformed to become the United Nations, with a primary aim to maintain global peace. There is, however, plenty of evidence that America has something of an obsessive-compulsive disorder to ensure that good triumphs over evil. This has manifested itself into military interventions overseas where, for better or for worse, America has played a significant role in many conflicts.

In fact, America has been involved in more battles than any other nation since the outbreak of World War II, yet has suffered only two major foreign attacks on home soil – at Pearl Harbor (1941) and New York (2001). There have been Cold Wars with Communist China and the Soviet Union, plus numerous covert wars where previous opponents have included Cuba, Vietnam, Korea, Japan and Germany. You do not have to be Sigmund Freud to analyse that there is something in the American psyche that has anger management issues. The world's biggest economy has the world's largest army, and spends a quarter of its annual budget on defence. America believes in its right to fight moral wars, which began with the War of Independence against the British, and continued with the Civil War to determine self-rule by the states and enshrine in its Constitution the values of freedom and democracy.

In the twenty-first century, America has instigated regime change in Iraq and retaliated against its perceived enemies in Afghanistan. Too often, however, this right to fight moral wars has been misinterpreted, notably under George W Bush's presidency. The global response was a loathing of American values, which led to 9/11, and was then made worse by the Republicans' aggressive knee-jerk response to it. Bush's war hawks were imbued with the political evangelism of good versus evil, creating the image of an American Crusade and a modern-day version of British imperialism, with America, and not the UN, becoming the world's unofficial police force.

Heroism and National Shame – Tuskegee, Alabama
The town that calls itself a city, Tuskegee where my Uncle Clarence studied, is a place of great historical significance to African-Americans.

It is the birthplace of Rosa Parks and is named after the Native American Creek tribe. Tuskegee is home to the prestigious Tuskegee Institute, now Tuskegee University, founded by Booker T Washington, and where he would develop as a teacher, academic and civil rights campaigner. The university has come a long way since its humble origins, and among the many buildings on the impressive campus stands Carnegie Hall, donated as a library in 1901 by the aforementioned Scotsman.

Tuskegee is also the place where, between 1932 and 1972, the government carried out experiments on over 600 local Black men. They wanted to know what would happen to the human body if they left the disease syphilis to go untreated without the aid of penicillin as a cure. The results were death, hereditary illnesses and a lasting legacy of mistrust of the government and health agencies among African-American communities. The Tuskegee Human Rights and Civil Rights Multicultural Center is dedicated to Fred D Gray, a local attorney who not only represented the Tuskegee victims in a successful lawsuit against the US government, but also was Dr King's and Rosa Parks's attorney. Inside, among the impressive historical exhibits, I watch President Bill Clinton on video giving a sincere apology on 16 May 1997 for the Tuskegee scandal, an apology his wife Hillary, as Secretary of State, was to follow in 2010 for similar American experiments in Guatemala.

Fighting for Freedom, Fighting against Oppression
The Black Soldier

Across many American airports, soldiers in combat fatigues can be seen travelling to or from America's wars. Although Obama officially ended the war in Iraq in August 2010, 50,000 soldiers remained to assist with training. At the official cessation of war in Iraq, over twice that number were deployed in Afghanistan.

The armed forces are excellent equal opportunities employers, and champion diversity as one of their key reasons for success. Ever since President Harry Truman desegregated the armed forces in 1948, the military, like any good soldier, has duly followed the order of its commander-in-chief and integrated its ranks to break down racial barriers. In recession-hit America there are not too many employers offering health benefits, housing, education and training opportunities in exchange for protecting the virtues of Uncle Sam.

Some of America's military conflicts have been major landmarks in the battle for racial equality. By offering to fight and die for America, and Britain, Black soldiers have helped to change perceptions of Black people. This is best summarised by the Tuskegee Airmen slogan I saw at its airfield: 'Fight for the right to Fight!'[119]

At the beginning of World War II there were no African-American pilots, and they served the armed forces in segregated all-Black units. Soon the clamour to utilise men and women who were willing to fight for their country mounted, and, supported by First Lady Eleanor Roosevelt, Black soldiers were allowed to fight in Europe. They undertook many missions, with Dr Roscoe Brown becoming the first African-American to shoot down a German pilot.

The story of the Tuskegee Airmen was made into a 2012 Hollywood film *Red Tails*, named after the wings of their P-51 Mustangs which they painted red, starring Cuba Gooding Junior and Terrence Howard. The story of the airmen's skill and valour is told in full at Motor Field, which is still used as an airfield, but also holds a museum as a tribute. Here you get the sense not just of the airmen, but of a whole team of mechanics, operators, teachers and servicemen and -women who put those magnificent men in their flying machines into battle against the might of the German Luftwaffe.

The American War of Independence

America's battle to rid itself of the tyranny of British rule was laced with irony. Jefferson blamed King George III for expanding the slave trade into the Americas, but would not grant freedom to his slaves. The British, however, promised to free slaves and grant land in Canada, West Indies and Sierra Leone to those who would take up arms against their slave masters. The slaves fought in the war, were spies, guides and cooks, and buried the dead. They developed a loyalty to the Crown, despite Britain's long-established history in the slave trade. One of the many evocative stories the historian Simon Schama recounts in his 2005 book *Rough Crossings* is of a battalion of 300 slaves who called themselves 'The King of England's Soldiers'. Just like the Maroons in Jamaica, they secured their own territory called Bear Creek, creating a village on the borders of the Savannah River that spanned the states of South Carolina and Georgia. In May 1786, three years after British surrender, an American militia burned down Bear Creek in a battle that lasted four days.[120]

The American Civil War

Slavery was hugely integral to the southern economy, and thus the Confederates' ability to wage war. Lincoln's Emancipation Proclamation controversially not only welcomed the four million slaves in the South to the free North, but encouraged them to join the Yankee Army. Up to 200,000 enlisted, paving the way for victory and freedom. Bob Marley would famously pen a song in tribute to the regiments of this period, who continued to serve in the US Army and were known as 'Buffalo Soldiers'.

World War I

During World War I, thousands of African-Americans played a part in the war, mainly in support roles due to the persistent myths that prevailed about their inadequate fighting abilities. At a time when America was gripped by economic decline, the war boosted the economy by selling armaments abroad, giving thousands work in the factories. The creation of the American war machine began a new wave of migration to the northern cities, with 500,000 people reported to have left the South during the decade beginning in 1910, and a further 750,000 leaving during the 1920s.[121]

America was going through a social revolution with the arrival of moving pictures and cinema. New prohibition laws on alcohol only succeeded in creating illegal clubs, famously known as speakeasies. These underground dance clubs gave birth to a thriving musical scene, with artists like jazz legends Louis Armstrong and Duke Ellington revered on both sides of the colour line. This time also heralded the birth of the Harlem Renaissance in New York, giving prominence to a new wave of writers, poets, artists, intellectuals, composers and musicians.

World War II

The biggest changes that affected both West Indian and Black American servicemen occurred in Britain during World War II. Thousands of West Indians signed up to defend their queen and, by association, their country. Ahead of the arrival of the *Windrush* Generation, servicemen and women from the Caribbean and the Commonwealth enlisted in the British armed forces and fought gallantly. America – with Churchill's approval – attempted to impose the Jim Crow segregation laws of the South on British soil. Gaining respect was at the core of the Black American GIs' struggles, and they adopted a slogan of 'Double V for Victory', tackling Fascism abroad and racism at home.

Vietnam

One of sport's greatest and most charismatic superstars, Muhammad Ali, went toe-to-toe with the American government by refusing to be conscripted into the US Army in 1967. He said, 'Why should they ask me to put on a uniform and go ten thousand miles from home and drop bombs and bullets on brown people in Vietnam while so-called Negro people in Louisville are treated like dogs?'[122]

His stance would not only see him stripped of his world title, but banned from boxing for over three years. He lost millions of dollars in earnings, and suffered the scorn and vitriol of the American establishment. Already having converted to Islam, Ali's principled stance encouraged the growing anti-war movement, and he spoke for a number of African-Americans. They, like Dr King, were becoming increasingly uncomfortable with the Vietnam War, which would see America unload more bombs on the tiny country than in both world wars combined. In percentage terms, Black Americans were over-represented in the numbers fighting and dying, as they were unable to find the financial means to 'dodge the draft'.

When Ali returned to the ring and regained his heavyweight crown in 1974 he became a global hero, for whom the acclaim continues today. A warrior in the ring, he became a colossus outside the ropes without throwing a punch.

General Colin Powell was born to Jamaican immigrants, and became the best exponent of overcoming racism within the Army. He fought in Vietnam, and was involved in the 1983 American invasion of tiny Grenada in the West Indies. He rose to become one of the highest-ranking military generals as the chairman of the Joint Chiefs of Staff during the first Iraq war. He then became one of the few respected voices in George W Bush's cabinet as Secretary of State, before being replaced by Condoleezza Rice. Despite serving under Republican presidents, Powell endorsed Barack Obama's presidential campaign as 'being the best person qualified for the job'.

As a senator, President Obama was a fierce critic of the Iraq War, and when he received his Nobel Peace Prize in December 2009, he praised the previous holders of the award, including his heroes Dr King and Gandhi. He spoke of the ongoing tensions between war and peace, and summarised America's foreign conflicts stretching back to President Woodrow Wilson:

> There will be times when nations – acting individually or in concert – will find the use of force not only necessary but morally justified. Whatever mistakes we have made, the plain fact is this, the United States of America has helped underwrite global security for more than six decades with the blood of our citizens and strength of our arms.[123]

A few months later he underscored this by authorising another troop surge to increase the US forces in Afghanistan.

America's Moral Maze – Fighting Wars to Keep the Peace

It has been America's post-World War II wars that have troubled me most, particularly when fought with such naked religious zeal as under George W Bush and the neoconservative hawks. This, alongside slavery, race and its treatment of its poor, heads my list of America's hypocrisies that sit uncomfortably with me on my travels. My American hosts smile warmly when I challenge them, and with a shrug tell me not to worry too deeply about these 'contradictions', as they call them. I know from the heated debates I have had at home when defending the United States that many see America's foreign policy as too aggressive, interventionist, and purely about financial gain in terms of securing oil fields and rebuilding contracts and arms deals. Whether Caped Crusader or imperialist invader, from Kabul to Kent or Beirut to Bristol, these flaws lie at the heart of how America is perceived. What Americans fail to understand is that these inconsistencies in their ideology feed their enemies, and give their friends little ground on which to stand to defend them.

While Obama has technically taken America out of two wars, he has authorised drone attacks, which daily kill the innocent in Pakistan and Afghanistan. An American presence remains in many countries in which it has fought. While Obama's election was welcomed across the planet as a change from the unchecked military excesses of 'Sheriff' Bush II and his warmongering team, Obama is still in charge of the biggest war machine on the planet.

Old problems are resurfacing in the Middle East, and new questions arise about Syria, Libya, Iraq, Iran, and even in Europe from the Ukraine. We shall see, as he completes his second term, what foreign policy legacy Obama will leave; much of the leadership seems to have been delegated to US Secretary of State, John Kerry. However, as the rest of the world knows, foreign policy and chiefly the decision to go to war are more complex than a Hollywood western, where the good guys wear white and the bad guys wear black.

Paul Stephenson and the Bristol Bus Boycott

There are few people who could link a peaceful bus boycott, serving in the military, becoming the first Black man to desegregate an Alabama hotel and enduring the full extent of racism in Britain during the 1960s – but Bristol resident Paul Stephenson is that person. His colourful life includes meeting legends such as Muhammad Ali, and also Nelson Mandela on visits to South Africa's townships before he was banned by the Apartheid regime. In 1963, he started the Bristol Bus Boycott, inspired by Rosa Parks's actions and the leadership of Dr King. As he was to find out, the repellent blend of racism and hypocrisy rife in the Deep South of America was also apparent in the south-west of England.

Bristol Omnibus operated the bus service in Bristol, and failed to employ a single Black worker. This was unlike their counterparts within London Transport who employed my father and hundreds of other Black workers. Bristol Omnibus blamed the lack of Black workers on the threat of industrial action from the Transport and General Workers' Union (TGWU) if they were to employ Black workers. This was known as the colour bar, and existed despite the TGWU publicly attacking the South African Apartheid regime.

Stephenson was working in the city as a youth worker, and arranged for nineteen-year-old Jamaican-born Guy Bailey to attend an interview for a role as a bus conductor. When Bristol Omnibus staff found out he was Black, Bailey was told there were no longer any jobs. Stephenson joined the West Indian Development Council and led a boycott of the buses by the Black community in April 1963.

The young, articulate local MP Tony Benn was an ardent supporter of the campaign, as was West Indian activist and former cricketer, Sir Learie Constantine. The campaign gathered support from students at Bristol University and from ordinary Bristolians, with many letters of support sent into the local newspapers. Like Dr King, Stephenson suffered death threats from racists, and concern from those in the Black community who told him, 'You can't tell a white man what to do in his country!'[124] For Stephenson, however, it was a matter of principle and a human right to being treated with dignity.

On 28 August 1963, the same day Dr King delivered his *I Have a Dream* speech, Bristol Omnibus announced an end to the colour bar of Black drivers and conductors on their buses, handing victory to the Bristol activists.

Stephenson continues to be a campaigner for civil rights in Britain. During an interview I had with him, he recalled vividly the day he was refused a drink in a city-centre pub because of his colour. He refused to leave, and was promptly arrested; however, he was later acquitted of all charges, and the pub landlord was sacked.

Stephenson's actions led indirectly to increased rights for Black and Asian people in Britain. In the same year that President Johnson signed a new civil rights legislation after Bloody Sunday in Alabama, Prime Minister Harold Wilson, who as the Opposition leader had supported the Bristol Bus Boycott, brought in the 1965 Race Relations Act outlawing discrimination in public places. This was followed, in 1968, by further legislation to outlaw discrimination in employment and housing.

Stephenson was the chair of the Bristol Legacy Commission, which raised money to tackle the educational inequalities between white and Black children. He has seen the biggest changes in Britain during the intervening years, as Black people are finally able to have their civil rights while making advances to gain economic and political strength. He published the book of his life, called *Memoirs of a Black Englishman*, in October 2011, and Bristol's dignitaries and wider local community turned out in force to honour him at the book launch in the city.

In 2013, I joined a team of volunteers that included authors Lilleith Morrison, who had co-written *Memoirs of a Black Englishman*, and historian Madge Dresser. The Bristol Bus Boycott 50 (BBB50) committee organised a series of events to commemorate its fiftieth anniversary, and brought together local volunteers, activists, artists and Bristol City Council officials. We garnered support from the Unite union, who used to be the TGWU responsible for the colour bar. The Unite union leader Laurence Faircloth expressed 'sincere regret' for what Paul Stephenson and the ethnic minority community in Bristol had endured half a century ago. 'It was completely unacceptable,' Mr Faircloth said. 'I can well accept the sense of injustice and pain that has been felt because of what happened in Bristol all those years ago. I hope the apology goes some way to righting a great wrong.' Unite also reprinted Madge Dresser's book *Black and White on the Buses: The 1963 Colour Bar Dispute*.

BBB50 also organised a year of events, which included talks and readings, and began a campaign to get the story told in schools. We rounded off with a gala dinner for Bristol's *Windrush* Generation, and a tour of the city on one of the green buses to celebrate and commemorate the Bristol Bus Boycott achievement. Roy Hackett and Guy Reid Bailey, who were involved in the actual boycott, attended. I chaired a lively debate at Bristol's M Shed, simultaneously broadcast on Ujima and BBC Radio Bristol, examining what had changed in Bristol regarding race in the fifty years since the boycott. Among the panellists were Toyin Agbetu of Ligali and Bristol's first female Somali councillor, Hibaq Jama, who answered questions reflecting the changing nature of race and immigration in Bristol and Britain, both of which have around sixteen per cent Black and minority ethnic populations. Stephenson was awarded an honorary doctorate in July 2014 by the University of Bristol.

Supported by both Bristol's first Muslim Lord Mayor Faruk Choudhury, and its first elected mayor, George Ferguson, Bristol Omnibus unveiled a plaque dedicated to the leaders of the Bristol Bus Boycott. It was unveiled on 28 August 2014 and I was the proud Master of Ceremonies, especially as it was on the same date as Dr King's *I Have a Dream* speech in 1963. There is also to be a national campaign to highlight the work of Dr King and his influence on British social justice campaigns, called Journey to Justice.

With pictures of Muhammad Ali holding his children jostling for wall space alongside his Freedom of Bristol award and a photo of him receiving his OBE from The Queen, Paul Stephenson is a proud and valiant reminder of the many influences of the civil rights struggles from the Deep South of America, and how they inspired those of shared African heritage in Britain and around the world.

Epilogue

Back to the Beginning

What initially began as a personal pilgrimage from where Dr King took his first breath in Atlanta to his last gasp in Memphis, Tennessee, has unfolded into a wonderful odyssey of discovery. The Deep South was proving a wonderful historical exploration field, at times disturbing and at others heart-warming, but never less than absorbing. Each of the first five Southern states I visited left me with a different experience, and in each state I found a personal resonance, plus answers to many burning questions. I have found out more than I ever could have imagined about the European colonisation of Africa, Asia and the Americas; the transatlantic slave trade; Bristol's past and how it continues to affect its present; the events that led to the American Civil War; the Civil Rights Movement; the power of the presidency; the importance of the Black church within Black communities; America at war; Dr King's life and more. Each major issue had taught me so much about how people can make a difference by mobilising, and, in some cases, sacrificing themselves, and all in the name of equality. Yet, I still felt there was much to investigate, learn and share.

I had begun by watching the first Black President of the United States of America being sworn into office, but since then, I have seen him condemned and defended, loved and loathed in unequal measure. Obama, with a difficult upbringing and a distant relationship with his father, too, had travelled afar to find answers to ghosts from his past. At times, raised by his white grandparents away from his mother, he experimented with drugs and alcohol and, by his own admission, at one point he would have preferred a career in basketball to that of the White House. Yet when he returned to America from Kenya – the land of his fathers – he returned with new resolve, soon married Michelle, and the rest, as they say, is history. Part of that history, Obama acknowledges, was influenced by Dr King. The acclaim for the civil rights campaign that Dr King led has only been heralded since his death. As more of the civil rights story has been told, so others involved in struggle, from the Bristol Bus Boycott to women's fight for equality, have found inspiration and prospered.

America is judged on the world stage by more exacting standards than any other nation. These standards are set by Americans themselves, as written into the Constitution for their 320-plus million people. That is why there is such contempt for America whenever it slips from those democratic values and doesn't follow its lofty principles. I have seen and heard this vitriol from critical friends of mine as well as seasoned political commentators. The list of issues about which they protest includes Guantánamo Bay, which, despite Obama's promises and efforts to close it, still remains an undelivered campaign pledge. Domestically, people are concerned about the imprisonment of so many of America's young Black men, 150 years after the country apparently set them free.

I, too, struggle with these glaring hypocrisies, but I have come to accept that, since its inception, the United States of America has been and always will be a nation of contradictions. This makes America deeply flawed, but never less than fascinating.

The Legacy of the *Windrush* Generation

On arriving in England, the *Windrush* Generation knew only hard work, toil and difficult conditions. Scrapping and scraping for every penny, they were specialists in making a little go far, but their efforts went largely unrecognised. Until my mid-twenties, I had been unaware of the full significance of the Black and white images of men and women disembarking from the *SS Windrush* in 1948, but having discovered Martin, Malcolm, Nelson, Harriet, Rosa and Maya, I subsequently discovered some new heroes a lot closer to home.

Perhaps we should rename their time the British Civil Rights Story. Their hard-won victories have led to a better and fairer Britain, which started with the 1965 Race Relations Act, making the *Windrush* Generation the first of the equality groups to gain legal rights. After successfully supporting the Bristol Bus Boycott in 1963, Tony Benn lobbied the then Opposition leader Harold Wilson to improve conditions for Black people in Britain. When Wilson became prime minister in 1964, the Labour government introduced the Race Relations Act, the first anti-discriminatory legislation in the UK, to be followed by laws banning discrimination against women, disabled people, LGBT (Lesbian, Gay, Bisexual and Transgender) people and religion. This has since evolved into the 2010 Equality Act – a fine epitaph to Tony Benn, former Bristol MP, personal friend of Paul Stephenson's and lifelong champion of the disenfranchised, who died on 14 March 2014.

*

My family has provided me with more than a platform to tell their story, and I am honoured to pay tribute to their roles. One uncle was inspired by Dr King to go to the highest level in his church, and another became part of London's 'Swinging Sixties'. Mum and Dad, like many of the *Windrush* Generation, played their part in building two major post-war industries: the NHS and London Underground. They had joined the quest of many to build a new life, and were preoccupied with negotiating the difficulties of this new land with racism a constant backdrop. Theirs was a stoic generation, ironically including the British stiff upper lip in their armour for braving a new environment. They rarely talked openly or publicly bemoaned their treatment, and never complained to their children about their experiences. However, we couldn't fail to notice their brooding sense of resentment and frustration, overheard in snatched conversations with their friends and family disputes, and compounded by punishments from employers for minor misdemeanours. We didn't realise it then, but they were showing their love, first by providing for us then by protecting us, while not knowing how to prepare us for a life that was Caribbean at home but British beyond their net curtains. It was new to them, as well as us.

What of us, the second generation of Black and brown skins born and raised in the UK into a society that appeared to distrust us and did little to understand us? Like our parents, there was no manual or Internet guide. The only precedent came from the combined factors of slavery, colonialism, globalisation and racism that had preceded our arrival into a hostile British environment. Some adapted and assimilated as best they could, others rebelled, while many sought their own way, embracing their Afrocentric roots. Now, with our third, fourth and even fifth generations of Caribbean heritage knowing nothing else but their Britishness, we can explain our parents' part in British history with many stories and pictorial evidence, and take a sense of pride as we follow in their footsteps.

With race inequality still a stain on its values, and for all the issues that has brought, Britain is seen globally as a vibrant, culturally diverse society. This has dramatically changed its sporting teams, music, fashion and even its food – a direct result of the immigration investment from the Caribbean, Asia and Africa it made at the end of World War II. Time will tell whether present and future migrants will be afforded any recognition and integrated into British society, or will history see them ostracised and scapegoated, as were our parents and many immigrant communities stretching decades before them?

Connections: Bristol, the Caribbean, Washington DC,
the Birth of Baby Olivia – 20 January 2009

My final tale from America involves one of my closest friends, Janet Allen, previously of Bristol. Janet, a former Gladiators champion and Bristol City Council employee, met her husband Rory Teape in Jamaica. In March 2005, they married in Jamaica, which is from where Janet's parents originated, and from where Rory, aged fourteen, emigrated to America. Together, they moved to Leesburg, Virginia, USA.

Despite only living an hour away from Washington DC, neither Janet nor Rory attended the inauguration of President Barack Obama. They do, however, have a special reason to remember that day as

Janet gave birth to their first child, Olivia. The next day, I went to the hospital and congratulated them both, and we excitedly relived our separate special days; Janet and Rory with a deeply personal significance, and me with a deeply historical significance.

There in my arms I held baby Olivia, and I felt all the connections from the past yet again swirling within me as I literally held the future. With Obama's words still ringing in my ears, this baby felt like a true bridge from the *Windrush* to the White House. What will Olivia's legacy from Obama be? I wonder. Will her children clamber over a monument to Obama in Washington DC, or understand her heritage from Bristol, the city of her mother's birth?

The Enchantment of the Deep South

A New Yorker once advised me in a cautionary fable that the Deep South is just about the *3Rs* – Racism, Rifles and Religion. However, I have uncovered that there is plenty more to the region than that. I had, in the first part of my journey, unearthed issues beyond the Hollywood images of the Deep South. I found it was neither idyllic, with the southerners wronged by a liberal President Lincoln as in *Gone with the Wind,* nor were there current plots by southerners to murder activists, as in *Mississippi Burning* – although they are all there in its past. What I did find in each state were issues, history and places as absorbing as they were enlightening.

I know I am not the first, nor will I be the last, to be beguiled by this captivating region. I met so many different people, from all backgrounds and races, and received all the legendary southern charm and kindness. Most people greeted me with warmth, but also a strange fascination at my English accent juxtaposed with my skin colour, mixing up their perceptions of both. As I engaged them in open conversation about their lives and America's history, I wondered to myself why they look so confused. They should be used to living with such complex contradictions – such as the fact that outside of the United States and United Kingdom, the first thing I get asked is '*Eres americano?*' '*Êtes-vous Américain?*' 'Are you American?'

Bristol elected its first mayor, George Ferguson, in October 2012, defeating candidate Marvin Rees who would have been Europe's first Black mayor. Obama won a second term in November 2012, and, like him, I felt I still had much unfinished business to complete in America. The aftermath of Hurricane Katrina in New Orleans, the fight for education of the Little Rock Nine in Arkansas, the murderous past of Mississippi, immigration in the 21st century, and the role of Black people in sport and music headed a list of subjects to be explored that included Obama himself. But that, as I say, is for another adventure.

I found my voice and told my story, their story and our story via the United States of America, the Caribbean and Britain, in an admittedly unusual direction of travel. I have brought these various themes together into a compendium of history, personal stories, cultural references, commentary and travel. Others have found their own voices through Africa, Europe and, increasingly, further afield. I encourage you all to tell your stories, and maybe let me know how you get on. As the African-American historian and geologist Professor Henry Louis Gates Jr, himself borrowing from ancient Greece, says, 'Know Thy past. Know Thyself'.

References

Chapter Four
Discovering My Roots via the Transatlantic Slave Trade

1. *Bristol, A Darker History, Swindles Scandals & Skulduggery*, Derek Robinson, Countryside Books 2005, p 10.
2. *The Atlantic Slave Trade*, Herbert S Klein, Cambridge Books 1999, p 6.
3. Olaudah Equiano, *The Interesting Narrative and Other Writings*. Penguin Classics. (1789), p 58.
4. *A Traveller's History of the Caribbean*, James Ferguson, Windrush Press 1998, p 110.
5. *The Trans-Atlantic Slave Trade*, Women in Slavery, Jennifer Lyle Morgan, Trans-Atlantic Slavery Against Human Dignity, Liverpool University Press 1994, p 64.
6. *The Hemingses of Monticello: An American Family*. Annette Gordon-Reed, Norton 2008.
7. *Slavery & the British Empire*, From Africa to America, Kenneth Morgan, Oxford University Press, 2007, p 56.
8. *Bristol, Africa and the 18th Century Slave Trade to America* Vol. 2 1730-1745, David Richardson, Bristol Record Society Vol XXXIX, p viii, 28 and 102/3.
9. *Capitalism & Slavery*, Eric Williams, André Deutsch Ltd 1944, p 34.
10. *Capitalism & Slavery*, Eric Williams, André Deutsch Ltd 1944, p 52.
11. *Bristol and the Slave Trade*, local history pamphlet, Professor MacInnes – Bristol Century Library, p 3.
12. Taken from the official website of Merchant Venturers, www.merchantventurers.com.
13. *Slavery & the British Empire, From Africa to America*, Kenneth Morgan, Oxford University Press, 2007, p 39.
14. *Slavery & the British Empire, From Africa to America*, Kenneth Morgan, Oxford University Press, 2007, p 81.

15. *Slavery & the British Empire, From Africa to America*, Kenneth Morgan, Oxford University Press, 2007, p 50.

16. *Slavery Obscured: The Social History of the Slave Trade in Bristol*, Madge Dresser, Redcliffe Press Ltd, 2007, p 110 quote of Benjamin Donn.

17. *Slavery Obscured*, Madge Dresser, originally from p 165 Vol 3, JF Nicholls and John Taylor, Bristol Past and Present, Bristol and London Arrowsmith, p 32/33.

18. *Rough Crossings*, Simon Schama, BBC Books 2005, p 175.

19. *Black Cargoes, A History of the Atlantic Slave Trade 1518-1865*, Daniel P Mannix & Malcolm Cowley, Penguin Books, 1962, p 172.

20. *Rough Crossings, Britain, The Slaves & the American Revolution*, Simon Schama, BBC Books 2005, p 24.

21. *Rough Crossings, Britain, The Slaves & the American Revolution*, Simon Schama, BBC Books 2005, p 204.

22. *The Longman Companion to History: Slavery, Emancipation & Civil Rights*, Harry Harmer, Pearson Education Ltd, 2001, p 74.

23. *Black Cargoes, A History of the Atlantic Slave Trade 1518-1865*, Daniel P Mannix & Malcolm Cowley, Penguin Books, 1962, p 151.

24. *Rough Crossings*, Simon Schama, BBC Books 2005, p 194/5.

25. *Olaudah Equiano, The Interesting Narrative and Other Writings*. Penguin Classics. (1789), 1995, p 169.

26. *Satan's Kingdom, Bristol and the Transatlantic Slave Trade*, Pip Jones, Past & Present Press, 2007, p iii.

27. *Black Cargoes, A History of the Atlantic Slave Trade 1518-1865*, Daniel P Mannix & Malcolm Cowley, Penguin Books, 1962, p 182.

28. Extract from Eli Whitney museum website, www.eliwhitney.org.

29. *Rough Crossings*, Simon Schama, BBC Books 2005, p 476.

30. *America Empire of Liberty*. David Reynolds, Allen Lane/Penguin 2009, p 137.

31. *The History of the Atlantic Slave Trade 1440-1880*, Hugh Thomas, Allen Lane/Penguin 2009.

32. *Trans-Atlantic Slavery Against Human Dignity*, Liverpool University Press 1994 (edited by Anthony Tibbles), p 73-77, section written by Anthony Tibbles African Resistance to Enslavement.

33. *Trans-Atlantic Slavery Against Human Dignity*, Liverpool University Press

1994 (edited by Anthony Tibbles), p 40 section written by Stephen Small and James Walvin.

34. *A Travellers History of the Caribbean*, James Ferguson, Windrush Press 1998, p 162.

35. *A Travellers History of the Caribbean*, James Ferguson, Windrush Press 1998, p 157.

36. *A Travellers History of the Caribbean*, James Ferguson, Windrush Press 1998, p 169.

37. *Colonial Latin America* (5th edition), Mark A Burkholder & Lyman L Johnson, Oxford University Press 2004. Original source p 116-119 Philip D Curtin, The Atlantic Slave trade. A census. Madison University of Wisconsin Press 1969, p 134.

38. *A Travellers History of the Caribbean*, James Ferguson, Windrush Press 1998, p 188.

39. Frederick Douglass, William S McFeely, W W Norton & Company 1991, p 141.

40. *Rough Crossings, Britain The Slaves & the American Revolution* Simon Schama, BBC Books 2005, p 483.

41. *Rough Crossings, Britain The Slaves & the American Revolution* Simon Schama, BBC Books 2005, p 477.

42. *Rough Crossings, Britain The Slaves & the American Revolution* Simon Schama, BBC Books 2005, p 229-236.

43. *Rough Crossings, Britain the Slaves & the American Revolution* Simon Schama, BBC Books 2005, p 471/2.

44. Professor MacInnes, *Bristol Gateway of Empire*, 1st Edition 1939, Arrowsmith 2nd Edition David & Charles, p 196/7.

45. Extract from *The Observer,* 7 March 2010 written by John Vidal.

Chapter Five
Personal Reflections of the Transatlantic Slave Trade

46. *Many Thousands Gone, The First Two Centuries of Slavery in North America*, Ira Berlin, Harvard College, 1998, p 359.

47. *The Autobiography of Martin Luther King*, Abacus Books, 1998, p 326.

48. *Eric Williams Capitalism & Slavery*, Eric Williams André Deutsch, 1944.

49. *Transatlantic Slavery – Against Human Dignity Anthony Tibbles.* Subsection

Stephen Small Racist Ideologies, Liverpool University Press 1994, p 107.

50. *Who Do You Think You Are?* Spike Lee, (US Version 2010) NBC TV

51. *A Traveller's History of the Caribbean,* James Ferguson, Windrush Press 1998, p 93.

52. *Slavery Obscured, The Social History of the Slave Trade in Bristol,* Madge Dresser, Redcliffe Press Ltd, 2007, p 97.

53. *Slavery Obscured, The Social History of the Slave Trade in Bristol,* Madge Dresser, Redcliffe Press Ltd, 2007, p 96-98.

54. BBC News website 25 March 2007.

55. Interview with Toyin Agbetu in The Guardian Newspaper 3 April 2007.

56. From the website of the anti-slavery movement, www.anti-slavery.org.

57. *America Empire of Liberty* – David Reynolds, Allen Lane/Penguin 2009, p 28.

58. Ibid.

59. *Slavery Obscured, The Social History of the Slave Trade in Bristol,* Madge Dresser, Redcliffe Press Ltd, 2007. Original Dunn Sugar and Slaves p 112-115, p 16.

60. *Words to Strange Fruit.* Written by Abel Meeropol. Sung by Billie Holiday.

61. *Slavery Obscured, The Social History of the Slave Trade in Bristol,* Madge Dresser, Redcliffe Press Ltd, 2007, Peros epitaph at Henbury/Blaise Castle also p 80.

62. Website changed in 2013 after being bought by private equity firm KSL Capital.

63. BBC News website 22 February 2006.

64. *The Autobiography of Martin Luther King,* Abacus Books, 1998, p 326.

Chapter Six
Power of the Presidency – Washington DC and Virginia

65. *America, Empire of Liberty,* David Reynolds, Allen Lane, 2009, p 11. [Original Columbus diary, 16 Dec 1492, In Julius E Olson and Edward G Bourne, eds the Northmen, Columbus and Cabot, 985-1503, New York: Charles Scribner's Sons, 1906, p182.]

66. *Days of Grace,* Arthur Ashe and Arnold Rampersad. Alfred A Knopf, 1993, p 101.

67. Richmond see full extract p 63-72 No Place Like Home, Gary Younge, Picador, p 69.

68. *The Great Virginia Triumvirate: George Washington, Thomas Jefferson, and James Madison*, John P. Kaminski, University of Virginia Press Books, 2010, p 15.

Chapter Seven
In Search of a King

69. Malcolm X, 28 June 1964 speech at the founding rally of the organisation of Afro-American unity, Audubon Ballroom, Washington Heights, Manhattan, New York City.

70. *The Autobiography of Malcolm X*, Alex Haley, Penguin, 1965, p 479.

71. David Reynolds, America Empire of Liberty, p 219.

72. *The Essential Frederick Douglass*, Frederick Douglass Wilder Publications, 2008, p 490.

73. *The Autobiography of Martin Luther King Jr*, edited by Clayborne Carson, Abacus 1998, p 58.

74. *The Autobiography of Martin Luther King Jr*, edited by Clayborne Carson, Abacus 1998, p 65/66.

75. *The Autobiography of Martin Luther King Jr*, edited by Clayborne Carson, Abacus, 1998, p 110.

76. *Martin Luther King*, Godfrey Hodgson, Quercus, p 59.

77. *The 7 Habits of Highly Effective People*, Stephen R. Covey, Simon & Schuster 1989, Habit 2 p 95-143.

78. *Interview with Andrew Young – Martin Luther King, Jr. A Documentary...from Montgomery to Memphis*, Norton 1976, p 65.

79. *The Autobiography of Martin Luther King Jr*, edited by Clayborne Carson, Abacus, 1998, from 'Letter from Birmingham Jail', p 193.

80. *From Montgomery to Memphis Martin Luther King, Jr. A Documentary... from Montgomery to Memphis*, Norton 1976, p 70.

81. *The Autobiography of Martin Luther King Jr*, Edited by Clayborne Carson, Abacus, 1998, p 206.

82. Martin Luther King, Jr. A Documentary...from Montgomery to Memphis, Norton 1976, p 72.

83. From Interview with Andrew Young – Martin Luther King, Jr. A Documentary...from Montgomery to Memphis, Norton 1976, p 66.

84. *The Autobiography of Martin Luther King Jr*, edited by Clayborne

Carson, Abacus 1998, p 148.

85. *The Autobiography of Martin Luther King Jr*, edited by Clayborne Carson, Abacus, 1998, p 237.

86. *The Autobiography of Martin Luther King Jr*, edited by Clayborne Carson, Abacus, 1998, p 235.

87. *The Autobiography of Martin Luther King Jr*, edited by Clayborne Carson, Abacus, 1998, p 81.

88. *The Autobiography of Martin Luther King Jr*, edited by Clayborne Carson, Abacus, 1998, p 326.

89. Charles Whitaker, 'Is Atlanta the Black Mecca?' Ebony Magazine March 2002.

90. Andrew Young on Atlanta, Charles Whitaker, 'Is Atlanta the Black Mecca?' Ebony Magazine, March 2002.

91. *The Autobiography of Martin Luther King Jr*, Edited by Clayborne Carson, Abacus, 1998, p 285. From The How Long, Not Long speech Montgomery, Alabama 25 March 1965.

92. Charles Whitaker, 'Is Atlanta the Black Mecca?' Ebony Magazine, March 2002.

93. Atlanta, Crown Jewels of the South. Ebony Magazine 1997 – Black Capital of America.

94. Earl Graves Senior, 40th anniversary of Black Enterprise Magazine 'Extraordinary Journey', July 2010, www.blackenterprise.com.

95. Roper Center Public Opinion Archives – www.ropercenter.uconn.edu/ elections/how_groups_voted/voted/_08.html.

Chapter Eight
The Foundation of Black America – The Black Church

96. *America Empire of Liberty*, David Reynolds, Allen Lane/Penguin 2009, p 582.

97. Americana BBC Radio 4. 10 Oct 2010.

98. Only in America, Matt Frei, HarperCollins 2008, p 164.

99. Ed Miliband interview with Nicky Campbell, BBC Radio Five Live 28 September 2010.

100. YouTube – https://www.youtube.com/watch?v=TYqrXVNfYUI

101. *Colonial Latin America*, Mark A Burkholder & Lyman L Johnson.

Oxford University Press USA, 1990, p 141.

102. *America Empire of Liberty,* David Reynolds, Allen Lane 2009, p 46.

103. *The Interesting Narrative of the Life of Olaudah Equiano*, Penguin Classics, 2003, p 132.

104. US Government National Park Service http://www.nps.gov/hafe/ historyculture/the-niagara-movement.htm.

105. *The Autobiography of Martin Luther King Jr*, Edited by Clayborne Carson, Abacus, 1998, p 359.

106. *Martin Luther King*, Godfrey Hodgson, Quercus 2009, p 80.

107. *Martin Luther King*, Godfrey Hodgson, Quercus 2009, p 78.

108. *Martin Luther King*, Godfrey Hodgson, Quercus 2009, p 156.

109. *Martin Luther King*, Godfrey Hodgson, Quercus 2009, p 163.

110. *The Interesting Narrative of the Life of Olaudah Equiano*, Penguin Classics, 2003, p 172.

111. *The Autobiography of Martin Luther King Jr*, Edited by Clayborne Carson, Abacus, 1998, p 6.

112. *America Empire of Liberty,* David Reynolds, Allen Lane 2009, p 246.

113. *America Empire of Liberty,* David Reynolds, Allen Lane 2009, p 246.

114. *Vivian Duffield Profile,* Andrew Anthony, *The Observer* 27th March 2011.

115. BBC Website http://www.bbc.co.uk/news/uk-wales-12692760.

116. *Martin Luther King*, Godfrey Hodgson, Quercus 2009, p 119.

117. *Only in America*, Matt Frei, HarperCollins 2008, p 181.

118. Nick Cohen, 12 September 2010, *The Observer* Newspaper.

119. Tuskegee Airfield, National historic site, Motor Field, Alabama, USA.

120. *Rough Crossings: Britain the Slaves and the American Revolution*, Simon Schama, BBC Books 2005, p 151-2.

121. *America Empire of Liberty,* David Reynolds, Allen Lane/Penguin 2009, p 329.

122. *King of the World*, David Remnick, Picador 1999, p 289.

123. No 28 Obama acceptance speech available on NY Times.com, 10 December 2009.

124. Various Interviews with Paul Stephenson 2010-2014.

Further Bibliography

Ashe, A & Rampersad (1993) *Days of Grace – A Memoir*, New York, Alfred A Knopf.

Belafonte, H (2011) *My Song A Memoir*, New York Alfred A Knopf.

Berlin, I (1998) *Many Thousands Gone – The First Two Centuries of Slavery in North America* Cambridge, Massachusetts, USA, Belknap Harvard.

Branch, T (1998) *Parting the Waters*. London, Macmillan.

Buckingham, JS (1842 reprinted 2006), *A Journey Through the Slave States of North America*, Charleston/London, Nonsuch Publishing.

Burkholder, MA & Johnson, LL (2004), *Colonial Latin America* (5th edition), Oxford, Oxford University Press 2004.

Cantor, G (1991) *Historic Black Landmarks – A Traveler's Guide*, Detroit, Visible Ink Press.

Carson, C (1998) *The Autobiography of Martin Luther King, Jr*, New York, Abacus.

Covey, S (1989) *The 7 Habits of Highly Effective People*, New York, Simon & Schuster.

Curtin, PD (1969) *The Atlantic Slave-trade A Census*. Madison, University of Wisconsin Press.

Dabydeen, (2007) *The Oxford Companion to Black British History*, Oxford, Oxford University Press.

Dhondy F (2001) *CLR James Cricket, the Caribbean and World Revolution*, London, Weidenfeld & Nicolson.

Douglass, F (1845) *Narrative of the life of Frederick Douglass An American Slave* written by himself, USA, Dover Publications.

Dresser, M (1986) *Black and White on the Buses – 1963 Colour Bar Dispute in Bristol, Bristol*, Press Gang Co-Operatives Ltd.

Dresser, M (2007) *Slavery Obscured – The Social History of the Slave-Trade in Bristol* – Bristol, Redcliffe Press.

WEB Du Bois (1994) *The Souls of Black Folks*, New York, Dover.

Equiano, O (1995) *The Interesting Narrative and other writings– 1745 Library of Congress*, London, Penguin.

Ferguson, J (1998), *A Travellers History of the Caribbean*, Gloucestershire, Windrush Press.

Haley, A (1964) *The Autobiography of Malcolm X*, London, Penguin.

Haley, A (1976) *Roots*, London, Vintage.

Harmer (2001) *The Longman Companion to History: Slavery, Emancipation & Civil Rights*, Harry Harmer, New York, Pearson Education Ltd.

Harris, S (1996) *The Timetables of African-American History* – New York, Simon & Schuster.

Hodgson (2009) *Martin Luther King*, London, Quercus.

James, CLR (1963) *Beyond a Boundary*, New York, Pantheon.

Jones, P (2007) *Satan's Kingdom Bristol and the Transatlantic Slave Trade*, Bristol, Past & Present Press.

Kaminski, JP (2010) *The Great Virginia Triumvirate*: George Washington, Thomas Jefferson, and James Madison, Virginia, University of Virginia Press Books.

Kerridge, R & Joseph, M (1989) *In the Deep South* – London, Joseph.

King, MLK edited Carson, C (1998) *The Autobiography of Martin Luther King Jr*, New York, Abacus.

Klein, HS (1999) *The Atlantic Slave Trade*, Cambridge, Cambridge Books.

Lee, Harper (1960) *To Kill a Mockingbird*, Philadelphia, USA, JB Lippincott & Co.

Local history pamphlets and references books from Bristol Central Library.

MacInnes, CM (1939) *Bristol Gateway of Empire* 2nd edition, Newton Abbot, David & Charles.

Mannix, DP and Cowley, M (1962) *Black Cargoes – A History of the Atlantic Slave Trade – 1518-1865*, London, Penguin.

McFeely, W (1996) *Frederick Douglass*, London, WW Norton.

McGregor JHS (2007) *Washington From the Ground Up* – Cambridge, Massachusetts, USA, Belknap Harvard.

Mitchell, R (2010) *Myths Facts, Feelings Bristol & Transatlantic Slavery*,

Bristol, Community Media South West Imprint.

Morgan, JL (1994) *The Trans-Atlantic Slave Trade*, Women in Slavery, Trans-Atlantic Slavery Against Human Dignity, Liverpool, Liverpool University Press.

Morgan, K (2007) *Slavery & the British Empire, From Africa to America*, Kenneth Morgan, Oxford, Oxford University Press.

Morgan, K (2007) *Slavery and the British Empire – From Africa to America*, Oxford, Oxford University Press.

Murphy D, Cooper K, Waldron M, (2001) *United States 1776-1992*, London, Collins Educational.

Obama, B (1995), *Dreams from My Father*, London, Canongate.

Obama, B (2006) *The Audacity of Hope*, London, Canongate.

Observer, The London various articles read and sourced.

Phillips, M & T (1998) *Windrush The Irresistible Rise of Multi-Racial Britain*, London, HarperCollins.

Reid, AR (2008) *The Hemingses of Monticello, An American Family*, New York, W W Norton & Co.

Reynolds, D (2009) *America, Empire of Liberty*, London, Allen Lane.

Richardson, D (1986) *Bristol, Africa and the 18th Century Slave Trade to America* Vol 2 1730-1745, Bristol, Bristol Record Society.

Robinson, D (2006) *Bristol, A Darker History, Swindles Scandals & Skulduggery*, Newbury, Countryside Books.

Schama, S (2005) *Rough Crossings – Britain, the Slaves and the American Revolution*, London, BBC Books.

Schulke, F (1976) *Martin Luther King Jr, A Documentary...Montgomery to Memphis*, New York/London, Norton.

Sparks, Allister (1990) *The Mind of South Africa* New York, Alfred A Knopf.

Stann (1998), *Deep South*, London, Lonely Planet.

Sullivan, A (2010) *America A Visual History From Then to Now*, New York, Life/Time Inc.

Thomas, H (1997) *The History of the Atlantic Slave Trade 1440-1880*, London, Picador.

Tibbles, A (1994) *Trans-Atlantic Slavery, Against Human Dignity, Liverpool*, Liverpool University Press.

Voice, The. London various articles read.

Walker, A (1982), *The Color Purple*, New York, USA, Harcourt Brace Jovanovich.

Williams, E (1964) *Capitalism & Slavery* – New York, André Deutsch/ University of North Carolina.

Wolfe, R (2009) *Renegade The Making of a President* – New York, Crown Publishers.

Woodson, CG (2002) *The Journal of African-American History* founded by Carter G Woodson 1 January 1916, Maryland US, Silver Spring.

Younge, G (2010) *Who Are We? And why should it Matter in the 21st Century*, London, Penguin.

Younge, G (1999) *No Place Like Home – A Black Briton's Journey Through the American South*, London, Picador.

Selected Film and Television

Civilisation is the West History?, Niall Ferguson, Channel 4, 2012.

Empire of Cricket, BBC TV, 2009.

Empire of the Seas, Dan Snow, BBC, 2010.

Eyes on the Prize, PBS, 1987.

Four Little Girls, Spike Lee, HBO Films, 1997.

In Search of Wilberforce, Moira Stuart, BBC TV, 2010.

Malcolm X, directed by Spike Lee, Warner Bros. Films, 1992.

Nothing But a Man, directed Michael Roemer, 1964.

Obama: Whatever Happened to Hope & Change, Presented by Andrew Marr, BBC Television, November 2010.

President Obama, Interview with Andrew Marr, The Andrew Marr Show BBC Television 22nd May 2012.

Roots, ABC, 1976.

The Civil War, Ken Burns, PBS America, 1990.

The Tea Party – On the road with America Right-wing Radicals, Presented by Andrew Neil, BBC TV, 2010.

When the Levees Broke – A Requiem in Four Parts, directed by Spike Lee, HBO, 2006.

Who Do You Think You Are? Featuring Spike Lee, NBC TV USA Version, 2010.

Acknowledgements

Thanks to my editor Emily Anderson for her guidance, memory prompts and eagle eyes, Dr Madge Dresser and Dr Edson Burton for historical and writing inspiration, and the staff at Bristol Central Library for their help in months of research on the Transatlantic Slave Trade.

Additional editing by Matt Rance, ProofProfessor in 2018.

Index

241